PSYCHE AND THE SACRED

Spirituality beyond Religion

Lionel Corbett

Spring Journal Books
New Orleans, Louisiana

Published by
Spring Journal, Inc.;
627 Ursulines Street #7
New Orleans, Louisiana 70116
Tel.: (504) 524-5117
Fax: (504) 558-0088
Website: www.springjournalandbooks.com

Cover design by:
Michael Mendis
24 Blackfriars Street
London, Ont. N6H 1K6
Canada

Cover photograph by:
Michael Busselle
Digital Vision Collection, Getty Images

Printed in Canada
Text printed on acid-free paper

Library of Congress Cataloging-in-Publication Data Pending

PSYCHE AND THE SACRED

Contents

Acknowledgments

I wish to thank the many people who gave me permission to discuss the experiences described in this book. I would also like to thank my wife, Cathy M. Rives, M.D., for her patience while the book was being written, especially for her understanding my need to spend long periods writing and reading. Without her support, this project could not have been completed. I am particularly indebted to Michael Mendis, whose close reading and editing of the text corrected errors, allowed me to clarify my thinking, and improved the writing. His comments made the book much better than it would otherwise have been. Any inaccuracies that remain are of course entirely my responsibility. I am grateful to Erin Barta and other reference librarians at Pacifica Graduate Institute for their help with literature searches. Finally, I would like to thank Nancy Cater of Spring Journal Books, who has been patient and encouraging throughout this long process.

Foreword

How can we understand the increase of fundamentalism that we see around the world today? Following Jung, I think we should recognize this as a very human response to modernity and to the absence of apparent symbols and mythic awareness that so prevails in our time, at least in Western cultures. The forces that we see at play so powerfully in the world at this time—globalization, the hegemony of the money complex over religious and cultural values of any kind, the disappearance of secular ideologies that earlier could capture the idealism of the young and give it direction and communal expression, the social and economic marginalization of so many people who no longer live in a place they can call home—are among the conditions that enhance the appeal of the fundamentalisms. Jung spoke often about "modern man in search of a soul," and the rise of the fundamentalisms can be read as a sharp response to the soullessness of the modern rationalistic and mechanistic, not to mention grossly commercialistic, *Weltanschauung.* Fundamentalisms offer people access to the archetypal images of the psyche. In these communities, there are numinous symbols and sacred spaces, and this holds a strong appeal to the religious yearning in humans. Also, their leaders are often the recipients of powerful archetypal transferences from their followers. I think Jung would see the retreat into fundamentalism as regressive, in the sense that it embodies a strategy for avoiding the emotional and spiritual demands forced upon us by modernity. Fundamentalism is not a way forward to greater human consciousness. It represents a retreat from modernity to an earlier type of religious consciousness. Jung would call it a regressive restoration of the self. On the other hand, it might turn out in the long term to be a regression in service of the self because it does draw attention to the spiritual hunger of humanity that is not being satisfied by modernity's offerings.

As a Jungian Analyst, Lionel Corbett presents in this work, using his understanding of the relationship between psychology and religion, another option to the person who feels at a loss about how to live responsibly within the context of modernity and still lead a life of deep spirituality. This involves an individual approach to spirituality. Jungian psychology studies and treats the individual, albeit also in relation to others and the collective. The religious traditions, on the other hand, address groups (the church or the congregation) and encourage the people in them to adjust and conform their thoughts, beliefs, attitudes, and feelings to the doctrines handed down by their specific teaching traditions. The traditions urge conformity; Jungian psychology suggests individuation as an alternative. That said, one must also recognize that Jungian psychology can make a positive, if also sometimes critical, contribution to people who still subscribe to a traditional religion intellectually and practically. It can help them find deeper connections to the symbolic elements in their religious traditions. For people who do not belong to a religion or who have fallen away from the religion of their childhood, however, the Jungian approach offers an alternative avenue for living the spiritual life (the "symbolic life" as Jung called it). It is to such people that this book is primarily addressed.

The great pioneers in depth psychology, Freud and Jung, established important modern viewpoints for understanding and practicing the relation between psychology and religion. Freud's writings on religion—*Totem and Taboo, Civilization and its Discontents, Moses and Monotheism*—are challenging, and tend to cleanse one of leftover childish naiveté about the Bible, religious practices, and belief in God and the afterlife. Freud thus prepares a person to be "modern." From Freud's perspective, religious thought, belief, and practice are seen as elaborate games of wish fulfillment, and the grown up (and modern) thing to do was to get over such needs and face the realities of existence with a sort of tough, stoic determination. Books by Jung, on the other hand, like *Psychology and Religion* and the late compilation of autobiographical reminiscences, *Memories, Dreams, Reflections*, bring a whole new and different approach to the psychological understanding of religion and its possible position in modern consciousness. What Jung did was to completely reinterpret the "religious" in human experience. Thus he could write in *Memories* that when he met Freud at his home in Vienna in 1907, he realized that the man was in the grip of a numinous power, a *daimon*, in fact a God, i.e., sexuality. This numinous power formed the basis of Freud's religion, and his God moreover was a jealous God who would brook no other. So this relocation of religious experience in one's enthusiasms, in one's passionately held convictions, experienced right in the midst of one's emotional and intellectual life and quite apart from organized religious structures and traditions, is a key insight into how the religious may enter modern consciousness in the guise of something quite other, of something like a theory about human behavior. Jung wanted to make this conscious. He also was able to break out of the intellectual straightjacket constructed by modernity and refute its easy dismissal of the religious as sheer superstition. In so doing, he relocated the ground of religious experience and spirituality in everyday life.

Jung, one might say, was both pre- and post-modern. He wanted to find a way out of the trap of the rationalism and the scientistic prejudices of our day. From the practical and therapeutic point of view, Jung felt that the human soul needs the religious in order to develop properly and to live a psychologically deep and meaningful life. To live without the spiritual, as Freud recommended, is to live a partial and split-off existence, in denial of and out of contact with what the theologian Paul Tillich so aptly termed "the ground of being." Such a life is not whole. Jung sought to investigate this ground in his scientific writings, and he actively promoted cultivating it consciously in his therapeutic endeavors. He thought it was healthy to live a "symbolic life," in addition to a well-adjusted and correct life of reason.

For Jung, as for Freud, the Gods of traditional doctrine and image were dead. God had moved out of his temples, not to return, and had transmuted into an inner Presence, the Self. In an after-dinner talk at Christmas, 1957, Jung spoke in his rough Baseler dialect of this sublimation of God as follows:

> At a festival like the one we celebrate today the master of the house would have poured a libation at the house altar for the gods above and the gods below. Unfortunately that whole wealth of custom has been lost, except for small remnants. The idea of the *offrande*, the sacrificial offering by which the gods are invited to partake of the festival, persists only in the Eucharist, in the Mass for Catholics and in Communion for Protestants. In the Mass a natural food is transubstantiated into a heavenly one, while in Communion it remains what it is. It is no longer a symbol; the mystery has become nothing but a feast of remembrance. And thus we eventually arrived at our modern rationalism and materialism, in which all the *numina*

xi

have disappeared from the great realm of Nature and man himself is nothing more than the *homo terrenus*, terrestrial man and Adam. But strangely enough, since the seventeenth century this new symbol involving true cultic practice has gradually become widespread throughout Christendom: the Christmas tree. It is an archetypal symbol which had already appeared in heathen tree-cults. It is an alchemical symbol, which signifies the genesis of the inward, the greater and nobler man, that is, the man who comes into being when a person has drawn all the *numina* out of the world and into himself. Then he notices that he contains a microcosm within himself, a 'treasure hid in a field.' Man and his soul become miraculous. To that let us drink as a *momento vivorum et mortuorum* (Aniela Jaffé, *C. G. Jung: Word and Image*, pp. 143-4).

Lionel Corbett's powerful work here is a significant contribution, offered from within the large Jungian movement worldwide today, to help modern people find that soul and discover the numinous presence of the divine within themselves as they live a busy life filled to capacity with secular activities.

Murray Stein
Goldiwil (Thun), Switzerland
March 2006

Introduction

This book has two aims. The first is to suggest ways in which we may live a spiritually meaningful life without the need to embrace any particular theology or religious tradition. The second is to show that depth psychology has matured to the point where we can now fruitfully view problems such as the existence of suffering and evil, which were once the province of religion, through a psychological lens.

The book came about because I found myself facing a dilemma shared by many people. Although I have a personal sense of the sacred, I cannot accept the teachings, doctrines, and stories of the religious tradition of my childhood. I feel deeply that there is a Reality that is the source of our being, but I cannot connect with that Reality by means of the rituals and liturgy with which I grew up. Like many people, I experience the sacred in my own ways, which do not correspond to the manner in which the Judeo-Christian tradition tells me the divine manifests itself. Those of us in that position find that our personal experience of the sacred is far more compelling than sitting in a place of worship reading a book that contains doctrines that we are required to believe in, or stories about someone else's experience of God. To many of us today, much of traditional religion seems empty, and we can establish no real emotional connection to it. Unless we find our own alternative, this lack of connection deprives us of an important source of meaning in our lives.

Those of us in this predicament may nonetheless find ourselves in a church or a synagogue at special times of the year, such as the Jewish High Holy Days, Christmas, or Easter. Deep down, however, we know that we are there only out of nostalgia, or because our family expects us to attend, or because we feel our children need a religious identity. We may be there out of guilt, and if we realize this, we may feel resentful at the same time. Perhaps we are moved by the familiar melodies, the smells, the sights, the sounds that take us back to our childhood and evoke important memories of family and belonging. Upon closer examination, we might discover that it is these memories themselves, and the emotions they arouse, that are truly sacred to us, rather than the images of the divine and the doctrinal baggage attached to them that are associated with the memories. As the great Swiss psychologist C. G. Jung put it, once the gods have left the temple, they never return. Sure enough, after the special day is over and the family dinner is done, the religious institution of our childhood—which we have long since ceased to take seriously—recedes into the background, and we return to everyday practical reality, where organized religion seems to have no part to play.

For many of us, the loss of a meaningful connection to our religious tradition is a tragedy. Especially is this so for those of us who feel a larger Presence in the world and want it to be part of our lives. How can we make it so, if traditional religion is no longer a portal to the sacred? We know that there is more to life than we see on the surface, because we feel a connection to a deeper love, a deeper power, and sense a call to a larger Life. For some of us, losing touch with this Reality is like being separated from someone we love. Without a felt connection to a larger meaning in life, we are left with a painful yearning that nothing seems to satisfy. Occasionally, we have glimpses of that Reality, but then, without realizing it, under pressure from our other commitments, in a moment of unconsciousness, we are drawn back into mundane reality and the despair it inspires. Almost everything around us inspires despair; while popular culture pays lip service to traditional religious values, it seems its real gods are money, celebrity, sex, outward appearances, power, youth, power, or status. These are the highest values in our society; on their altars we sacrifice our energy, our health, our happiness, our children, and sometimes even our lives. In the service of these values, millions of human beings are routinely deprived, exploited, or simply ignored. This state of affairs is a sad testament to the ineffectiveness of traditional religions in making any significant difference in dealing with the problem of human suffering.

Many have given up on traditional religion because they feel that its doctrines and imagery are no longer relevant. Tragically, in the absence of any viable alternative, some have abandoned the spiritual quest altogether and have turned their energies to secular pursuits and the temporary distractions they offer. We become even more skeptical about religion when we read, with ever increasing frequency, about sexual and financial scandals among the clergy and other religious leaders, and we realize that religious teachings have not been able to help these individuals deal effectively with their personal problems. Organized religion is beginning to have less and less significance for many of us because we feel that its response to the needs of our time is inadequate. In the face of the increasing complexity and difficulty of modern life we can no longer believe that there will always be a happy ending or that technology will solve all our problems. Stories of heaven seem like fairy tales—mere mental pacifiers, or bribes—and stories of hell come across as threats; both play upon our emotional vulnerability.

People today often give up on traditional religion because it appears to offer no help in a serious life crisis. In the last 30 years of my practice as a psychiatrist and psychotherapist, I have worked with many people who are going through periods of intense suffering. Some of them had very little conscious interest in spirituality until they began to suffer. When they turned to the religion of their childhood for help, many of these distressed people were unable to find solace there. Their ministers, priests, and rabbis had little to offer except platitudes that were of no help. When the suffering person would ask why terrible things were happening to her or him, the typical response would be either an exhortation to faith, a brief lecture on the inscrutable mysteries of God, a claim that suffering is an aid to spiritual development, or a baffled silence. Many of my patients were deeply frustrated by these stereotypical "Father-knows-best" or "pray-it-away" or "it's-good-for-you" or "it's-all-a-mystery" approaches to their suffering. Many prayed for relief, but often none was forthcoming. Occasionally, the clergyman would suggest that the sufferer lacked sufficient faith. This is a classic tactic for dealing with one's sense of inadequacy: one blames others for what is really a failure on one's own part. Instead of admitting that the tradition he represents has a very limited repertoire of responses to the problem of suffering and evil—or even to ordinary everyday practical problems—the clergyman castigates the individual and exhorts him or her to greater faith. But that did not make the suffering go away for my patients.

In some cases, I saw that suffering alienated people from traditional religion because they felt cheated by promises that their religion had made but not kept. They had been told that God is loving, good, and benevolent, and would help them in time of trouble. They had attended worship services regularly and had convinced themselves that they believed what they had heard—but when suffering erupted, none of their religious observance was of any use. What they thought was an authentic faith was merely a belief system indoctrinated into them in childhood, and it simply crumbled under the onslaught of grief and pain.

Faith may arise spontaneously as an act of grace, but for most of us, faith is most soundly based in direct experience of the sacred, which leads to *knowledge* that there is a transcendent reality, rather than mere *belief* in it. No amount of preaching, reading of scripture, or worship services will have any effect in the absence of real emotional resonance with the teachings of the tradition. One can want to believe and try to believe and hope that faith will happen. But often it does not. If one does not experience the sacred in the way a particular religious tradition says one should, one may not belong in that tradition. As the Sufis say, there is no God but the experience of God.

Although an appeal to traditional faith in the midst of despair was often futile for these suffering people, what did help some of them were sacred experiences that spoke directly to their pain and loss. These experiences did not usually take a recognizably religious form. Nevertheless, the power of the experience was such that the individual felt quite sure that he or she was in touch with the transcendent realm—and so was I, as I listened to my patients' accounts. Just listening to these individuals relate their experiences gave me a vicarious sense of awe, and the healing effect on both them and me was sometimes quite profound. Yet the experience was often radically different from the traditional Biblical accounts of contact with the divine. Occasionally, some of my patients would tell their minister about their experience, only to have it labeled as "demonic," "hysterical," or "insane," because it did not fit into the traditional mold of encounters with the divine. The minister's thinking appears to have been restricted by a rigid image of the divine, which did not allow for a spirituality that manifests itself in novel ways, even when it was clear that the traditional ways were not working any more.

If the ministers are right, are we then doomed to a choice between a set of desiccated beliefs and a spiritual vacuum? In this book, I offer another alternative. If we develop a spirituality based on our own personal experience of the sacred, and find a workable way of speaking about the Unspeakable, there is no need to fall back on ancient traditions and the experiences of people long ago. Their experiences were influenced by the presuppositions of the times in which they occurred, and the passage of time consolidated these experiences into a tradition, which prescribed them as the standard by which all experience of the sacred is to be judged. However, each generation needs to articulate its own way of speaking about the sacred, because times change, and with them, the way we perceive ultimate reality. The prophets addressed the issues of their time within the consciousness of their time. But in the last one hundred years alone, the inner and outer dimensions of our lives have opened up into vistas that are radically beyond anything the Bible writers could ever have imagined. We have a different perspective on reality, not to mention a totally new set of world problems. Surely, even if we accept that some truths are eternal, our way of thinking about the divine must take these developments into account. If we are no longer satisfied with the old "explanations" for the origin and nature of the universe, why should we be satisfied with the traditional views on the nature of the divine?

As this book demonstrates, not only does the sacred appear to us in unexpected ways, but it forms part of the deepest structure of our personality. The great Christian mystic Meister Eckhart said, "God is closer to me than I am to myself," but such esoteric statements have to be made practical and applicable to everyday life. One powerful approach to doing this and understanding the manifestations of the sacred in our lives has arisen within the field of depth psychology, especially in the work of C. G. Jung. His ground-breaking and provocative approach to spirituality has given us a new way of articulating sacred experience. This approach is of great importance to our times because it provides a new vocabulary, which makes it possible to say things that were previously difficult to articulate. Jung showed that our spirituality and psychology interpenetrate and can even be viewed as two aspects of the same thing. This means we can now speak of our spiritual experiences in psychological terms and vice versa.

Following the Judeo-Christian tradition, Jung understood our relationship with the transpersonal dimension to be dualistic, that is, he saw the human and the divine as being somehow fundamentally different. However, his insight that the Self is also the Totality of consciousness leads inevitably to the conclusion that at this level there is no radical separation between the human and the divine, and that the two belong to a unitary whole. Although this unitary view is slowly gaining ground, most Westerners still experience the divine as an Other. This is especially true of people with a devotional temperament. I believe that both approaches are equally valid, depending on the individual personality, and there is no need to privilege either one or cast the two in opposition to each other.

Recent research[1] reveals that when it works for the individual, religious faith can have important health benefits. Authentically religious people are less depressed and anxious, less likely to commit suicide, and less likely to engage in substance abuse. Religious faith can enhance an individual's overall sense of well-being and happiness. Studies[2] show that older people who participate regularly in some form of spiritual practice live longer and have better general health than their peers. It is not clear to what extent this is the result of their spiritual practice itself, their personality, or the support they get from being part of a caring community. What is clear is that if we want to have a spiritual life and belong to a community of like-minded people, the difficulty we have in accepting the teachings of traditional religions may deprive us of the benefits to be gained from regular spiritual practice. Hence the pressing need for a viable alternative.

Human spirituality is about to make a great stride forward. Just as we have evolved biologically and socially, so, too, our consciousness and our spirituality have evolved. The next stage in our spiritual evolution is now emerging. The new spirituality requires the development of a personal connection to the sacred, unencumbered by doctrine, dogma, or preconceived ideas about the divine. It also involves approaching problems such as the existence of evil and suffering with all the new insights that developments in depth psychology can bring to bear on this and other human predicaments.

This book is divided into two parts. Part 1, "Meeting the Mystery: Developing a Personal Spirituality," describes a depth psychological approach to personal spirituality. Chapter 1—perhaps the core of the book—describes a variety of spiritual experiences, some of which are anything but traditional. Here I describe the particular quality that makes them recognizable, and I discuss the ways in which they are related to the psychology of the individual. Chapter 2 describes the irreducible reality of the psyche and Jung's controversial notion of the archetype, here considered to be a spiritual organizing principle within consciousness. Chapter 3 explains some of the connections between the type of spirituality we choose and our emotional difficulties. Part 2, "Through Psyche's Lens: A Depth Psychological Approach to Spiritual Questions," applies the principles of depth psychology to understanding traditional religious notions. Chapter 4 considers the ideas of salvation, redemption, soul, and spirit, which are found in one form or another in most religious traditions. I indicate the ways in which these ideas can be stripped of their metaphysical baggage, revealing important human needs that can be addressed psychologically rather than doctrinally. Chapter 5 describes a depth psychological approach to the problem of evil, and Chapter 6 discusses a psychological approach to the seemingly intractable problem of suffering. Here, I contrast the psychological approach to these problems with that of traditional teachings. Using the Biblical story of Job as an example, I discuss the relationship between personality, one's image of the divine, and the ways in which both of these may be transformed by suffering. In Chapter 7, I discuss some approaches to spirituality and personal spiritual practice that are not based on the God-images or theology of any particular religious tradition.

It is my hope that this book will help to meet the needs of those people whose needs are not being met by the established religious traditions. Welcome to spirituality beyond organized religion.

PART ONE

———————————

Meeting The Mystery:
Developing a Personal Spirituality

CHAPTER ONE

The Numinosum: Direct Experience of the Sacred

INTRODUCTION: WHAT IS SACRED EXPERIENCE?

This chapter describes a variety of ways in which we may experience the sacred, many of which do not conform to traditional Judeo-Christian expectations. We all have moments in life when we know we are touched by a force that is larger than ourselves, something very real that transcends our experience of the ordinary world. Such encounters are much more common than we have been led to believe. Consider the experience of a woman who was gathering flowers when suddenly:

> I looked at the large bunches we had gathered with growing amazement at their brightness. ... A wonderful light shone out from every little petal and flower, and the whole was a blaze of splendor. I trembled with rapture—it was a "burning bush." It cannot be described. The flowers looked like gems or stars ... so clear and transparent, so still and intense, a subtle living glow ... what a moment that was! I thrill at the thought of it.[1]

This woman was given an experience of the sacred quite different from the traditional images of the divine with which she was raised. She had been uncomfortable in her Church all her life, because the Biblical God worshipped there seemed to have no connection to her profound feelings for nature. As a child she felt like a wicked skeptic, all the time hiding a deep vein of sadness from her family. She knew that something was missing in her life because she could not reach the depths of her own nature. She yearned for something more, like a creature that had outgrown its shell yet could not escape from it. Eventually, exhausted by her search, during a period of surrender, she was confronted with experiences of the sacred irrupting as a holy Presence pervading nature. She was enrapt in the fragrance of flowers, and describes the experience as follows:

> The pleasure I felt deepened into rapture; I was thrilled through and through, and was just beginning to wonder at it when deep within me a veil, or curtain, suddenly parted, and I became aware that the flowers were alive and conscious. ... The feeling that came to me with the vision was indescribable.[2]

This experience filled her with "unspeakable awe." She had never been satisfied with the traditional images of God with which she had grown up, but here was the real thing. The crucified Christ and the sky Father of the Hebrew Bible did not reflect her personal experience of the sacred. However, her experiences of nature gave her a sense of an authentic spiritual ground. The power of an experience such as this is overwhelming and convincing.

Most of us do not expect to encounter the holy in our gardens. Traditional religions want us to experience it instead through prescribed rituals and prayers. Yet this woman knew that this was an experience of the holy because of the special feelings it produced. In his 1917 book, *The Idea of the Holy*,[3] Rudolf Otto used the word "numinous"[4] to describe this unique quality of the encounter with the sacred. Otto felt that the word "holy" had lost its original meaning and had come to indicate merely a feeling of moral self-righteousness. He pointed out that direct contact with the sacred produces a particular type of experience that forms the basis of all religion. He described this experience using the Latin phrase *mysterium tremendum et fascinans*, a mystery that is at once tremendous and fascinating, and thus produces the sense that we have been addressed by what he called the "wholly Other."[5] We feel stunned, astonished, and filled with wonder because we have been addressed by something uncanny, not of our ordinary world, something very difficult to put into words. We may be cowed by the experience because its sheer force overpowers us, making us feel very small. Or we may feel entranced, captivated, and transported. Contact with the numinosum (whatever it is that produces the numinous experience) may also produce a profound sense of union or oneness with the world and with other people. At such times we may feel unworthy, or perhaps blessed. Another possible reaction is the realization that much of what we have worried about is actually trivial. We are fascinated by our contact with the numinosum because it stimulates a kind of spiritual desire within us, a longing for the holy and the promise of love and peace that it holds out. If we were not too terrified by it, we long to experience it again. The crucial point is that experiences of the sacred may occur in novel ways that do not correspond to the expectations of traditional religions.

Our religious traditions have used stories such as those of Moses and St. Paul to illustrate how the divine can be experienced directly in a way that permanently changes the person who has the experience. While tending sheep, Moses is drawn by the sight of a bush that is burning but is not consumed by the flames (Ex. 3:2-6). He then hears the voice of God speaking to him out of the bush. On the road to Damascus, Paul sees a blinding light and hears Jesus say, "Why do you persecute me?" (Acts 9:1-9). This numinous experience produces a radical change in Paul—he stops persecuting Christians and becomes an apostle of Christ. However, numinous experiences are not confined to special people. They may happen to anyone at any time, and they are more common than is generally acknowledged.[6] There are various vehicles or portals through which they may be expressed.

THE NUMINOSUM IN DREAMS

Personal experience of the sacred does not depend on doctrine, dogma, or sacred texts, and it may actually *contradict* the authority of organized religion. For example, Father Tom had been a traditional priest for many years, although never quite happy with the Church. During a period in which he was questioning his vocation, he had the following numinous dream:

> I am Melchizedek. A radiant, blue image of the Venus of Willendorf looms over me. The Goddess is five times larger than I am. I am holding a chalice up to her left breast, and milk is flowing into the

13

chalice. I am deeply aware that I am in the presence of something intensely holy.

This numinous dream had an electric effect on Father Tom. Since he was a Biblical scholar, he knew that Melchizedek was the high priest who blessed Abraham.[7] According to tradition, Melchizedek became a priest by divine appointment, long before Moses' brother Aaron was appointed high priest for the Israelites wandering in the wilderness; his exact origins are unknown, but his name means "King of Righteousness." In the dream, the dreamer is given this name as a title, as if to reassure him that he need not worry about his vocation because the priesthood he belongs to is of a truly ancient line—one could say that his priestly vocation came from the soul, not from the Church.

A dream such as this carries its own authority because of its emotional power. Father Tom realized that he had not been happy in the Church because it did not sufficiently recognize the feminine aspect of the divine. The dream tells him that the milk of the Goddess—her nourishment— is sacramental to him. He realized that he had been trying to force-fit his spirituality into the Church's official container, but in fact what was truly sacred to him was highly personal. The dream tells him that the divine appears to him in a feminine form that is much older than the God-images of the Bible. The Venus of Willendorf is one of the oldest religious images known to us, dating back to about 20, 000 B.C.E., when the Goddess was understood to be the source of life. Clearly, this dream does not fit with traditional Church teaching. But it is typical for numinous experiences to disregard traditional norms, especially when the experience is relevant only to the concerns of a particular individual. Numinous experience allows us to discover our authentic spirituality by giving us a *personal* symbol of the sacred, in contrast to collective symbols such as the cross.

In this case, the numinosum appeared by means of a dream. According to Jung, such a dream does not arise from the personal levels of the mind. The psyche can be thought of as analogous to an iceberg. The visible tip of the iceberg represents the personal field of consciousness that we call the ego, or the sense of "me." Below that is the personal unconscious, which consists of experiences that are unique to the individual, such as events from childhood that are too painful or traumatic to recall. Deeper still, a transpersonal or archetypal level of consciousness links us all. Jung called this level the collective unconscious or the autonomous psyche.

However, it is important to immediately note that the personal and the transpersonal aspects of the psyche do not exist in discrete layers, but are intimately and inextricably intertwined. (See Chapter 2 for a fuller discussion of the structure of the psyche.)

Jung theorized that numinous dreams, such as Father Tom's, arise from the autonomous psyche. Father Tom's dream is then the modern equivalent of the dreams that Biblical writers believed were sent by God. Examples are Joseph's dream that Mary had conceived by the Holy Spirit (Matt. 1:20) and the dream that told Joseph to flee to Egypt because King Herod was about to destroy the baby Jesus (Matt. 2:13). The notion of the dream as divinely created for the dreamer has faded within the Judeo-Christian tradition,[8] but numinous dreams still occur with astonishing regularity. They give us the impression of a larger Intelligence that has its own message for the dreamer.

I hope it is clear, in both this dream and in the examples that follow, that numinous experience is often specifically relevant to the psychology of the individual who experiences it. Such specificity, although striking, is not necessarily *proof* that the experience arises from a transpersonal dimension of the psyche, since it can be argued that the personal psyche could produce the necessary imagery in an attempt at self-healing. A prior spiritual commitment might make us interpret a numinous event in terms of contact with the transcendent, while people who do not have a religious outlook on life might see such an event purely as one's own inner voice, a manifestation of the personal unconscious.[9] However, every aspect of the psyche contains both personal and transpersonal elements, and a rigid separation between them is impossible. It is therefore not surprising that a numinous experience would contain features of both. To argue that numinous experience arises purely from within one's own psyche makes an artificial distinction that ignores Jung's insistence that an element of the divine is located deep within our subjectivity. For Jung, unlike for Rudolf Otto, the divine is not wholly Other, because there is no sharp distinction between a transcendent divinity and what Jung refers to as the Self, an innate image of the divine. This level, which is the core of our being, is the ultimate source of numinous experience.

Given that a debate exists about the extent to which a numinous experience provides adequate reason for believing in a transcendent realm, it seems that the choice of whether to accept a spiritual or a non-spiritual understanding of numinous experience depends on which of these explanations feels most in keeping with one's own psychology. My personal commitment is to agree with Otto and Jung[10] that spontaneous numinous experience is a real seat of faith. Such experience feels as if it arises from the transpersonal unconscious, which is the reason Jung claims that the psyche has an "authentic religious function."[11] Here we must bear in mind that we do not know the nature of the unconscious; this word only means that aspect of the psyche that is unknown to us.

THE HEALING EFFECT OF THE NUMINOSUM

Numinous experiences often have a healing effect.[12] The following experience happened to Rebecca, a woman who had suffered an extremely bleak, abusive childhood in which she was often neglected and hungry. As a result, she was tempted to lose faith and give up on life—in her words, to be "small and hard and rageful." In the midst of a period of questioning the meaning of what had happened to her, this numinous vision irrupted into her life:

> One night, when the moon was dark and my bedroom lay in inky blackness, I sensed a presence in the corner of the room. I was afraid. I knew I was not dreaming. The presence grew and grew, until, pulsating, it filled the entire room, throbbing within the confining walls. The whole room seemed to tilt, as if accommodating itself to another dimension. I lay in terror, with my eyes tightly closed. A voice, deep and gentle, said, "Love; the whole thing is love." Slowly the energy ebbed from the room, leaving me in paralyzed terror in the darkness.

Although Rebecca's felt experience was one of fear, she reported that the event had "called me back to life," and to the challenge of discovering what "love" means. This is a good example of the way in which a numinous experience can affect one's behavior in everyday life. It is of course not new to stress the importance of love. However, when a teaching about love is given directly to someone from such an emotionally deprived background in the form of a numinous encounter, its impact is enormous. It is through this kind of experience that we develop an authentic spirituality.

In contemporary society, numinous encounters such as Rebecca's and Father Tom's are often considered to be hysterical, the product of an overheated imagination, or frankly insane.[13] Because of this societal prejudice, people are reluctant to speak of them, so we really do not know how common they are. Many people have told me that it was years before they could share their numinous experience with another person, because they were afraid they would be disbelieved or ridiculed for holding on to something that was to them precious and holy.

Although numinous experiences may come to us with no preparation, they can also be consciously invited by intense ascetic practices. In the Bible, long periods of isolation and fasting typically precede the appearance of the numinosum. Think of Moses on Mt. Sinai, fasting for 40 days before receiving the Ten Commandments (Ex. 34:28), and Jesus fasting for 40 days in the wilderness before his encounter with Satan (Matt. 4:1-11). It seems that severe deprivation or exhaustion can provide an opening that allows the numinosum to overwhelm our everyday consciousness and irrupt into our awareness. Numinous experiences may also occur during an illness—the sacred does not appear only to healthy people. Starvation or high fever may produce visionary experiences, which materialistic thinking would dismiss as merely the result of a disordered brain. Yet it is equally possible that serious illness and overwhelming stress can render the brain incapable of sustaining ordinary consciousness, with the result that the transpersonal dimension has a better opportunity to get through to us.

The feelings of awe, dread, and amazement that accompany a numinous experience are important not simply because they help us to identify the experience as sacred. These emotions tell us that the experience has been embodied. Emotions are felt in the body as a result of the action of the autonomic nervous system. They make the heart beat faster, make us pale, and produce muscle tension and sweating. Our hair may stand on end, and a variety of hormones may be secreted. A powerful emotional reaction provokes the response of the whole organism. William James, the great scholar of religious experience, also emphasizes feeling rather than concepts when discussing the essence of religious experience. James thought that theological formulas are secondary to the primacy of feelings,[14] and he realized that feelings "are genuine perceptions of truth."[15] That is exactly why we stress the emotional quality of experience of the sacred. We know an experience is numinous not only by its content but also by the way our bodies respond to it.

Sometimes a numinous experience does take a specifically Christian form, in which case the Christian tradition is still alive for that individual. A man was walking down a dark passage when suddenly

> ... a light shone on the wall of the passage with a cross clearly displayed, as though intense sunlight was coming through a window with the cross casting an intense shadow. There was in fact no window or source of light to account for what I saw. The curious factor to me was that although in those days I was nervous of the dark and very impressionable, I had a curious feeling of comfort and a deep feeling of intense emotion.[16]

This vision presents a Christian message, confirming the validity of this tradition for the man who experienced it, since it contains the uniquely Christian symbol of the cross and the typically Christian imagery of light and darkness.

THE NUMINOSUM EXPERIENCED IN NATURE

The following is a typically numinous experience of the natural world:

> At the foot of our garden was a very old large pear tree, which at the time was crammed with white blossoms, and at its summit a blackbird was singing, while beyond the tree a meadow sloped up to a marvelous sunrise. As I looked at this someone or something said to me: "That is beautiful," and immediately the whole scene lit up as though a bright light had been turned on, illuminating everything. The meadow was a more vivid green, the pear tree glowed, and the blackbird's song was louder and sweeter. A curious thrill ran down my spine.[17]

Because our sense organs can perceive only a limited range of signals, they normally act as a veil that filters out much of reality. In this visionary experience, however, for one precious moment, it is as if the veil is lifted, revealing a larger dimension of Reality. Unfortunately, today we rarely experience reality at this level. Especially since the Scientific Revolution, in contrast to pre-industrial cultures, we have lost the sense that the natural world is sacred, and this has made it easier for us to exploit it. A person in contemporary Western society might therefore hesitate to express intense feelings for nature for fear of being ridiculed, although such feelings could actually serve as a private form of spirituality.[18]

Conscientious adherents of the Jewish or Christian faiths might also conclude that such a numinous experience of nature is a form of pantheism, which holds that God and nature are identical. Religious traditionalists in the West believe that this type of experience cannot be a real experience of the divine, since Ultimate Reality is somehow above and beyond nature. But an experience of the divine often occurs through some kind of medium. That is why William Blake was able to "see a World in a grain of sand, / and Heaven in a wild flower,"[19] and Walt Whitman declared: "Was somebody asking to see the soul? / See, your own shape, countenance, persons, substances, beasts, the trees, the running rivers, the rocks and sands."[20] Because the Bible presents God as the creator of the universe, Bible believers have thought of the universe as somehow separate from God. We foster this split when we see God as a power outside the universe that gives rise to nature. Logically, the creator and the creation must be different entities. From this perspective, God remains removed from the world, even if he occasional intervenes in its affairs. However, this view imposes an anthropomorphic projection onto the divine in which God is seen as a kind of celestial engineer in the background who runs the machinery of the universe.

Even so, the Christian tradition contains a powerful strand of nature mysticism, which acknowledges the power and presence of the divine within the natural world. Meister Eckhart, the famous fourteenth-century Dominican mystic, emphasizes the presence of God in creation,[21] and Jakob Boehme, a seventeenth-century Protestant mystic, wrote: "In this light my spirit saw through all things and into all creatures, and I recognized God in grass and plants."[22] Because of his sensitivity to animals and the environment, St. Francis of Assisi is often thought of as the patron saint of environmentalists and ecologists. A similar strand of thought within the Jewish mystical tradition is expressed by Rabbi Abraham Isaac Kook, who believed that all of nature is a manifestation of God in many individual forms, the plurality of which is unified in God. Today, however, these voices are more likely to be associated with the ecological movement than with Judeo-Christian thought.

The vision of the illuminated pear tree reveals the divine manifested in nature. Within this numinous experience, nature is seen to be permeated with light, one of the oldest symbolic expressions of the divine. Nature thus becomes, for the woman who had the vision, the specific medium through which she can have an authentic experience of spirituality. This is not to suggest that she should worship nature in a literal way. Her experience simply tells us that a form of spirituality based on official liturgical worship of the divine is not the sum total of her spiritual experience; she can be in touch with the numinosum while hiking in the wilderness just as easily as she can in church.

The nature mystic has his or her spiritual feelings triggered by the natural world, not primarily by religious services in a place of worship. Some nature mystics are poets, such as William Wordsworth, for whom there is "a motion and a spirit, that impels … all objects of all thought, / And rolls through all things. Therefore am I still / a lover of the meadows and the woods."[23] Similarly, consider Walt Whitman's "… I too have consciousness, identity / And all the rocks and mountains have, and all the earth."[24] Or Thomas Traherne's "The green trees when I saw them … transported and ravished me; their sweetness and unusual beauty made my heart to leap, and almost mad with ecstasy, they were such strange and wonderful things …."[25] Such poets are found in all traditions.

Some nature mystics are practicing Christians who exalt the natural world as the creation of God; others regard themselves as atheists; still others as pantheists who worship an impersonal God. The twentieth-century naturalist and wilderness advocate Sigurd Olson had intended to become a missionary until he realized that he was more interested in saving the world's wild places than in saving souls. After a long period of distress and disorientation resulting from his loss of faith in the teachings of his Church, Olson discovered a sense of mission as an advocate for the spiritual value of the wilderness. This discovery resulted from experiences such as the following, described in his book *The Singing Wilderness*, which occurred while watching a sunset:

> The sun was trembling now on the edge of the ridge. It was alive, almost fluid and pulsating, and as I watched it sink I thought that I could feel the earth turning from it, actually feel its rotation. Over all was the silence of the wilderness, that sense of oneness which comes only when there are no distracting sights or sounds, when we listen with inward ears and see with inward eyes, when we feel we are aware with our entire beings rather than our sense. I thought as I sat there of the ancient admonition "be still and know that I am God," and knew that without stillness there can be no knowing,

20

> without divorcement from outside influences man cannot know
> what spirit means.

This numinous experience is of the type that produces gnosis, or direct intuitive awareness of the transcendent realm. Because the natural world stimulated this kind of experience in him, Olson became an apostle of the idea that there is a transpersonal power to be experienced in nature.

The English naturalist Richard Jefferies (1848-1887) also realized that the transcendent level of reality might break through as an experience of the natural world. For his devotions, he used every leaf and blade of grass, every bird feather, the hum of insects and the color of butterflies, the soft warm air, and flecks of clouds. Yet he did not believe in design or providence—he thought that the idea of a creator God was an "invisible idol,"[26] only a stepping stone to the Totality of the Beyond. Prayer for him was the yearning of his being for this Totality, not a conversation with a heavenly Personality.

For many people, personal experience[27] of the sacred is vastly more important than any doctrine or dogma. These are simply abstract concepts that depend for their validation on the authority of a Church hierarchy. Compare the effect of merely *asserting* that there is a divine life force in nature with the power of the following actual experience, reported by a young graduate student:

> As I ran across the grass, I could feel that each blade of grass had a life force, that the ground has a life force, that everything was bound together in this wonderful and horrible dance. I could feel my feet crushing the blades of grass, I could hear the crunch, I could feel the pain the grass felt. ... From this experience of expanded consciousness—which came totally unbidden and unexpected in that moment—I realized that I was something more than this pocket of flesh and mind wandering and searching. ... This is what I had been searching for ... I knew that there was really a power and presence that was all-inclusive, and that it included me as well.

This was a direct experience of life's spiritual dimension and its energy coursing through the world. According to Jung, following Cicero's understanding of the origin of the word, "religion" is the practice of "paying careful attention" to such experiences.[28] An experience is much more convincing than a theological assertion. The Christian concept of the Trinity, for example, is not based on personal experience, and there is no

Biblical concept of a Trinitarian God. The Church simply expects people to believe it. Today we question any kind of arbitrary authority, but an experience such as the one described above is compelling, although one must bear in mind the potential pitfalls inherent in subjective reports.

THE NUMINOSUM IN THE BODY

One of the most misunderstood and neglected manifestations of the numinosum occurs when it is expressed through the body, exemplified by the following experience, related by Dr. Bonnie Greenwell in her book *Energies of Transformation*:

> While meditating I felt suddenly as if I had broken through a layer of ice and could feel myself dancing above an ocean of bliss, feeling my toes touching it, feeling intense thrills, warm, flowing from my toes up through my body, flowing everywhere. Then I was plunged into this ocean and lost awareness of what was happening. It was indescribable ....[29]

Within the Christian tradition, the body has often been devalued in favor of disembodied spirit. At its best, the tradition has regarded the body as a temple of the Holy Spirit, while at its worst the body has been considered an instrument of the devil. However, a more realistic approach would be to think of mind-body as an indivisible unity that expresses the same Consciousness in two different ways. This Consciousness, which is felt in the experience described above as "an ocean of bliss" in the body, expressed itself as the light around the pear tree in the previous example. It also produces the imagery of dreams and visions, the intense emotions produced in the body by numinous encounters, and the vital or energic body that we feel within the physical body. This somatic energy, known in the East as *chi* or *prana*, is as much a manifestation of our spiritual source as any other numinous manifestation.

The Western religious traditions have denied what many other cultures have understood—that sexuality is an important vehicle for the expression of our spirituality. Thanks to two millennia of Christian influence, sexuality has come to be viewed as shameful. We have lost the sense that, as Jung[30] put it, sexuality is "a genuine and incontestable experience of the divine, whose transcendent force obliterates and consumes everything individual." Sexuality can provide an opportunity for ecstatic union with the divine, an experience during which our sense of separateness disappears. Following a night of intense lovemaking, a young woman described her numinous experience of heightened spiritual awareness as follows:

> ... I stood outside of time. It was as if time normally flowed in a horizontal plane, and I had somehow stepped out of this horizontal flow into a timeless state. There was absolutely no sense of the passage of time. To say there was no beginning or ending of time would seem irrelevant. There was simply no time ....[31]

To feel outside of time is to step beyond one's everyday personality, or the ordinary sense of self. Much spiritual practice is devoted to attaining exactly such a state of mind; this is why pre-Christian societies revered sexuality and made it sacramental, re-enacting ritually the union of the Goddess with her consort. In the pre-Christian temples of the Goddess, it was understood that sexuality can be a portal to communion with the divine.

THE NUMINOSUM IN RELATIONSHIPS

For most people the numinosum is encountered in relationships. The mystery of connection to others is vital and compelling, sometimes to the extent that it feels as if peace of mind can be attained only by means of relationships. Nothing is more important. Some people will go to any lengths to maintain their connection to others, no matter how much sacrifice is required to do so. This urgency cannot be explained away solely by saying that it results from their being deprived of adequate relationships in childhood. Such deprivation may account for the intensity of this need, but not the need itself, which is universal. Relationships are important to all of us, for many reasons. At the biological level, we are social animals who need each other for physical survival. Psychologically, we also need other people to hold us together, to comfort us, to validate how we feel, and to support our sense of self. Relationships act as a mirror in which we can develop more self-awareness.

We also invest certain relationships with profound spiritual significance. This is not surprising: we feel as if we are separate beings, but this is true only at the level of everyday, conventional experience. At a deeper level we are all contained within a transpersonal field of Consciousness that Jung refers to as the Self, the element of the divine within the personality. Here, we are deeply connected. We experience ourselves as separate from one another at the physical level because we have our own bodies, personal life stories, and memories, but the same Self is expressed through all of us. We sense this numinous field at moments of profound connection with others, and the experience is powerfully enlivening and life-affirming. Unfortunately, as we are growing up, we are not taught to recognize the divine in others. Whether we are taught to compete with others or to treat them kindly, there is always the implication that they are separate from us. Yet sometimes the experience of the Self arises spontaneously when we are with others, producing an unmistakable sense of sacred unity. Often it is this sense that people are referring to when they speak of love.

Modern communications technology, such as cell phones and the Internet, has proved to be a double-edged sword. It allows us to express our intense need for connection with each other, and we can quickly know what is happening all over the world, allowing unprecedented solidarity between people who care about the same issues. However, this technology tends to literalize the spiritual dimension of relationship, and the capacity for perpetual, instantaneous connection may discourage the experience of silence and self-reflection that is spiritually important. In moments of quiet contemplation, we feel our deep connection to others, but it is all too easy to use communications technology to drown out the "still small voice" that arises during these moments. We may use our technology to distract ourselves from this voice, partly because it may whisper uncomfortable truths about ourselves and sometimes because silence, or the experience of being alone, produces too much anxiety. Many people need periods of temporary disconnection to become conscious of this voice.

Although we have individual preoccupations, our most fundamental concerns are universal. All human beings are concerned with the experience of suffering, loneliness, confusion, pain, fear, and joy. At this level of experience we are not separate from one another at all. The differences in our skin color, language, personal history, and culture pale by comparison with the overwhelming similarity that exists in the way we relate to these and other feelings. That is why Krishnamurti[32] can say, "You are the world," or "The world is not different from us." Unfortunately, in our society our essential sameness at the spiritual level is obscured by a mythology of "rugged individualism," which is only benign if it implies that we can assert our individuality while also remaining conscious of our connection to others. If carried to extremes, this attitude may become antithetical to our innermost nature. Our deep level of connection is discouraged when our industrialized urban society predisposes us to feel separate by evoking feelings of competitiveness, acquisitiveness, and aggressiveness, which are also part of our nature. On the surface, these potentials seem to militate against connection to others, but they are in fact a perverse form of staying connected without acknowledging the need for connection. At the same time as we need each other, we have evolved with a deep distrust of strangers, for fear they might harm us. While this tension between need and distrust makes it difficult for us to be constantly mindful of our spiritual connectedness with others, it also provides us with an ongoing opportunity for a lifelong spiritual practice—the striving to become aware of the sacred in others, even as we become aware of it in ourselves.[33]

EXPERIENCES OF UNITY

One major reason why we do not sense our connectedness with all things at the deeper levels of Consciousness is that our reliance on the teachings of classical Western science has colored the way we perceive reality. Yet, the very importance of science emphasizes the gap between our perception of reality and its actual structure. As yet however, the insights of quantum physics have not had much effect on our social attitudes, especially with regard to the importance of consciousness and the underlying symmetry and interconnectedness of reality at a deep level.[34] As well, we are trained from childhood to think of ourselves as separate, a training that is reinforced by a set of personal memories which form the basis of our "identity." The result is a sense of personal boundaries. But innumerable people have been able to transcend these boundaries and thus have numinous experiences of union with the larger psyche. In such moments, the world and the personal self seem to flow into each other, both part of a greater unity, with no sense of separation or personal identity. This may happen as a result of spiritual practices such as meditation, or it may occur spontaneously, for no apparent reason. In such an experience, the personal self is lost in the larger Consciousness of the Self, revealing our essential continuity with it. These descriptions are found in the mystical literature of all the world's religions. Such an event is a normal numinous experience that must not be confused with a psychosis. There are many differences between a normal experience of the numinosum and a psychotic state. A numinous experience is transient, and the person soon returns to the consensual world of everyday reality. No lasting abnormality of perception, thinking or judgment occurs, and the individual can function normally in the ordinary world. In fact, whereas psychosis causes disruption or distortion of the personality, numinous experience is actually beneficial. Not only does it soothe anxieties, it enhances spiritual growth and makes the person aware that there is an unseen world of which he or she is a part, even though some numinous experiences are difficult to integrate into one's ordinary life, and it may be difficult to live up to what one has experienced. In unstable personalities, a numinous encounter may be emotionally overwhelming, sometimes even triggering a psychosis. But by and large, rather than viewing numinous experience as a *distortion* of reality, we can think of it as an experience of reality outside the boundaries imposed by our sense organs.[35]

THE NUMINOSUM AND CREATIVITY

The artist Marc Chagall is reported to have told his granddaughter, "When I paint, I pray,"[36] presumably meaning that for him painting was a spiritual practice. Our creativity is an important portal of access to the sacred. It is no accident that the ancient Greeks understood creative inspiration to come from divine figures personified as the Muses. Creative inspiration does not originate within the personal self; the ideas often come as a surprise because they seem to come from nowhere. Consequently, creative products usually come as a revelation, even to the artist. We must, of course, learn the techniques necessary for painting, writing, dancing, or making music, because only technical mastery allows us to express the Intelligence behind the creative product with a high degree of skill. Given that the creative process often involves a painful and prolonged struggle, when it finally arrives, inspiration for creative work seems to be received from a source quite unrelated to technique. When the creative artist feels in touch with that source, the artist senses a deep stream flowing through him or her that does not arise from his or her everyday personality.

RECEPTIVITY TO THE NUMINOUS

I believe that we all have an inherent ability to recognize an experience of the transcendent dimension, although skepticism, or the fact that the experience does not conform to our preconceived idea of the way the transcendent should appear, may prevent our recognizing it. Children are particularly receptive to numinous experience because their sensitivity has not yet become blunted by exposure to social expectations. They lack the prejudices of adulthood and are still permeable to transpersonal experience. They are therefore not surprised if they meet a fairy at the bottom of the garden or are visited by angels. A child might feel excitement or awe when he or she is in nature, with animals, or involved in art, music or dance. Any activity that is a source of passionate concern in the child's life may be numinous, whether friendships, sports, nature, reading, or learning a particular subject. But this potential for numinous experience may be suppressed. If caregivers ignore or belittle something that is naturally sacred to the child, the child will find it difficult to express its importance, or may feel ashamed to do so. For example, the potential dancer, artist, poet, or musician is told that to be practical, to earn a living, he or she must go to law school or medical school. What is felt innately to be sacred is thereby pushed underground, and the child has to make do with what he or she is *told* is sacred by the family, church, or synagogue. It is a tragedy when a child's spiritual potential is forced to attach itself to whatever the family and the culture insists is sacred, when this is not his or her natural inclination. It is a further tragedy when children are inculcated with images of the divine that stress guilt, punishment, and damnation, based on the projection of human feelings onto a God-image.

Unfortunately, if our natural means of contact with the transcendent have been suppressed or discounted in childhood, we may just go along with the religion practiced in our families out of a sense of guilt or loyalty, or from a desire to avoid hurting them. We may then become nominal Christians or Jews, but with a deeply uneasy or dissatisfied spirituality. If we do not submit to the suppression or distortion of our spiritual potential, we might reject the religion of our childhood and try to discover what is sacred to us in our own way. We may then begin a lifelong search to fill the need for contact with the transcendent, perhaps finding a spiritual home within another tradition.

In fact, there are multiple ways to experience the sacred without recourse to the sacraments or rituals of any established tradition. Those of us who prefer the spirituality that emerges from direct experience are more interested in the way the sacred actually appears to us than in images of God dictated by fiat, custom, or hearsay. These tend to reflect others' experiences and fantasies of the divine rather than our own. The approach based on personal experience does not create a new religious tradition, in which the divine is said to appear in only one particular form. Instead, we honor the many unique ways in which the divine appears to us individually, and we emphasize that the same mystery underlies all of them.

We do not try to define the essence of this mystery. Its nature remains unknowable. During meditation, it sometimes appears as pure Consciousness or Awareness with no content,[37] but sometimes it produces powerful imagery and emotions of the kind described above. Inevitably, our personal and cultural conditioning and the limitations of our language will affect our understanding of numinous manifestations. The best we can do is to allow the experience to speak in its own terms, as far as possible without imposing preconceived assumptions onto its meaning. We hope that its meaning will emerge as we are present to it, as we witness and pay careful and detailed attention to it.

In summary, I suggest that our reactions to numinous experiences are reactions to events that are normal, spontaneous, and real in their own right. I do not believe that numinous experiences can be dismissed as merely imaginary or pathological, or that they can be reduced to psychological factors such as a need for protection when we feel vulnerable, or that we can dismiss them as the result of some peculiar brain aberration.[38] I make this claim for various reasons, not only as an act of faith that numinous experiences emerge from the transcendent dimension. Numinous experiences may prevent a person from committing suicide,[39] produce a religious conversion, radically affect our feelings about ourselves and our behavior towards others, and sometimes change the course of our life. They may have an impressive healing effect, they invariably give the impression that they arise from a larger Intelligence than that of the subject, and their form and content is always a complete surprise to the empirical personality, sometimes giving information that was unknown to the subject. These experiences cannot be learned or taught, and they cannot be deliberately induced, no matter how much we wish to have one. Talking about them may not convey the full impact of their effect to those who have not experienced them.

THE NUMINOUS IN DISGUISE

An approach to spirituality based on direct experience widens our understanding of the ways in which the transcendent dimension may affect us. The numinosum may express itself in a disguised form, as, for example, when we feel gripped by something such as a passion for creative work that is totally absorbing. Such activity causes us to lose touch with ordinary time and plunges us into sacred time.[40] A kind of energy moves through us that seems to come from somewhere else. For the moment, we forget our sense of separateness, so that there is no distinction between ourselves and the work in which we are engrossed. Because these activities are usually considered to be secular rather than spiritual pursuits, creative work has become an unconscious—or at least a private—form of spirituality in our culture.

We may also experience the numinosum in a darker form. It may appear as an addiction, as anxiety, depression, or low self-esteem, problems that may cause much suffering. In Jung's psychology these emotional difficulties are thought to be caused by "complexes." When a complex is activated, we find ourselves flooded by feelings such as rage or panic, or our behavior becomes uncontrollable so that we act in ways that make no sense to us or to others. These kinds of emotional problems have two aspects to them. In part they may be the result of experiences in childhood, and they may have a numinous core to them, which adds to their gripping power. (Jung's idea of the archetypal or transpersonal core of the complex is discussed further in Chapter 2.) For many people, the driving need for power, money, sex, fame, status, substances, or some other intense preoccupation takes on the highest value within the personality. These things become unrecognized gods, in the sense that they come to dominate our lives and we are willing to sacrifice other parts of our lives—and even our loved ones—to them. In our culture, these aspects of our lives are labeled as purely secular. In fact, most traditional thought would consider it outrageous even to suggest that the sacred could be found in something compulsive, such as an addiction. Yet, without minimizing the problems of addiction, it is possible to see the addict as someone in search of ecstatic relationship with the divine through intoxicating substances.[41] One implication of this approach is that the development of an intense spiritual life may be therapeutic for such a person. This is one reason for the remarkable success of 12-step programs, which typically emphasize the need for a relationship with a "higher power" to prevent relapse.

It may seem strange to think of emotional difficulties as spiritual problems, or to regard them as manifestations of the numinosum. We are not accustomed to thinking of them in such terms. But notice their similarities to more traditional manifestations of the numinosum. The driven behavior, the addiction or the compulsion, is like a mysterious Greater Presence that has its own power over us, with its own fascination and allure. When we are in its grip, we feel as if something outside of us is in control of our actions. Later, we ask ourselves what came over us, and we resolve to control the problem the next time; but the next time we again find that the force is too great to resist. Similarly, when the numinosum appears, we have no choice in the matter; it chooses us. It is no wonder that pre-technological societies regarded such states of mind as possession by a demon or a god.

Within mainstream psychology and psychiatry, and in the eyes of the culture, problematic behavior is thought of *only* as a sign of emotional disorder. Seen as a manifestation of the dark side of the numinosum, the same behavior *also* takes on a spiritual significance not recognized before. Thus, a period of depression could also be viewed as a spiritual crisis, a "dark night of the soul." However, ministers of some religious traditions may be dismayed at the idea that the holy can be manifested through an abnormality or a mental illness, because they define the holy as associated *only* with that which is good and loving. They would protest: How can these disturbed emotions contain an element of the sacred? Why muddy the spiritual waters with the idea that an emotional problem could be considered a manifestation of the numinosum? Surely this area is the province of psychiatry or psychotherapy, and not spirituality. But I see no reason to assume that the divine may only appear in ways that *we* believe to be wholesome and healthy. Unless we insist on the traditional metaphysical position that the divine is only good, we may also see it within our pathologies and sicknesses, which is an equally valid attitude, and of course equally one that cannot be proven.

The divine does not only speak to those of us who are emotionally and physically robust. Consider the connection between piety, masochism, and mystical experience. For example, the Blessed Henry Suso, a fourteenth-century mystic, wore an undershirt studded with sharp nails that pierced his skin, and wore gloves with sharp tacks in them. He slept on a cross with nails that protruded into his body. In the winter he slept on the freezing cold bare floor of his cell, parched with thirst. He said that he endured these and other torments for his love of God. His piety seems authentic, but he may have also suffered from a masochistic character structure, which may have helped him gain access to the numinosum. Similarly, St. Teresa of Avila, a leading figure in the Counter Reformation and one of only three female Doctors of the Church, used to flagellate herself as part of her spiritual practice. The boundary between pathology and sanctity is often culturally determined. In medieval Europe, religious women who refused food were considered to suffer from "holy anorexia," a condition that today we would regard as an illness.

So far we have seen that the numinosum may manifest itself in many ways. Over time, our numinous experiences accumulate, though we may not always describe them as sacred; perhaps we simply think of them as special or compelling moments, or we use phrases such as "peak" experiences[42] or moments of extreme clarity of awareness. Gradually, these powerful events reveal certain themes that become deeply important to us.

SOME DIFFERENCES BETWEEN TRADITIONAL AND EXPERIENTIAL APPROACHES TO THE SACRED

An approach to spirituality based on direct numinous experience is different than many of the traditional ways of speaking of "God." The experiential approach does not treat God as a celestial personality or as a type of entity. This approach does not depend on a list of descriptions of God, or on a list of God's attributes or God's likes and dislikes. It does not suggest that particular rituals are the "right" way to contact God. It does not say that God has intentions for humanity. (Although it must be admitted that numinous encounters may give us the *impression* of an intention, we are probably projecting what we imagine that intention to be.) The experiential approach does not say that God is love, or that God is one, or that God is a trinity, or omnipotent, or personal, or eternal invisible spirit, or especially strongly present in a certain building in Jerusalem. These types of statements about what the divine is like or where it is to be found are simply abstractions, hearsay, unless they arise from personal experience. We may believe them because we are accustomed to hearing them, but for many of us they are just assertions that are emotionally empty.

Neither does spirituality based on personal experience of the numinous rely on a pre-formed scheme of salvation. It does not say: "Follow this recipe for life and you will be saved and go to heaven." Instead we ask: "What is your direct experience of the sacred? What form does it take in your life? How does it affect your behavior, and how does it influence how you feel about life and other people?" This approach does not encourage us to simply believe in a prescribed mythology; it asks us to discover our own living story. Just as we cannot choose arbitrarily between the truths put forward by the followers of Yahweh, Christ, Allah, Shiva, Vishnu, Kali, Kuan Yin or, for that matter, Quetzalcoatl, so we cannot dictate the mythology that most appeals to the individual. Very often, numinous experience is overlaid with cultural or doctrinal coloring, but this is not particularly important to the experiential approach. It does not matter whether the numinosum is experienced as a personal God, the Void of the Buddhist, or the absolute Consciousness of Brahman. The numinous experience of people of different cultural and psychological backgrounds has different names and contents, even though the effects of the experience on the personality and its emotional quality may be very similar. Whatever form it takes, experiences of the numinosum are a reality, and we cannot dismiss them because they do not fit with our expectations or our metaphysical theories.

All traditional religions are founded on someone's direct experience. The world's great monotheistic traditions are based on the experiences of their leading figures—Jesus, St. Paul, Moses, Abraham, Mohammed, and the other great names in our religious history. The problem is that over time the experiences of these few special individuals have become codified and handed down as though they applied to everyone. However, different psychological constitutions need different forms of spirituality, since one person's numinous experience may leave another unmoved. Having one's own experience of the numinosum is often more important than reading about someone else's experience. Second-hand accounts, such as the experiences described in the Bible, are valuable because they provide us with the history of our collective spirituality and they give us an idea of what we *might* expect. But they do not have the power of *direct* contact with the numinosum. We may doubt that events in the Bible happened in the way they are described, but in general, there is no denying our own reality, even if others refuse to believe us.[43] Neither should we let anyone tell us what is and what is not numinous; the image of the crucified Christ does not satisfy everyone's spiritual longings.

For many of us, the teachings of the Jewish and Christian traditions do not resonate with the deepest layers of our personality. We engage deeply in our outer lives only with what is inwardly important, with what corresponds to who we really are. When religious ideas do not speak to the psychology of the person, they are not taken seriously. We may pay lip service to them, but underneath the surface something is missing. We find many current and historical examples of this phenomenon in countries whose official religion is Christianity but whose behavior is anything but Christian. By contrast, when the Christian story corresponds to the dynamics of an individual's personality, an emotional resonance with Jesus' teachings occurs and the person then truly belongs in that tradition. We know that Christianity is an authentic path for such a person because his or her behavior and feelings are radically altered, not just the rhetoric. Such a person would not be found committing atrocities or war crimes, and the Sermon on the Mount would not be ignored when it was politically convenient to do so. The teachings of Jesus would fit naturally and instinctively into his or her behavior— they would not need to be reinforced by threats of eternal damnation and they require no hierarchy.

THE PROBLEM OF UNDERSTANDING NUMINOUS EXPERIENCE

Our understanding of a person's numinous experience must be in keeping with his or her personality and background. Sometimes the meaning of the experience is clear, as we saw in the case of the woman who heard a voice saying, "The whole thing is love." Her experience did not need interpretation. But at times the meaning of a numinous experience is extremely obscure, as we see in this dream:

> I was in a chemistry laboratory. I felt a tiny movement in my left ear, and with my finger I scooped out a tiny snake with the wings of a bird. I dropped the snake into a flask, and immediately there was a beautiful, lush forest in the flask. This happened again with

a second flask. Suddenly, a much larger winged snake flew out of my left ear, followed closely by a second one just like it. Blood came from my ear. Then my skin started to shed, and a huge winged snake came up through my throat and burst out of my mouth as my face fell backwards and began to slide down over the body of the emerging snake. It felt as if I would die, since this snake was much bigger than my body. I woke up afraid before my body had been completely shed.

Since a numinous experience like this cannot be squeezed into a doctrinal box, there is a danger that the event will be dismissed as being of demonic origin.[44] There is no need to be burdened by such preconceived ideas. The dream is so numinous we accept its authenticity without judging it as good or evil. We initially try to understand such numinous imagery in terms of the person's life story, taking into account her development, personality, and cultural setting. However, this snake dream cannot be understood in purely personal terms or in terms of our contemporary culture. It requires an excursion into the mythic history of humanity for its full significance to be grasped. There is no reason to impose a specifically Christian interpretation on the dream, either negatively, seeing the snake as the Tempter of the Garden of Eden, or positively, in which case the snake would represent the wisdom of Christ. In pre-Christian antiquity, the serpent represented healing, renewal, wisdom, and often the Great Mother, or the Goddess. The dream can be understood in terms of these energies possessing the dreamer. Since the dream serpent has wings, as a combination of snake and bird, the dream image suggests that the spiritual and the earthbound are united—we experience this as a teaching dream.

Faced with this kind of imagery, one becomes aware of the problem of how to choose from among the many different approaches to dream interpretation and to the psyche in general. No theory of the psyche is complete on its own. Psychology can never have a theory of everything, since the psyche cannot be contained in the net of conceptual thought. Consequently, one inevitably falls back on personal preferences. My own practice is to use a combination of various types of depth psychology. I find that Jungian theory is most powerful in understanding numinous experience, while various psychoanalytic approaches are important for understanding more personal material.

PITFALLS OF THE EXPERIENTIAL APPROACH

Whichever psychological system we use to approach spiritual experience, we have to be wary of certain pitfalls. We must not explain away the experience of the sacred as if it were merely a product of the personal levels of the mind. Neither should we use numinous experience to build a new system of theology that will be universally applicable. Because personality structures vary, people will always need an individual approach to the sacred rather than a one-size-fits-all approach. Another potential snare is that we may identify with the experience, using it for narcissistic purposes, to enhance self-esteem or prestige. There is also a danger that we will seek out unusual experiences instead of concentrating on everyday spirituality, expressed in our behavior in the world. There is a risk that we may use numinous experience as a kind of narcotic, as part of a search for certainty or security, and become attached to it as if it could give us some permanent Truth. Neither can one claim that any particular experience is more valid than any other. At most, a numinous experience is a pointer, and expresses the sacred as an image or symbol. Therefore, it is important for us to let go of the experience, realizing that all it can be is a stepping stone. No experience can be a complete experience of Reality, and all experiences occur to a personality that is limited. Thus it is that the Eastern traditions point out that "I" cannot experience enlightenment, because at the level of the Totality there is no discreet entity, no separate "me." Nevertheless, numinous experiences are of relative value to the person, especially if we remember that at the deepest level of our being we are not separate from the experience—we *are* the experience. Numinous experiences reveal aspects of our true nature of which we had no prior inkling. They always produce something new; they are not necessarily a product of what we have learned or what we have been told is true. In the model of spirituality proposed in this book, symbolic material such as the Venus of Willendorf and the winged snake arise spontaneously from the depths of the soul. We do not choose these manifestations; they are like visitors that appear from the Unknown.

Our language and theories tend to determine what we can observe. We may not even consciously see what we cannot speak about, or we may dismiss as irrelevant what our theory does not explain. Today it is well recognized that all languages and all theories, including those of religion, reveal some aspect of reality and conceal other aspects. Consequently, we must be suspicious of those who claim to have absolute spiritual authority. Authority is often divisive and a source of conflict, but Reality is undivided. There is no room here for competing notions about which traditional ideas of God are the most correct.

Various caveats are in order at this point. When we consider an event to be numinous, there is always the possibility of self-deception. What seems to be direct contact with transpersonal Reality may actually represent the projection of our own preconceptions or biases, so reasonable skepticism is in order. Another objection to the experiential approach to spirituality is that it runs the risk of validating any form of spirituality, even those, like Nazism, that are manifestly evil. Is this a spirituality in which anything goes, as long as we can claim that it is numinous to the individual? Surely, we can overvalue our personal experience to the exclusion of the collective wisdom of humanity. In its positive aspects, the shared cultural mythology found within our religious heritage has facilitated social stability and given meaning to many lives. However, for many of us, it is no longer possible to believe in an overarching myth that applies to everyone. Accordingly, as Jung pointed out, those of us who have lost faith in traditional religion must now discover a personally meaningful myth to live by. Jung's approach to religion is a kind of counter-myth that John Dourley claims is currently "in the process of supplanting, even as it appreciates, Christianity and other monotheistic mythologies."[45] Jung's myth radically relocates our sense of the divine deep within the psyche, rather than in a transcendent Beyond. Our form of access to the transpersonal has therefore changed; we now experience it through the immediacy of the psyche rather than by means of a traditional religious container. This situation produces some anxiety, because it makes a tremendous moral demand on us; it is axiomatic that even the most numinous dream does not tell us what to do. We have an ethical responsibility to respond to the experience, but we remain responsible for our behavior, so that the advice to "test everything; hold fast what is good," (1 Thess. 5:21) remains very important. According to Jung, the psyche contains the potential for both good and evil; we must suffer the tension between them, and it is up to us which of them we incarnate. The psyche critiques or challenges our conscious attitudes by means of dreams, leading to the ethical demand to confront the dark side of the personality—a far cry from a moral free-for-all. No matter how numinous the shadow feels to us, it is crucial to this approach that we become conscious of it and we try to assimilate it.

Jung's stress on the symbolic manifestations of the unconscious has been harshly criticized as an approach based on revelation rather than the scientific method. In the words of Philip Rieff,[46] because there is no arguing with revelation, Jung's approach is "beyond the danger of being invalidated by argument or contrary experience ... against the democracy of the scientific intellect, he [Jung] represents the aristocracy of emotional profundity." Elsewhere, Rieff writes: "Because it offers no criteria of validity, other than the therapeutic experience of conviction, Jungian theory amounts at once to a private religion and an anti-science."[47] Jung's approach has often been accused of being too mystical and of "repudiating rationality,"[48] and of standing "in strong contrast to the rationalism and determinism characteristic of Western thought in general and of modern science in particular."[49] It is true that Jung would say that numinous or mystical experiences (the two are not necessarily the same) are encounters with the unconscious. However, these experiences are, I believe, an empirical reality, and surely they are of considerable value for the expansion of our consciousness. It is important to balance, and if necessary hold the tension between, a spiritual outlook on life and a rigorously scientific approach. Whether these are incommensurable is at present a matter of opinion. My own belief is that we do not yet have an adequate scientific approach to numinous experience, and we may never have one. However, numinous experience is psychologically true for the one who experiences it, whether or not it can be validated scientifically.

Finally, it is important to remember that while numinous experiences are impressive, the sacred reveals itself in the ordinary if we have eyes to see it. There is no need to "seek after a sign" (Mark 8: 12) or pursue ecstatic experiences. If such experiences happen, we are grateful, but one may live a profoundly spiritual life, and realize one's essential unity with all other beings, without such experiences.

CHAPTER TWO

The Reality of the Psyche: The Archetype as a Spiritual Principle

THE REALITY OF THE PSYCHE

Our experience of the world is fundamentally psychological. The psyche, which for me is synonymous with consciousness and its contents, is the indispensable medium through which all our experiences, including sacred experiences, occur.[1] Without consciousness, we would not know that we exist, and we could not reflect on ourselves. Thus, to ignore what is known about the psyche when discussing spiritual experience would be like trying to understand astrophysics without taking into account Einstein's Theory of Relativity. Consequently, it is essential to discuss the structure and dynamics of the psyche before we attempt a psychological approach to spirituality. I should say at the outset, though, that I do not think we can understand consciousness fully. I believe that consciousness is a mystery that cannot be explained simply in terms of the workings of the brain. Nevertheless, we can study its effects even if we do not understand its exact nature, just as physicists can study the effects of gravity without understanding the exact nature of the gravitational force.

Jung believed in the existence of a *psychic* reality, whereas our modern science-based culture holds to the position that only *physical* reality is real. To demonstrate the existence of a psychic reality that includes both mental and physical experiences, Jung pointed out that, in psychic terms, the fear of ghosts is just as real as the fear of fire, whether or not ghosts exist in the objective sense that fire does.[2] The images and figures in our dreams are compellingly real in this sense, because they have such a powerful impact on us emotionally.

In this view, when we say that psychic experiences are as "real" as physical ones, we do not mean that every experience that we have can be proved to be "true" in the way that science can prove the existence of objects and their properties in the physical world. Unless one is a committed materialist, "real" does not have to mean "provable by observation of the five senses." Many experiences that science cannot explain—such as falling in love—are important emotionally and it would be absurd to dismiss them as not real just because they cannot be demonstrated rigorously by the scientific method.

From the psychological perspective, it does not matter whether an experience occurs in the physical world or in a dream. We know that an experience is real because we feel its effects in our bodies and in our behavior. Thus, it is a mistake to dismiss dreams as "only psychological," meaning that they are not real because they are not something we can examine with the five senses. Dreams may seem to be private and "inner," yet it is not unusual for some people to dream of an event, such as a plane crash or a death, before it actually happens in the outer world.[3] The separation between "inner" and "outer" reality is much too shortsighted, as is the separation between psyche and matter. Both are aspects of the same unitary reality; they represent different ways of experiencing it.[4]

Because the psyche is the organ of perception for all our experiences, we can never study the psyche from outside it, with the detachment and objectivity of a scientist. We have no alternative but to use the psyche to study the psyche, from which we cannot escape, somewhat as if we are in a hall of mirrors in which wherever we turn we see the psyche reflecting on itself. Consequently, psychic truth is not the same as scientific truth, because there are no extra-psychic standards by which psychic truth can be judged. Whatever is experienced is true, in the sense that the truth relates to the fact of experience itself. Thus, for Jung, the experience of UFOs is true, even if the fact of UFOs cannot be proved. Such experiences are psychic images, which according to Jung mediate or bridge between subject and object (or between ideas and things) to create our sense of psychic reality. As Paul Kugler puts it: "Psychic images signify something that consciousness and its narcissism cannot quite grasp, the as yet unknown depths, transcendent to subjectivity. ... What the image signifies cannot precisely be determined ...."[5] In this way, psychic images "provide a bridge to the sublime, pointing toward something unknown, beyond subjectivity." Therefore, when we try to describe numinous experiences or when we make metaphysical statements, according to Jung, we cannot know what they rest on—"we only know that something is there. ... I am satisfied with the statement that I have seen a divine image, but I am unable to make out whether it is God himself. Outside this image and its dynamic qualities, it is utterly impossible for me to make out anything about the nature of God."[6]

THE COMPONENTS OF THE PSYCHE

The Ego

Although consciousness is indivisible, we experience the psyche as if it had different parts, to which we give different names. The ego is the name given to that aspect of the psyche associated with our sense of a "me," the feeling that I am a separate person with a private sphere of consciousness. Beginning at birth, the ego begins to develop gradually as our genetic endowment interacts with our environment. Gradually we accumulate knowledge, experiences, and memories within our individual bodies, and eventually we form a mental image of ourselves. The personality that results has a range of knowledge that is necessarily incomplete and highly conditioned by family and culture. Over time, a change occurs in our sense of who we think we are—the ego is not our essential identity. Our body ages, new memories and attitudes accumulate, and some of the old ones fall away. Values, ideals, and goals change. Eventually our image of who we were thirty or forty years ago appears entirely different from the current image of ourselves, even though we recognize that there has been no break in the continuity of our existence and that our essential core remains unchanged. It is as if the ego is a painting on a canvas that the artist works over on an ongoing basis, sometimes scraping off old paint, sometimes just adding more paint on top of what is already there. Each change produces a different picture of what I call "me." The canvas upon which the ego is painted, the actual Ground of consciousness that contains all this information, is one of the great natural mysteries.

The Personal Unconscious and the Objective Psyche

Below the level of our ordinary conscious awareness is a vast area of the psyche that we cannot access at will—an area known as the unconscious. This understanding of the structure of the psyche has given rise to the term "depth psychology," which implies that the psyche has hidden depths, much like an iceberg, most of which is hidden beneath the surface of the water. In the Jungian understanding of the psyche, the unconscious has two levels. The first level, the personal unconscious, consists of material that has been pushed out of our conscious awareness because it is too painful or too traumatic to hold in conscious memory. It is personal because it consists of things that have been experienced by the individual. This is the level with which traditional psychoanalysis concerns itself. Jung, however, pointed out that beyond the personal unconscious there is a deeper, transpersonal field of consciousness in which we all partake. If consciousness were like an ocean, the personal level of the mind, which we call the ego or the individual sense of self, would be like the crest of each of its waves (Fig. 1). Above the surface of the water, the waves appear as separate formations, but at their base they all merge into the larger ocean. Similarly, in its totality the psyche encompasses far more than just each individual's experiences. Though we usually have the sense of being separate individuals, we are all nonetheless connected to each other at the transpersonal level of the psyche—even if we are not aware of it. Consciousness as a whole is seamless; each individual's consciousness draws upon and is continuous with the underlying totality of consciousness, just as each individual breathes air into his or her lungs and is at the same time surrounded by the air in the atmosphere, which permeates everything.

In the Hindu tradition, the transpersonal level of consciousness is known as Brahman; in the West, we might call it the Mind of God.[7] In Jungian psychology, this larger field of consciousness is referred to as the "objective psyche" or the "autonomous psyche." (Jung originally called it the "collective unconscious," but this term is not commonly used today.) The larger psyche is called "autonomous" because it acts independently of human consciousness. We can experience it, but we cannot control it. For Jung, the autonomous (objective) psyche is either the *medium* for the transmission of numinous experiences from a transcendent divinity beyond the psyche, or numinous experience may be a direct encounter

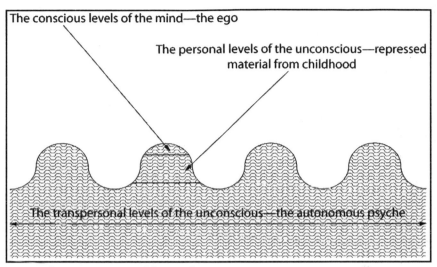

The conscious levels of the mind—the ego

The personal levels of the unconscious—repressed material from childhood

The transpersonal levels of the unconscious—the autonomous psyche

Fig. 1: The Components of the Psyche

with the autonomous (objective) psyche itself—we cannot be sure which of these possibilities is correct. In practice, the distinction is not important. When we have a numinous experience, we feel as if we are being addressed by a consciousness that is different from our own. At a deeper level, however, just as the wave is part of the ocean, the experiencing ego is not really separate from the larger Consciousness.

The notion of a transpersonal or spiritual dimension of the psyche is one of Jung's major contributions to Western psychology. We participate in this dimension in much the same way that fish live in the ocean. We are immersed in the psyche, but we do not know how far it extends. As far as we know, the transpersonal psyche may permeate the entire world of nature, and even the entire cosmos. We often refer to it as "deeper" than the personal psyche, or as representing a "higher" level of consciousness. But words like "deeper" and "higher" are misleading, because consciousness is not spatial in the ordinary sense. The "depths" are not really hidden; they are on the surface, in the sense that they are immediately present—we simply do not experience them regularly. Even to say that the personal and the transpersonal strands of the psyche intertwine is to imply a separation between the two that does not exist.

There is considerable resistance to the idea that our personal consciousness is actually continuous with, or is an aspect of, a larger

43

consciousness. Many schools of psychotherapy deal only with the personal level of the mind. Many psychologists still refuse to accept Freud's idea that we are not the masters of our own psychological house because the unconscious influences our thoughts and feelings. No wonder it is impossible for them to accept the existence of yet another level of the psyche that transcends the individual entirely. This sounds too religious for many mainstream psychologists who are struggling to be "scientific." It is difficult for them to accept that the relative importance of the human ego is further reduced, once it is placed within this larger perspective.

THE ARCHETYPES

We are born into a world in which the psyche operates according to certain natural laws, just as the material world operates according to the laws of physics. Jung calls these transpersonal ordering principles in the psyche "archetypes." For Jung, the archetypes are simply a given; they are natural constants, pre-existent, self-organizing forces within the psyche whose origin is unknown. Like the laws governing our physical universe, archetypal processes are not specific to any particular place or time. We see the operation of the archetypes during typical human situations, when the psyche responds with inherent patterns of imagery and emotion.

During a period of turmoil, a man dreamed:

> I follow a young girl to an old adobe house in a village nearby. When we enter the house the front room is softly lighted and its walls are bare. Suddenly the girl is suspended on the wall like a crucifix. I am shaken. Her body then begins to disassemble, and her separated limbs, torso and head rotate on the wall. Her limbs look very ancient for a moment. She then quickly reassembles and is standing beside me. I am overcome with awe and run out to tell the people in the village what has happened. They become very joyful and say how fortunate for me and them that I have seen this miracle.

The theme of dismemberment is archetypal,[8] closely related to the theme of sacrifice. Dismemberment imagery is found in the initiatory experiences of shamanism, where it points to a death-rebirth process, in which the initiate's old identity must die before rebirth into a totally new state of being. Dismemberment was also a favorite theme of the alchemists when they tried to depict the experience of the personality broken down into its component parts in order to be reconstituted in a more whole way. In other words, this dream indicates that a radical process of reorganization and transformation is taking place in the dreamer, and part of him may feel crucified by the experience. By seeing his situation in these archetypal terms, the dreamer is given a larger perspective on his situation. The dream allows him to see that he is participating in a universal human process, one that has more than purely personal aspects. Archetypal imagery always has this kind of alien, impersonal or even fantastic quality about it, and often contains mythological or religious motifs.[9]

In this dream, we see the effects of the archetype, but not the archetype itself, which Jung believed was not observable. The archetype-as-such is a predisposition in the unconscious for certain types of ideas and images to emerge into consciousness in particular life situations, just as the instincts are predispositions for the emergence of certain types of behavior under certain environmental conditions. Each person expresses an archetypal predisposition in his or her own way, when particular life circumstances foster its emergence. Jung believed that the underlying archetypal form itself is empty, but consciousness fills it with material so that it can be recognized. In his words, "... archetypal ideas are locally, temporally, and individually conditioned."[10] That is, the archetype determines the form of a dream such as this, but the setting and the context of the dream are filled in by the dreamer's own life and the culture in which he lives.

It is important to note, that, according to Jung, we do not inherit archetypal ideas themselves; we inherit the "functional disposition to produce the same, or very similar, ideas."[11] Archetypes are "inherited with brain structure—indeed they are its psychic aspect."[12] However, it is not clear in what way the archetypes are inherited or transmitted. In his early work, Jung[13] thought that the archetypes resulted from the deposit in the psyche of the constantly repeated experiences of humanity, as if constant repetition left imprints or "engrams" in the psyche that would produce analogous images in later generations. There were two problems with this idea. One was the chicken-egg question: how could the archetypes both result from previous experiences and also condition these experiences? The other difficulty was that this idea implied that acquired characteristics could be inherited, a theory that has been discredited. In his later work therefore, Jung abandoned this idea in favor of the notion that the archetypes are simply part of the inherent nature of the psyche, whose origin is unknown. The question of whether the psyche and its archetypal constituents ever "originated" at all is a metaphysical problem[14] that cannot be answered directly, since the archetypes "entered into the picture with life itself."[15] There is no Archimedean point from which to observe them. Jung therefore left the mechanism of transmission unspecified. Fortunately, questions about the nature and origin of the archetypes are not relevant in practice, since we can observe their effects without being aware of their source.

In Jung's words, the archetypes are "not mere names, or even philosophical concepts. They are pieces of life itself—images that are integrally connected to the living individual by the bridge of the emotions."[16] That is, they are real processes, not just maps of reality or convenient ways of talking about patterns of observations. The archetypes inform our psychological and spiritual development just as our genes determine our physical form. If one can identify a human activity that is truly universal, found in all cultures at any time in history, one has discovered an archetypal process. In the body, this kind of behavior is referred to as instinctual,[17] and in the psyche the archetypes produce imagery and symbolic material that correspond to the instincts. For example, all normal women may become mothers, and all cultures have their own preferred form of mothering behavior. The archetype of Mother corresponds to a deep structure in the psyche,[18] while the mothering style of the individual woman or society supplies its conscious manifestation. The deep or archetypal structure has the potential to be expressed in many different ways by particular people and societies. A human mother is therefore not the Mother archetype itself; she embodies in herself the archetypal process of mothering in time and space. She gives a human face to the transpersonal quality of mothering. This "humanizes" the archetype, that is, brings it down to earth.

The archetypes make it possible for certain types of ideas to appear universally, such as the notion of divinity; but the local form and name that a given divine being takes is determined by the culture in which the archetype is expressed. In this way, culture fleshes out the deep structure of the archetype into specific images. In some traditions, God-images are masculine, in others they are feminine or androgynous. In the case of feminine God-images, local folklore gives the goddess different dress, and names her differently—Isis in ancient Egypt, Oshun in Nigeria, Pele in Polynesia, Demeter in ancient Greece, Kali or Quan Yin in the East, and the like. All of these names point to the same underlying archetypal principle.

ARCHETYPES AS SPIRITUAL PRINCIPLES

In addition to their psychological importance, archetypes also constitute a *spiritual* principle in the psyche.[19] In antiquity, archetypal processes were often personified as gods and goddesses. Typically, mythological systems have a trickster-god, a god of war, a god of love and beauty, a divine child, a redeemer figure, and so on. Archetypal patterns are also represented in mythological stories in the form of recurring motifs such as death-rebirth, the descent into the underworld, the heroic quest, or the confrontation between good and evil. These themes are still being depicted in our times, in contemporary theater and in movies such as *Star Wars*, and this attests to their archetypal quality.

The Great Mother archetype is expressed in religious traditions and mythology as the Queen of Heaven or the Goddess. We experience this archetype both personally, humanized in our own mother, and also spiritually, in mythic or religious images of the feminine aspects of the divine. In Catholicism, the mother archetype takes the form of the Blessed Virgin Mary. Like many religious symbols, and many archetypal principles, Mary as an object of Catholic faith unites within herself a series of apparent opposites or contradictions. In the Catholic tradition, she is both perpetual virgin and mother, handmaiden and "Queen of Heaven," a simple carpenter's wife, and even for some Catholics the woman "clothed with the sun" in the Book of Revelation.[20] In Catholicism, Mary is classically depicted as innocent, sexless, pure, and humble before God. She is also the grieving mother, resigned to the death of her son and to the will of a loving heavenly Father, but then she is glorious and triumphant after the Resurrection, the mother of God himself. Catholics see her as able to mediate between humans and God and intercede with him on their behalf, and she acts as protectress of the faithful. In view of the ongoing devotion to Mary among Catholics, and the fact that she still periodically appears to the faithful, it can be concluded that this particular version of the archetypal image of the Queen of Heaven must meet important emotional needs for a great many people. This is *not* to say that Mary is merely an illusion, but rather that the archetype always takes on forms that people can recognize.

THE ARCHETYPE IN ITS CULTURAL MANIFESTATION

Cultures change gradually and express archetypal processes in new ways over time. Thus, to many contemporary Catholics, the image of the Blessed Virgin Mary is no longer as satisfying as it once was, so the image of Mary has begun to change. In our time, people draw upon the power of the Great Mother archetype when they project strength and determination onto the image of Mary in order to make her more relevant to our present-day concerns. For example, the doctrine of her perpetual virginity is re-interpreted by some in terms of the independence of the liberated woman. She has also been seen as a champion of the oppressed and the marginalized. In Guatemala in the 1980s, Mary became such a powerful symbol of liberation theology's social justice movement that the government banned the public recitation of the *Magnificat* (Luke 1:46 55)—a song in which Mary proclaims that God will bring down the mighty, raise the lowly, and feed the hungry—on the grounds that this (quintessentially Christian) idea was politically subversive. However, true to its nature, the symbol of the Virgin Mary has continued to embody opposites, and the Catholic establishment has also appropriated Mary as a way of upholding its own traditional values.

The image through which an archetype manifests itself is greatly affected by both cultural factors and the individual personality, which are often inextricably connected. In medieval Europe, society at large could not absorb the idea of a woman being both maternal and sexual, perhaps because the mixing of these two qualities would produce undertones of incest. Hence arose the Catholic portrayal of Mary as both sexless and a perpetual virgin.[21] The Catholic use of the word "mother" in speaking of the Church as "Mother Church" only deepened the separation between motherhood and sexuality, and shifted the idea of "mother" even further into the spiritual realm. The Madonna-Whore dichotomy implies that a woman can be one or the other, but not both at the same time.

Some modern women view the Catholic dogma of Mary's perpetual virginity as a denigration of womanhood and as a devaluing of the female body; for them, if Mary is to be a model of womanhood, she must be a *complete* woman. They challenge the idea that a woman must deny her sexuality in order to be pure and holy. However, the Roman Catholic Church must at least be given credit for restoring the role of the divine feminine in spirituality by raising Mary to the status of Mother of God, and by promulgating the dogma of the Assumption, that is, the teaching that after Mary died she was taken body and soul into heaven. By contrast, traditional Protestantism does not have any means of acknowledging the feminine qualities of the divine, since in Protestant theology Mary is not given any importance other than as the earthly mother of Jesus.

From a psychological (rather than a theological) perspective, the Virgin Mary in Catholicism plays a role similar to that of the goddesses of the pre-Christian world, since both meet similar needs, even if they express different aspects of the archetype. Today, we see the power of the archetypal feminine expressed in many ways—most notably in the resurgence of goddess- or earth-based spirituality, and in the dreams of individuals who are devoted to her.

Any manifestation of the divine feminine is an expression of the same underlying archetype. In Egypt the Great Mother was called Isis, in India Durga, Kali, and many other names. In the Greek pantheon, the representation of this archetype ranges from the life-giving Demeter to the relationship-loving Aphrodite to the virginal hunter Artemis. In the Jewish tradition, Wisdom was seen as a feminine power that radiates from God, and makes it possible for humans to have understanding and knowledge of the divine. While the feminine aspects of the divine remain largely unacknowledged within mainstream Judaism today, in the Kabbalah, a mystical form of Judaism that arose towards the end of the 12th century C.E., the divine has a distinct feminine component, especially in the classic Kabbalistic text, the *Zohar*. Here, the *Shechina* is a female essence or radiance that represents the presence or immanence of God in the world. She seems to correspond to a profound psychological need for a feminine element within the Godhead.

The archetype cannot be contained within the boundaries of any single manifestation or any one religious doctrine. It expresses itself differently in different cultures. Therefore we cannot rely solely on the Jewish or Christian tradition in trying to understand the manifestation of the archetypal feminine. The whole of world mythology is needed to depict the Goddess in the fullness of her archetypal role, and any combination of her manifestations may be found within the psyche of the modern man or woman. The divine feminine has innumerable names and images because each religious tradition dresses her in its own folklore and superimposes its own theology onto her. All of these cultural manifestations are simply images that point to a spiritual reality in the psyche. Exactly like human women, in her positive aspect the divine feminine is nurturing and protective, but in her negative aspect she is rejecting, devouring, and death-dealing, like the wicked witch or jealous stepmother of fairy tales.

Similarly, the Father archetype is represented in mythology as a male sky-god such as the Greek Zeus, the Norse Thor, or the Hebrew Yahweh. Like all archetypal forces, the father-gods can be either positive, as guides and guardians of law and order, or negative, as tyrants and warlords. Just as human parents may have a mixture of positive and negative qualities, so the gods and goddesses may be either benevolent and gracious or arbitrary and punitive towards human beings. While these qualities have given rise to a multitude of gods and goddesses with different names in various cultures and traditions, they always relate to some kind of archetypal (that is, spiritual) process or idea, such as birth and death, law, beauty, love, war, healing, or fertility. The monotheistic traditions eventually gathered up all of these processes and ideas and attributed them to one single God.

The gods and goddesses of mythology depict archetypal processes within the psyche. Since the archetypal level of the psyche is common to all human beings, stories with the same themes appear in the myths and fairy tales of very different cultures.[22] For example, the story of Cinderella focuses on the experience of a child who is at first abused, neglected, and devalued, but eventually comes into her own. There are several hundred variations of this story, found in cultures across the globe; the story is so common because it deals with an archetypal human situation: many children are treated like Cinderella was in childhood.[23] We are moved by such a story because it strikes a powerful chord within us and arouses latent feelings—we instinctively recognize its trueness to life. Even though the events in the story may never have happened literally, the story itself is always true—it is eternally relevant because it keeps happening psychologically in the lives of people everywhere. When we read a myth or fairy tale that resonates with us, we ask ourselves, "How is this story like my experience?"

Archetypal patterns within the psyche form part of the human condition; in typical situations, people react in typical ways because psychologically we are all built in the same way. Just as all bodies have common anatomical and physiological structures, so the psyche has recurrent themes and images that are common to everyone. The archetypal level of the psyche reveals its inner workings by representing these recurrent motifs in the form of stories that are similar across cultures. The details of what appears to be "my" story can also be found in stories that reflect the larger experience of humanity—our heritage of mythology and folklore—because my personal psyche cannot be divorced from the psyche of the human race as a whole. For example, many people today sacrifice their children in the service of ambition or in the drive for success. The mythology of many cultures includes the theme of child sacrifice; it is not just the Bible that contains stories such as Abraham almost killing his son Isaac as an offering to God, or God sacrificing his son Jesus on the Cross. Homer tells us that as the Greek fleet was preparing to set sail for Troy, the wind suddenly veered in the wrong direction, as if the gods were working against the Greeks. A soothsayer revealed that the goddess Artemis had been offended, and was demanding a human sacrifice—King Agamemnon's daughter, Iphigenia. Another such story of child sacrifice involved Idomeneus, a Greek general and one of Agamemnon's most trusted advisors. On his return trip home from the victory of the Trojan War, his ship was caught in a severe storm. Idomeneus vowed that if he returned home safely, he would sacrifice to Poseidon, the god of the sea, the first living thing he encountered on his arrival. This happened to be his son, who had come to meet him at the shore to welcome him. (One version of the story says that he sacrificed his son; another says he refused to do so, with the result that the gods sent a plague to torment the island of Crete.) Like the theme of child sacrifice, the motif of the hero can be found in the myths of all cultures, but each hero behaves according to the standards and expectations of his own culture. Sir Galahad is rather formal and English in comparison with the very Greek Ulysses.

The archetypes are analogous to the skeleton structure around which a building is erected. Two buildings may have different façades and different contents and yet be based on the same basic structural design. Likewise, local folklore and customs may differ widely and yet be variations of the same deep archetypal pattern. The development of religious systems is thus a form of archetypal human activity, springing from archetypal processes such as the urge to connect with the divine in worship and ritual, the telling of mythic stories and the reading of sacred texts, the impulse to visit sacred sites in pilgrimage, or the need to develop a code of ethical behavior. Local culture and traditions determine the ways in which these activities are carried out.

ARCHETYPAL MASCULINITY AND FEMININITY

Nowhere is the cultural coloring of an archetypal process more evident than in the way a society creates its images of ideal masculinity and femininity. In this controversial area, it is particularly important to distinguish between the archetypal *potential* for a pattern of behavior and the specific cultural *contents* that actualize this potential. If we do not make this distinction, we are likely to misunderstand the nature of masculinity and femininity and end up depicting them as stereotypes rather than as a set of potentials. Until recently, our cultural images of masculinity and femininity defined in rigid terms the roles and behavior of men and women. According to this definition, masculinity involved being assertive, authoritarian, penetrating, clear thinking, and logical, while femininity was described exclusively in terms such as passive, receptive, relational, nurturing, and intuitive. In the early years of Jungian psychology, it was assumed by some writers that these qualities were expressions of the essence of maleness and femaleness. In fact, while the difference between masculine and feminine is archetypal, and a particular combination of qualities and traits are associated with each, there is no particular need to label any specific human quality in terms of gender. Both men and women have the potential to experience both archetypal femininity and masculinity. We have opposite-sex figures in dreams, and it is important to try to become conscious of these aspects of the personality, as Jung suggested in his concept of the animus and anima.

We associate mothering with women and fathering with men, because of the biological differences between men and women. But a cultural prejudice is present here when it comes to defining exactly what mothering and fathering involve. Both men and women have the potential for embodying either the Mother or the Father archetype and this potential may be highly actualized in some men and women but not in others. The psychological differences between men and women are proving to be more subtle than was once thought. Archetypal masculinity and femininity, then, are not necessarily what we have been told they are. In some personalities, the question of gender is not prominent at all. Important archetypal potentials such as healing, love, wisdom, compassion, violence, envy, and hatred may have little to do with the gender of the personality in which they manifest themselves. Children of both genders try to develop self-esteem, a cohesive sense of self, and many other aspects of being a person that make us more alike than different.

RITUAL PROCESS AND THE ARCHETYPE OF INITIATION

The fact that all religious traditions have rituals suggests that human beings are archetypally predisposed to engaging in ritual behavior. Simply stated, a ritual is any symbolic action that we invest with sacred meaning and that has emotional significance to us. Ritual emphasizes the physical world as a medium of connection to the divine. Ritual is a complex phenomenon, and scholars disagree about its role in human behavior. Very often the participants in a ritual find themselves unable to explain why they are participating in the ritual, only that they feel powerfully moved to do so.

We feel the need for ritual especially when we are in the throes of a life crisis or a major life transition. At such times, ritual gives us the means by which to express feelings and ideas that cannot easily be put into words. Ritual then provides structure in situations that are confusing or intimidating. When illness or a natural disaster strikes, we feel as if we have been assaulted. In antiquity, people would ask which god or goddess they had offended, or which deity had to be approached for help with the situation. In psychological language, this question can be rephrased as: What archetypal process is at work, and how can we engage with it? A suitable ritual would be one response.

Ritual symbolically links the unconscious with consciousness, using the body as the means of connection. The body itself becomes a symbol. Including the body in this way counteracts any tendency to separate mind from body, affords the archetype a degree of conscious expression, and opens us to the possibility of discovering meaning within the situation. Thus, ritual has a healing effect. Because ritual expresses deep feelings non-verbally, it is closely related to art of all types, especially theater. We use ritual not only when we are trying to express a common feeling or experience, but often also when we are trying to bring something new into life, to articulate what has not yet been expressed.

Ritual's main instrument is the body, since it can express in movement what is often difficult to express in words. It is no accident that both Islamic prayer and Tibetan Buddhist practices involve prostration. Dance is spiritually powerful for many people, such as the Native American Indians and the Sufis. Some of the most beautiful verses of Rumi, the Sufi mystic, came to him as he whirled in an ecstatic dance. The urge to engage in ritual may begin with our impulse to express ourselves in the language of action when words fail us because they are inadequate. We *perform* ritual, rather than speak it. In ritual, the physical movement is the most important thing, as is the case with dance, in which the whole body is used to symbolically express a feeling or a story. Ritual does not only commit the body to action; in some cases it uses the body itself as the ritual object, as is seen, for example, in ritual body piercing or in circumcision, in which a part of the body is sacrificed in a symbolic act that is connected in some way to the mythic history of the tribe.[24] Not only is this kind of ritual action a substitute for words, but we do not need to be aware of the myth that is being enacted for a ritual to have its effect on us. Because rituals are pre-verbal, the emotions stirred up by the ritual seem to penetrate us quite directly, so that ritual may have a powerful effect even when its meaning cannot be put into words. Like any symbol, ritual mobilizes energy and expresses the otherwise inexpressible. For example, placing flowers on a grave or just kneeling in a church can be symbolic acts that are charged with emotional energy. Situations of this kind may feel as if they possess a sacred dimension of their own, while at other times our intention to ritualize the action imbues it with sacredness.

Religious rituals often enact a mythic story, such as the events of the Last Supper, which form a basis for the Christian Eucharist. The ritual is not simply about the history of the event, but about its sacred quality. The ritual makes the event come alive again in the here and now, making it possible for the celebrants to partake in transcendent reality. When a ritual is used to express a myth, it may have many levels of meaning, even when the origins of the practice are unclear. Exactly where and how the practice of baptism began, for example, is unknown, but the first followers of Christ adopted it as a rite of admission into the Christian Church. While the Christian practice of baptism has mythic associations to the story of Jesus being baptized by John the Baptist in the River Jordan before he embarked on his mission, it originates specifically in the command that Jesus gave to his disciples to "teach all nations, baptizing them in the name of the Father, and of the Son, and of the Holy Ghost" (Matt. 28:19). Jesus himself used baptism as a metaphor for intense suffering that reaches deep into the soul (Mark 10:38). St. Paul added other levels of meaning to the ritual by suggesting that baptism symbolizes dying to sin and rising again to a new life (Rom: 6: 3-4; Col. 2:12). Paul also saw baptism as signifying the elimination of all differences between people: it affirmed the equality of all humans before God; in his theology, everyone who is baptized into Christ participates in the same spirit (1 Cor. 12:13; Gal. 3:27-29). As well, for St. Paul, baptism symbolized membership in the New Covenant, under which circumcision was unnecessary—thus he saw the ritual of baptism as a replacement for the ritual of circumcision (Col. 2:11-12). The Roman Catholic tradition added to this complex of meanings the teaching that baptism removed the guilt of Original Sin. Today, parents have their children baptized simply because they want to make the child formally a member of the Church

The meaning of a ritual may change over time. Hallowe'en, for example, is now a secular ritual, even though it has religious roots going back to pagan times. Hallowe'en was originally the evening (e'en or eve) before All Hallows' Day (or All Saints Day), November 1st, hence the name "Hallowe'en." All Saint's Day was instituted by the Catholic Church as a counterweight to the pagan belief that on one day of the year all the devils and demons and other forces of evil were let loose upon the earth for one single night. Over time, Hallowe'en became secularized and commercialized, and the spelling of the word changed (the apostrophe—which is essential to the meaning of the word—was dropped), further obscuring the origins of the celebration. Today, the ancient religious significance of the celebration has been lost, even as the ghosts and goblins have been retained—a social sanction for the experience of horror rather than the original pagan confrontation with evil. Other examples of rituals whose meaning has changed radically over time are those associated with Christmas and Easter. The Christmas tree and the rituals surrounding it originate in the pagan celebration of the winter solstice, while Easter egg hunts derive from pagan celebrations of the spring equinox. These rituals were incorporated into Catholic tradition and invested with Christian meaning in order to make Christianity more appealing to pagans, who never quite gave up their old rituals when they converted to Christianity. In our distant past, when rituals were related to the cycles of nature and tied to the seasons and seasonal human activity, they made a great deal of sense. Today our lives are not controlled by the seasons, and seasonal rituals do not make much sense at the collective level, but they persist under a different guise.

In its positive aspect, ritual makes us aware of the sacred dimension of our lives amidst the humdrum routine of everyday activity. It has the added effect of binding us to the religious tradition within which it is performed, and at the same time strengthening our ties to the other members of that tradition. However, when a ritual is repeated constantly, it may lose all meaning. If they are carried out mechanically, rituals, such as the saying of the blessing before meals, the Mass, the Rosary, the recitation of the Torah, and the lighting of the Menorah, can be turned into something that simply has to be done, without much devotion or sense of the presence of the numinous. Constant repetition makes the ritual all too familiar and thus robs it of its numinosity by reducing it to the level of the ordinary, even as it purports to celebrate the sacred. Ritual can clearly become ossified and institutionalized to the point where it becomes emotionally meaningless, and may even develop into an addiction. Institutionalization of this type has a deadly effect on spirituality by robbing it of its sense of newness and by forcing everyone to experience the sacred in the same manner. Ritual then becomes a collective activity at the expense of individual experience.

Historically, the establishment of ritual was the first step in the shift from spirituality to institutional religion. Every spiritual movement becomes a religion once it establishes fixed rituals. For, with the establishment of the ritual come prescriptions for how it should be performed, whereupon attention becomes focused on following the prescriptions or making sure that the ritual is performed in the right manner, while the spiritual experience itself recedes further and further into the background. The spiritual practice becomes increasingly rigid precisely because the ritual has to be performed in the same way each time by each performer in order for it to be a ritual and not just an isolated one-time spiritual experience. Ritual then makes *form* more important than *content*—and this is the death knell for spirituality. Martin Luther recognized this and tried to get rid of the deadwood of Catholic ritual when he established his own denomination. For him, content was more important than form, and he tried to keep ritual to a minimum. In some traditions, ritual persists precisely because of its narcotic effect: ritual may numb the mind, dull the senses, and put the worshipper into a light trance. Not only is this phenomenon seen in Catholicism, it is also a feature of Russian and Greek Orthodoxy, and especially of Orthodox Judaism, as witnessed in the rocking motion that accompanies prayer. Trance states *can* lead to numinous experiences, but this rarely happens during the Catholic Mass or synagogue prayer, precisely because the trancelike state descends on the worshippers like clockwork, right on cue, whereas mystical experiences do not. While genuine trance states and meditation can expand consciousness, mechanically performed ritual does exactly the opposite. When it is repetitive and unvarying in performance, although it may express devotion ritual may also produce unconsciousness. As such, it is the very antithesis of *spirituality* although it is the essence of *religion*.

It is important to note that any action (spiritual or otherwise) repeated often enough becomes ritualized (or "stylized"). When actions are required to be repeated frequently, they can safely be done by the brain's autopilot; but if the autopilot is in control of the action, there has to be a fixed formula, a standard way of doing the action, since the autopilot has no will of its own. Thus, in matters of spirituality, one has to make conscious the process by which actions become ritualized so as to avoid slipping into automatic behavior. To drive a car on autopilot is fine, but to make contact with the divine on autopilot is not real spirituality. The way to prevent spiritual practice from becoming automatic is to avoid excessive repetition and stylization and resist the mind's natural tendency to standardize. Otherwise, ritual can easily become a living fossil, and risks becoming fundamentally inimical to spirituality. Eventually, meaningless ritual practice leads to the rejection of ritual, which we see in the teachings of the Hebrew prophets, of Jesus, of the Buddha, and of Reform Judaism. Reformers always insist that there is no point in ritual for its own sake.

When ritual does perform its proper function, because of the numinosity of the archetype that is activated during ritual performance, the location where the ritual takes place is felt to be sacred space, and the time during which it is performed becomes sacred time. The Romanian-born professor of religion, Mircea Eliade, defined the difference between sacred and profane space and time in the most well-known of his works, *The Sacred and the Profane: The Nature of Religion.*[25] Ordinary, or profane, space is homogeneous—it has no orienting center, as sacred space does. Thus, sacred space, the space in which the numinous is manifest, feels qualitatively different from profane space—one reason why Moses, for example, took off his shoes when he approached the burning bush, which filled him with a sense of awe. It felt to him that this space—otherwise quite ordinary—was now full of spiritual power. While the Israelites wondered in the desert for forty years, wherever they set up the Tabernacle became a sacred space, during the time it was there. The Most Holy Place was in several different locations during those forty years. At each of these locations, the spot was ordinary before the Tabernacle was set up, and it became ordinary again after the Tabernacle was dismantled and moved on to the next location. The presence of the Tabernacle conferred sacredness upon it. Eventually the Most Holy Place was fixed in Jerusalem when the Temple was built during the time of Solomon. Once again, a particular place in Jerusalem became holy when the Temple was dedicated. Before that it was ordinary ground.

Christ spiritualized sacred space completely and divorced it from physical space. When the woman of Samaria at the well asked him about which was the right place to worship, the mountain in Samaria or Jerusalem, he replied, "Woman, believe me, the hour cometh, when ye shall neither in this mountain, nor yet at Jerusalem, worship the Father … but the hour cometh, and now is, when the true worshippers shall worship the Father in spirit and in truth …." (John 4:21-24). With this statement, Christ made the point that sacred space is not located in any physical location on earth, but within the individual. One's physical location was unimportant; Jerusalem was no more sacred a place than the mountain in Samaria. The early Christians had no sacred places and did not subscribe to such a notion. Thus, in a way the reinstitution of sacred places, the building of shrines, grottoes, and churches, and the establishment of places of pilgrimage, are a reversion to paganism.

Christ's denial of the importance of sacred space is very much in keeping with the idea of the transpersonal. Just as the transpersonal transcends gender, it also transcends time and space, and thus there are no physical locations on earth that are particularly sacred in and of themselves. Sacred places derive their sacredness from the "set apart" value that is ascribed to them by human beings rather than from anything inherent in them. The sacredness of a spot may have nothing to do with the divine in the traditional sense of the word. A purely secular spot can assume sacredness and not have any religious sentiments attached. Thus, the Jewish and Christian views of sacred places have nothing in common with the understanding of sacred places in New Age spirituality, with its idea of energy vortices, nor does it have anything to do with geomancy in general. In these cases, in a supposedly sacred place, there is a special quality or property inherent in the topography of the land itself. Even then, the sacredness of the spot derives not from the properties of the land, but from the human response to these properties. The special properties of the land are perceived as having a numinous quality and the spot is therefore invested with sacredness.

From the ritual's point of view, sacred space has a center, which orients us to absolute reality; places such as Jerusalem or Mecca, for example, are considered to be orienting centers, places of spiritual power. Sacred space makes it possible for humans to communicate with the divine realm, as is illustrated in the dream of Jacob in the Bible, in which Jacob sees a ladder connecting heaven and earth, the ladder representing the orienting center. Within sacred space and time, we feel that we pass from our profane mode of being into a sacred mode. Unlike time in the profane realm, sacred time moves in circles and is therefore actually timeless; thus, Jews partaking in the Passover Seder are able to think of themselves as being freed from bondage in Egypt along with their ancestors, and at Easter the Christian faithful sing, "Christ the Lord is Risen Today." Sacred time, therefore, suspends literal, physical time and space.

The term ritual is commonly restricted to religious practices, in which the focus is primarily on the sacred. However, we may also think of ritual as any behavior that is carried out in a fairly fixed, prescribed manner. Thus we have *social* rituals such as shaking hands on meeting someone. Rituals of this sort are taken for granted as matters of convention and politeness—they control social behavior. All social conventions are ritualized; all cultures have prescriptions about how to act in certain situations. Social rituals pervade our culture, as is seen in the ceremonies and conventions that form an essential part of institutions such as the government, the military, and the law. Social rituals fulfill an important individual and collective psychological function in that they preserve shared beliefs and values and promote group solidarity and cohesiveness. Social rituals reduce our anxiety about how to behave and reinforce our sense of self by reaffirming that we belong to a group of people who are similar to us. Because they prescribe behavior that is both officially approved of and stereotyped, social rituals reinforce a sense of community, the structure of society, and social order. Thus, it seems that a certain amount of ritualizing of social behavior is necessary. If there were no speeches, toasts, and handshakes at an important occasion, the event would lose some of its sense of importance. Even though such behavior is stereotyped, its very existence suggests there is an archetypal need for such enactments to mark the passage from one state to another. We feel these behaviors to be necessary, although in many cases social rituals are nothing more than meaningless habits that sacrifice individuality.

For some people, social rituals are so important that they seem to take on a spiritual significance. Indeed, the boundary between religious rituals and social rituals is not a sharp one, because many of our social rituals unconsciously honor the gods of our culture. We have rituals that honor the god of money, for example, such as the ringing of the opening bell at the Stock Exchange every weekday morning. Millions of people have a devotion bordering on reverence to the Super Bowl, the lighting of the Olympic flame, or the Academy Awards. The United States Congress has a well-defined set of rituals, and some Americans even speak of the Constitution as if it were a sacred text. The medical profession has its own rituals surrounding death in hospitals, such as the monitoring of vital signs, so that due reverence is shown to the god of science. When a birth or death occurs naturally, the experience is intensely numinous for everyone present, but our medical rituals sanitize and standardize these life transitions and thus rob them of their archetypal force.

Religious rituals either invoke the presence of an archetype or represent unseen powers symbolically. In either case, unless the spirit is present the ritual is empty; it degenerates into mere ceremony, and one can sense the difference quite easily at an emotional level. Civil pageantry, for example, is ceremonial; it is about protocol rather than about connection to the sacred. A military parade for a visiting head of state is a ceremony that indicates respect for and good relations with another country. Ceremonies are mostly for the sake of appearances and tradition—no one is trying to invoke spiritual powers. When the Queen of England opens Parliament ceremonially, for example, no transformation takes place; no new insight is arrived at. Like all ceremonies, the official opening of Parliament serves to maintain the existing social order. Religious ritual may degenerate into mere ceremony; we may, for example, take part in a Passover Seder or attend a Church wedding without feeling that we are in the presence of the sacred. We are then simply relating to the event on a social or practical level. Rituals are spiritually empty when we participate in them without any meaningful connection to the values they express, or when we approach them without drawing upon the unconscious or the archetypal energies involved. For example, during peacetime, we may see the flag being ceremonially raised and lowered and not be especially moved by it, but during a war, with all its archetypal overtones, the sight of the flag may affect us profoundly.

The human tendency to create rituals reflects our instinct to invest events and objects with sacred significance. Not surprisingly, then, even though religious ritual has been almost done away with in Western Protestant and secular culture, it is still found in Catholicism, Judaism, and the Greek and Russian Orthodox traditions, as well as in all pre technological societies. Some psychologists believe that the rituals of pre-industrial societies grow out of the closeness that these societies have to nature. Far from looking down on these societies as "primitive," we must thank them for preserving ritual practices that are only now beginning to be appreciated by Western culture.[26] The West lost its connection to ritual when the Protestant Reformation, and later, Enlightenment thinking in general, diminished the importance of ritual on the grounds that it was pagan and not in keeping with Christian beliefs or with reason. According to this view, ritual is antiquated and springs merely from superstitions— after all, the rationalist would argue, we cannot prove conclusively that ritual has any real effect on our daily lives. The rationalist does not believe, for example, that a rain dance actually causes rain to fall. This literalistic interpretation of ritual, however, does not take into account ritual's psychological and spiritual effects on the participants.

In traditional cultures, only an initiated person may act as the elder who leads a ritual, because only after our own initiation do we become conscious of our transpersonal nature, of our connection to the Self. It takes a ritual elder to locate and consecrate a sacred place and to create the essential boundaries for it to be preserved. Only those who understand the powers that are involved are able to guide the group in the performance of the ritual. They are the culture's medicine men, priests, or shamans. The shadow side of this system is that it sets up a split between the priesthood and the laity, between the experts (those who have special knowledge) and ordinary people (those who do not). There is a constant danger that, in an effort to maintain their hold on religious power, those who know will exploit the ignorance of those who do not.

There are many types of rituals, each with its own purpose: to bring about healing, to greet or bid farewell, or to mark important transitions, such as the change of the seasons. Bereavement rituals, for example, such as a wake, or the Jewish seven days of ritual mourning, are intended to provide a means for the expression of grief. Pre-industrial societies use rituals of initiation whenever there is going to be a transition from one social status to another, for example, when a boy is about to achieve the status of a man, or a girl a woman. In such societies, one does not simply become a man or woman by default. A ritual is necessary to activate this process.

RITES OF PASSAGE

Rites of passage, such as those marking birth, death, or marriage, facilitate safe transition from one state to another. The Flemish anthropologist Arnold van Gennep identified the common elements, that is, the archetypal form, that underlies many types of rites of passage, not only in tribal cultures but also in Roman, Greek, Near Eastern, Hebraic, and Islamic rituals.[27] All such rites occur in three stages. First, the initiate is separated from his or her normal life in society. Then the person enters a "liminal" or threshold phase, which puts him or her into a marginal state, in which he or she has neither the new status nor the old one. Jesus' 40-day fast in the desert represents such a liminal state. Finally, the initiate is re-incorporated into society in the new social position, and normal life begins again. This three-part sequence is found in every rite of passage, whether it relates to inducting a person into the priesthood, conducting a funeral, or initiating a young person into adulthood.

During the ritual process, the transitional or liminal period of the ritual is particularly important. At this time, the usual social hierarchies and roles are dissolved, so that human relationships take on a particular quality of social equality, which the anthropologist Victor Turner has called *communitas*.[28] This is a state of mind in which there is a sense of a common humanity, a deep feeling of oneness that unites all of the participants in the initiation, without the hierarchical differences that are usually found among people. In our culture, *communitas* is found mostly among chronically marginalized people, who make contact with others like themselves outside the bounds of the normal social structures. *Communitas* may break out during a communal crisis such as an earthquake, or for the duration of events such as the Olympics or the Super Bowl, which have the character of a mass ritual.

The rituals of tribal societies are brutal by our standards.[29] Sometimes the novices die in the process. Boys' initiation rites typically involve ordeals such as circumcision, beatings, terrorization by elders dressed as demons, sleep deprivation, symbolic death and rebirth, and dietary restrictions. A Southern African tribe initiates boys into manhood with circumcision after an initial rite of separation from their mothers in which the boys must jump over a fire. After the operation, they are marginalized by being segregated in a special hut until the wounds heal. During this liminal period they learn tribal songs and wear special clothes. This transmission is an important part of the rite, for it typically passes on the sacred knowledge that is the foundation of the culture. Eventually the boys are returned to the village in stages. Upon their return, their mothers are not allowed to touch them until they emerge in their new social status and assume their full social role as adult males. During this process, the boy learns secrets of the tribal mythology. In its positive aspects, from the ordeal there emerges a man who knows about courage and self-denial in the face of danger, but who has also mastered these strengths and can now apply them for the greater good of the community, a man who knows how to relate to other people and how to work harmoniously as part of a group.

Early anthropologists and students of comparative religion assumed that the purpose of such rituals was to produce a spiritual rebirth. Contemporary scholars are skeptical of this interpretation,[30] suggesting instead that ritual symbolizes a social transformation that has already occurred. In the example just given, boys have been preparing themselves for adulthood throughout their childhood, and the ritual is only the final step to ensure that the transformation has been complete. In this view, the ritual is mainly about connection to society rather than to the divine. The ritual is actually a social enactment of a process of maturation that has occurred naturally. Its purpose is to ensure that members of the society conform to social expectations. The frightening aspects of the ritual are a form of indoctrination that shocks the initiate into compliance with social norms. The ritual artificially simulates contact with the numinosum as a way of maintaining social cohesion, which is why tribal cultures were able to remain unchanged for thousands of years. The problem with such initiation rites is that they narrowly define what it means to be a man. They make no allowances for people who may be temperamentally different or too physically handicapped to participate in or survive the rigors of the ritual. These individuals are marginalized, and the status quo is never questioned.

Women's rites too can be painful and dangerous. Among the traditional Nootka people of Vancouver Island, B.C., the rite of passage of girls into womanhood involved their being taken far out into the ocean and left to swim to shore. Prayer, chanting, and support from the tribal elders surrounded the event. This act of courage was said to transform the girl into a woman by means of a symbolic rebirth from the water. After successfully completing the test, she was eligible to marry and have children in the clear knowledge of who she is.[31] Other initiation rites for girls involve scarification of the body, a process in which symbols of the tribe's mythology are carved into the girl's flesh.[32] Because the body has been permanently altered, the initiate realizes that she is no longer a child. The Dyaks of Borneo isolate young girls for a year in white cabins, dressed only in white and eating only white food. Among some groups, such as the Apache, passage into womanhood is celebrated with a long period of feasting, singing, drumming, and dancing. During these initiations, the young woman is instructed in tribal beliefs about menstruation, sexuality, pregnancy, and birth. For the girls, these beliefs are shrouded in mystery until initiation. Rituals such as rites of passage therefore mediate between the demands of society for stability and the demands of nature for biological rhythm and change.

The young person has to prove his or her ability to withstand fear and pain, and this demonstration bonds the person to his or her peers and facilitates the formation of an adult identity. Overall, such ritual is used to connect people to each other and to the cosmos, to express the mythology of the tribe, and to propagate the knowledge that the tribe needs for its continuance. In those cultures where coming to adulthood is thought to coincide with entering into spiritual maturity, the rituals may also initiate the young into the mysteries of safe contact with the invisible powers. The person then has a clearly defined position in society, and this serves to bind the individual and the group into a cohesive unit. In some cultures, these rituals also give the initiate access to the sacred symbols of the culture, because initiation into adulthood entitles him or her to be told the sacred stories and secrets of the tribe, such as the names of the secret gods. The rites enable the individual to move into the new status supported and acknowledged by his or her society. The initiate is made radically conscious of his or her new status and is given a place in an ordered cosmos, along with all the attendant responsibilities. Initiation ceremonies are therefore the guardians of traditional ways of doing things. Such rituals are felt to be divinely sanctioned, but a skeptical view of these rites of passage suggests that this feeling, induced in the young by the elders of the tribe to ensure compliance, is a misappropriation of the divine for social purposes. Rites of passage also suffer from the drawback of preventing the individual searching for identity in his or her own way. By maintaining the status quo they prevent social renewal.

Because of its capacity to arouse extremely powerful emotions, contact with the numinosum can be dangerous, and ritual actions must therefore be undertaken with proper regard for their sacred nature. Following a ritual procedure ensures that the archetype will enter consciousness in a contained manner, without overwhelming it. Ritual then acts as a kind of valve that regulates how much of the unconscious is allowed to enter consciousness. This regulation is necessary for the protection for the ego, which might otherwise feel swept away by the power of the unconscious.

Erich Neumann, a student and colleague of Jung's, suggested that ritual acts like an irrigation system that allows the unconscious to flow into the personality in a controlled manner.[33] The ritual both irrigates and at the same time prevents flooding. When the unconscious enters consciousness in the right amounts, we experience a spurt of creativity, but pathology results when the unconscious floods consciousness. The danger of flooding is seen in obsessive compulsive neurosis. The sufferer feels an overwhelming internal pressure to carry out a certain ritual behavior such as repeated hand-washing or counting, or feels compelled to ruminate constantly on a painful thought. The sufferer knows that his or her ritual is irrational and not necessary from a commonsense point of view, but he or she cannot stop doing it. The actions that the obsessive compulsive person feels driven to carry out are like private rituals that have to be done properly or else tremendous anxiety results. In traditional psychoanalytic thought, obsessive compulsive disorder is thought to be caused by a combination of unconscious problems such as conflict and guilt about aggression and sexuality, the tension between compliance and rebellion against authority, and a very harsh internal critic. The obsessional ritual prevents this material from flooding consciousness and binds the anxiety that would otherwise be generated.

Freud noted that the rituals of this disabling illness represent a caricature of a private religion, and that, conversely, religious rituals are required to be carried out with obsessional attention to correctness. Accordingly, neurosis is a form of individual religiosity and "religion [is] a universal obsessive neurosis."[34] Without actually equating neurosis and religion, Freud pointed out that obsessional neurosis is the "pathological counterpart of the formation of religion."[35] However, although Freud pointed out the similarities between the two types of ritual, he did not dwell on their differences. The person in the grip of a powerful obsession has no control over his or her ritualistic behavior—it is a compulsion that he or she must obey, or else face unbearable anxiety; on the other hand, those who engage in religious ritual do so by choice, in a conscious attempt to make contact with the numinous level of the unconscious. The Jungian view understands obsessional or pathological ritual in terms of the presence of a powerful complex in the psyche, in which a particular unconscious archetypal image dominates. This archetypal element determines the content of the compulsive behavior. For example, the psychoanalyst Karl Abraham,[36] a colleague of Freud's, described two women who were afraid that they were going to die during the night. Both had bedtime rituals in which they had to arrange their hair in a special way and be careful that their bedclothes and nightdress were as perfectly arranged as possible. One of the two women would repeatedly wake up after sleeping for a while and rearrange everything. She did all of this in case she died in her sleep; she did not want to be found in an untidy state. The other patient also observed a strict nighttime obsessional ceremony, which involved taking great care with her appearance in order to make herself look attractive. She also felt compelled to lie down with her arms folded across her chest, and forced herself to lie as still as possible. Because Abraham's patients associated these behaviors to sexuality, chastity, and marriage,[37] in their correspondence Freud and Abraham called this ritual the "bride of death ceremonial."

The archetypal element in these obsessional rituals is suggested by the fact that in many cultures death is likened to a marriage. Abraham's patients' private rituals are reminiscent of a ritual that was carried out in ancient Greece for young women who died without ever having been married.[38] Such a woman was considered to be the bride of death, and she was ritually identified with Persephone, the mythological maiden who was abducted and forced into the underworld by its ruler, Hades. An unmarried girl who died was thought to have been snatched away and forced to marry Hades, while an unmarried man who died was thought to have taken the earth as his bride. In some rural Greek communities, the same songs are sung at both weddings and funerals, even today. In rural Romania, when a young woman dies unmarried, a "bride of death" ritual is still performed, in the belief that an unfulfilled soul can cause trouble for the living. The young woman, dressed in full wedding regalia, is given a symbolic wedding at her funeral in order to satisfy her soul. We cannot know whether Abraham's two female patients were familiar with the funerary customs of ancient Greece, perhaps from a study of Greek tragedy, where marriage to death was a frequent theme. But the compulsive nature of their behavior would suggest that they were possessed by demands from the unconscious—the demand, for example, to die to their current lives and connect with the realm of the soul. Instead of experiencing consciously the need for radical transformation in their lives, they concretely and compulsively enacted literal death.

RITUAL AND PSYCHOTHERAPY

For centuries, shamans and healers of all types have used rituals to bring about wholeness, so it is not surprising that there are parallels between traditional ritual practices and the techniques of modern psychotherapy. In both cases, strong belief in the underlying mythology (read theoretical orientation) and faith in the practitioner and the process help to increase the ritual's effectiveness.

Because psychotherapy, by its very nature, invokes archetypal forces that may need to be contained, psychotherapy includes subtle elements of ritual. The release of these forces results from the stimulation of the transference and various complexes within the therapeutic relationship.

The presence of a healing intention and the therapeutic setting of the relationship also stimulate archetypal energies. The Jungian analyst Robert Moore[39] has described some of the similarities between psychotherapy and ritual process, even when the participants do not think about what they are doing in these terms. At the same time, ritual and psychotherapy have important differences: ritual in general tries to control change for the benefit of the society, in predetermined ways, while psychotherapy tries to facilitate change for the benefit of the individual in ways that are highly personal.

One of the common features in all healing rituals is the arousal of intense emotion while new ideas are being introduced. This combination of factors is often present during psychotherapy. During a ritual process, the intense emotion is induced artificially by the ceremony and will eventually subside naturally. However, people in psychotherapy are often suffering from powerful feelings that arise spontaneously and need therapeutic containment because they otherwise may never subside. The psychotherapist tries to explain and understand these feelings, which are gradually worked through therapeutically. In these ways, for people undergoing major life transitions, the psychotherapist can provide the type of ritual guidance that is lacking in our culture. These transitions may be difficult to negotiate without help, which is why psychotherapy may be useful, since our Western culture generally expects individuals to make such transitions unaided by socially instituted means.

Often, a psychological crisis is at the same time a spiritual crisis, and psychotherapy provides a space and time that can be sacred if it is approached in the correct spirit. By means of the regularity and structure of the work, its "frame," the therapist provides the necessary boundary conditions, or a safe container, for transformation or initiation into a new status. Psychotherapy provides the experience of *communitas* in a setting where the usual hierarchies do not apply, where the participants can behave in ways that would not be allowed in the everyday world of normal society. *Communitas* is especially likely to be experienced in the setting of group therapy, where a shared emotional state develops among a group of people going through the same kind of experience. By facilitating the undoing of old behaviors and the development of a radically new sense of self, psychotherapy provides a safe opportunity for enactment, containment, and understanding. Psychotherapy thereby fulfills some of the same psychological functions as ritual once did, but it does so at the level of the individual rather than the collective. Although psychotherapy has its own dangers, its focus on the individual avoids some of the dangers of traditional ritual. In contrast to traditional ritual, psychotherapy does not try to maintain the status quo; it facilitates the client's attempt to change in his or her unique way, in the context of our expanding human consciousness.

The therapist may facilitate the adoption of private rituals, if such a need emerges spontaneously. The ritual must be compatible with the client's worldview and belief system, and can be as creative as the client wishes. For example, a woman is having difficulty letting go of her recently deceased husband. She is angry with him, and too many things have been left unsaid. She writes a letter to him that says everything she feels. The letter is then ritually and prayerfully burned, and the ashes scattered on a river as a symbolic farewell. The healing value of such a personally constructed therapeutic ritual can be enhanced by a therapist who understands the basic nature of ritual and is able to locate the personal ritual in its larger spiritual and psychological context for the client.

Psychotherapeutic ritual, or symbolic enactment, must be carried out with a high degree of awareness and attention to detail, and must involve some kind of behavior that is outside the normal routine. Various elements of traditional practice may be felt to be necessary. Sometimes a ritual "purification" ceremony is used; this may involve simply washing the hands or bathing before the ritual is performed, or it may extend to wearing special clothes or fasting. A statement of intention is also sometimes made in order to focus attention on the purpose of the ritual. The ritual may make use of dream imagery, a personal altar, art work, movement, or dialogue with inner figures. An object that has special meaning, such as a ring or photograph, may form the centerpiece of the ritual. The person performing the ritual may call upon a guiding figure of some sort, an unseen power, a numinous figure from a dream, or simply the Self. To end the ceremony, a ritual of closure is needed; this must involve specific symbolic gestures, expressions of thanks, and a return to everyday reality.

Finally, it is important to remember that ritual is not always used for the good, and the psychological effects of ritual are not necessarily all benign, since ritual may encourage regressive behavior. Traditional ritual may prevent people dealing with archetypal forces in an individual manner and discourage newer forms of spirituality. Ritual can also be used with the intention to harm to others, as it is in black magic. The Nazis used ritualistic elements to great advantage at their huge rallies, where the sights and sounds had a hypnotic effect on the crowds. Another danger is that while ritual can contribute to social stability, it can also lead to social disintegration and other harmful effects, as was the case with the rituals of human sacrifice among the Aztecs and Maya. During the Middle Ages, the rituals of bonding, homage, and fealty by which a vassal swore allegiance to and became a member of the feudal lord's family propped up feudalism for almost a thousand years. These rituals kept Europe in relative stagnation until the Renaissance came along and broke through the barrier that was blocking advancement with its new ideas of humanism and the dignity of all individuals. Analogously, new forms of spirituality are born of struggle and change, not simply preservation of the past. Established religions try to maintain stability and seek to impose it by maintaining a closed system of rituals, whereas true spirituality thrives on instability, recognizing that the universe is in a state of constant flux. Thus, spirituality is in harmony with nature, while established religion tends to work against it. When ritual imposes uniformity and resistance to change, it serves the interests of established religion rather than individual spirituality.

SPONTANEOUS INITIATION IN ADOLESCENCE

Some archetypal processes have hardly any acceptable cultural outlets, even though they persist in the psyche. The archetype of initiation is one such pattern that is neglected in our culture, with the result that it has to operate unconsciously, and this often causes trouble. We have seen that rites of passage are needed whenever we reach a point in our life when we must move on into a new stage, or else remain stuck and even regress to an earlier stage. Here it is important not to confuse the content of the ritual (which varies with the culture) with the underlying archetypal potential for initiation into a new status (which can be achieved in many different ways). As with all other archetypal processes, each tradition colors and gives content to this potential in its own way, so that a Bar Mitzvah has a different content from a First Communion, even though both are archetypal expressions of initiation into a new religious status. Apart from the formalized initiations into adulthood of traditional religions, such as Confirmation and Bar Mitzvah or Bat Mitzvah, there are several informal social initiatory experiences that mark a young person's passage into adulthood in Western society: having one's first sexual experience ("losing one's virginity"), getting a driving license, leaving home to live on one's own, "coming out" at a debutante ball, undergoing a hazing, and voting for the first time. But these experiences are generally relatively superficial and they are not necessarily transformative. Most of them do not have the spiritual intensity of the rites of passage of tribal cultures—they are not numinous. Our culture ensures social compliance by means other than the induction of emotionally powerful initiation ceremonies. We socialize children during a long period of education, and we have many social rewards, punishments, and legal restrictions for maintaining social cohesiveness. Because our world is constructed so differently from that of tribal peoples, highly ritualized tribal-style initiations would be out of place in our society. For many of us, transitions into different phases of life are made gracefully, and happen naturally, although it is well known that the move into a new developmental period, such as adolescence, can predispose one to emotional instability.

In the absence of socially sanctioned forms for its expression, the archetypal need for initiation does not simply go away, but instead finds its own outlet, sometimes without ritual. The unusual or unconventional behavior that can be seen among adolescents in the West may represent the spontaneous emergence of this archetypal process in an unconscious form. Puberty, the transition from childhood to young adulthood, is a time when initiation is helpful, since the change is a particularly dramatic one. Because the psyche has innate archetypal patterns built into it, the behavior of adolescents in Western cultures, which have no formal rites of passage, can serve the same purpose as the initiatory practices of tribal cultures. Adolescents in industrialized societies behave in ways that may seem inexplicable until one realizes that these young people are unconsciously trying to initiate themselves into adulthood. In the absence of any socially organized, pre-packaged form of initiation, the archetype expresses itself spontaneously, but in our society it does so in an individual manner without any formal ceremony.

Some form of symbolic death, or the risk of actual death, occurs in many traditional rites of passage. Among adolescent boys today, the search for an initiatory experience is seen in the pursuit of activities that require some sort of physical ordeal, often to prove worthiness to their peers or to adults around them. Such activities usually require a combination of bravery, strength, and agility in the boy, and involve an element of danger. To this end, the adolescent takes on a dare or challenge, which may be dangerous, and if the process goes awry actual death may occur. It may not be a coincidence that some adolescents seek out body piercing or other bodily modifications, inspired by the fact that these are common features of traditional tribal rituals for initiation into adulthood. However, whereas adolescents in tribal cultures have little opportunity to rebel against the established ways of doing things, our teenagers are constantly pushing for more freedom. They resist both the imposition of traditional ways of doing things and values that they consider unacceptable. That is, by seeking initiation in their own ways, our adolescents reject the type of pressures that would have forced them into conformity within tribal cultures. This leads to a "trial and error" approach to initiation that may be different for each adolescent, but one that seems to work most of the time in our culture.

It is of interest that a Church of Body Modification now exists,[40] which teaches that spirituality can be expressed "through what we do to our bodies." That is, instead of being part of an initiatory rite that happens once in a life time, body modification has itself become a religion, thus taking on an entirely new significance. Practitioners continue to modify their bodies in stages, throughout their lives. Those who tattoo themselves continue to do so for many years, until the body is fully covered—tattooing becomes a way of life. Unlike the way in which ritual was used in tribal cultures, the ritual has then become the religion itself—an idolatrous use of ritual.

This behavior illustrates some of the ways that a religion may act as a container for emotional difficulties. Clinicians find that constant body modification has a variety of psychological underpinnings. Some people who frequently pierce themselves are dissociated when they do so—they are in an altered state of consciousness, a self-induced trance state, and not fully aware of their bodies. Some are so disconnected from their bodies that they view the body merely as a piece of art work. Other frequent body modifiers are masochistic, and develop an intense relationship with the person who carries out the tattooing or piercing. Some pierce or tattoo themselves in order to belong, as part of a "twinship" transference to their peers—the need to feel the same as others, or to feel accepted by them.

Some adolescents act in this way to defend against depression, while others do so to cope with painful feelings of numbness or emptiness. One young woman who frequently burns herself with cigarettes has flowers tattooed around the burn, in order to "transform pain into beauty." In other words, even when body modification is described in spiritual terms, it also serves various unconscious psychological ends, which is why people who carry out constant body modification cannot give a conscious explanation for their behavior.

It is well established that a lifelong spiritual search often begins in adolescence[41] and sometimes results in adolescents' attraction to cults, which are often destructive.[42] Many reasons have been suggested for this phenomenon, such as the adolescent need to rebel, the need to find a pack to travel with, to be devoted to a cause, to find an identity, to find a substitute family, and to find direction and purpose. An additional possibility is that the archetypal search for initiation becomes active at that developmental period.[43]

Any numinous experience, any contact with the sacred, is potentially powerful enough to perform the function of initiating the individual into a new level of consciousness and moving him or her into a new status. In a sense, then, all contact with the numinosum produces an initiation. In the absence of initiation by the culture, the Self may take the lead in initiating the person by means of a numinous experience, either positive or negative. For example, a young man, in a painful quandary about the direction his life should take, had the following dream, which he described as "unbelievably clear":

> I'm sitting on a hillside overlooking the ocean, under a big tree. It's night; I look up, and the stars move to form a message in a script and a language I do not understand. As they move, a voice, which seems to come from every direction, says: "You are blessed to have this choice. You have the opportunity to be of service to other people." The voice also speaks an unknown language but the odd thing is that I understand it with no difficulty. The sense is that the stars and the voice say the same thing, which is that I have the opportunity to do a great deal of good if I pick a career that allows service to others.

This experience left him with a sense of clarity about his life. He went into training in a helping profession, at which he is now very successful. The dream is an example of an initiatory experience coming from the Self,

73

from the level of the autonomous psyche. Because this young man was in a state of turmoil over the transition he was required to make, with no direction from the outside, this archetype became activated. Again we see the theme of numinous experience providing specific help with an emotional problem. Any form of suffering, either due to a difficult life situation, mental or physical illness, or generated in the crucible of relationships, tends to facilitate the experience of initiation and may produce the necessary radical change of consciousness.

IS GOD SYNONYMOUS WITH PSYCHE? THE "NEW DISPENSATION"

In view of this kind of experience, which we now approach psychologically rather than theologically, Edward Edinger[44] suggested that we are entering an historical period characterized by a new religious dispensation. We now experience divine grace entering the world in a new manner. In contrast to the dispensation inaugurated at Mt. Sinai, in which the law was handed down cast in stone, or the Christian dispensation, which requires a redeemer, our felt sense today is that there is a dialogue emerging between human consciousness and a larger Consciousness. Numinous experiences seem to emerge from a transpersonal level of consciousness, although it is possible that such experiences arise from a level of divinity that is *beyond* the psyche, in which case the psyche is simply the agent of transmission. But these conceptual problems are not relevant to our focus on experience. The idea of something "beyond" the psyche may not be meaningful to us, since we are contained within psychological reality, and it is impossible for us to imagine what might be beyond the psyche. Our ego-oriented spatial and temporal distinctions would not apply in that realm. It is therefore impossible to know to what extent "God" and the transpersonal psyche are in fact synonymous. What matters is our felt sense that we are dealing with a greater Intelligence than our own, which manifests itself to us in the form of numinous experiences. The rest is speculation, or a matter of faith.

What is important to the psychological approach is that the way we experience the numinosum, and the content of the experience, is closely related to our personality and our emotional difficulties. It is to these matters that we now turn.

CHAPTER THREE

Personality, Psychopathology, and Personal Spirituality

INTRODUCTION

The type of spirituality to which we are drawn is not a matter of chance, since we are born with a particular spiritual constitution that radically affects our spiritual orientation. Although we all have some spiritual concerns in common, other aspects of our spirituality are as individual as our personality. Our spiritual constitution, which is the same as our archetypal constitution, is as unique as our biology and its genetic make up. In fact, the archetypes and the genes fulfill analogous functions. The way we are constituted predisposes us to respond to the world in particular ways.[1] Physically, we respond according to our genetic make-up; psychologically, we organize and respond to what happens to us through archetypal processes. It is as if the body and the psyche act as refracting lenses for the light that comes from our spiritual Source, which enters the world of time and space by means of archetypal patterns and bodily behavior, some of which we regard as pathological. As a result, even though Ultimate Reality is a unity, each human being expresses that Reality in a unique way, rather in the way that snowflakes are all made up of frozen water droplets, but each one appears in its own unique shape.

Standard psychology textbooks tell us that our personality is formed gradually through childhood, as our genetic constitution interacts with the environment.[2] However, I believe that this model is incomplete. Many depth psychologists with a Jungian orientation believe that a spiritual blueprint, an archetypal ground plan, also contributes to the formation of our sense of self. The set of talents, abilities, and liabilities with which we are born are influenced both by genetic and archetypal components. A good example is Mozart's gift for music, which was an archetypal potential that showed itself early in his life. Mozart's father exerted tremendous pressure on his son Wolfgang,[3] but in the absence of an archetypal genius for music this environmental contribution to his musical ability would not have had the same effect. There are many such archetypal qualities within the personality. We may be more or less studious, religious, communicative, loving, aggressive, esthetically oriented, and so on. These abilities are both genetically and archetypally determined: that is, they have a basis in our biology and they are also expressions of our spiritual life.[4] The archetypal level of our being is a dimension of our spiritual Source, and so is "outside" of time and space in the ordinary sense of these words. It is therefore not a part of the developmental model of human growth, yet paradoxically participates within it.

Just as the body has organs that carry out various functions, so the psyche's archetypal processes behave like "organs" within consciousness. Just as our bodies reflect infinite variations on the same general plan from one individual to the next, so too our individual archetypal potentials express themselves with different intensities and combinations, and in particular directions. For example, we all have the capacity to communicate, and we can all be aggressive. If these two archetypal potentials are linked, a person will speak vigorously and assertively, but if these potentials have little connection to each other the individual's speech will tend to be dull and flat. If one's passion is linked to creativity and an appreciation of beauty, given the necessary talent and ambition one may become an artist, but if one's passion is instead linked to a strong desire for justice, one may employ one's passion in the fight for one's ideals.[5] Throughout the life cycle, our unique combinations of archetypal potentials increasingly express themselves in our behavior. As they become part of our activity in the world, they move from being purely spiritual potentials to being concretely realized in time and space. This means that throughout our life cycle, we continuously incarnate spirit. Therefore, it is true to say that our personalities are organized spiritually, since the archetypes are so important to the way we are organized. As our archetypal potentials incarnate, we become more and more conscious of the deeper levels of our identity. Bear in mind that the deepest level of our nature has no form or content and shades into the Absolute, being a part of it. Consequently, our nature cannot be fully explained in terms of development, since development implies time and space, and the Absolute cannot be limited to these categories. Although our ego and the personal contents of the unconscious develop within time and in space, in response to family and culture, some aspects of the personality just seem to rise or fall away for no obvious reason.

ARCHETYPES AND COMPLEXES

Starting with Freud, all depth-psychological theories have tried to describe the ways in which our early experiences with caregivers affect our development and our sense of who we are. The way we think about ourselves is shaped largely by our early relationships and by what people said about us in childhood. We store memories of our interactions with parents and siblings not only in our minds, but also in our bodies, as patterns of tension in our muscles. Our experience of these childhood interactions may have been positive or negative, so our memories of them are always emotionally colored, whether pleasantly or painfully. Memories, thoughts, and images from childhood, and the emotions that belong to them, are grouped together into what Jung called complexes. For example, we speak colloquially about an "inferiority complex," meaning the sense of inadequacy that we feel in comparison to others, or we speak of the Oedipus complex, meaning the attraction that a child may have for the parent of the opposite sex. In fact, there are many possible complexes, which may be conscious or unconscious to varying degrees.

Our complexes are formed in childhood, but they heavily color our adult relationships, because we tend to view life through the lens of our complexes. If one's father was negative or abusive, for instance, one may experience all older men or authority figures as difficult and demanding. If a child is devalued, shamed, unloved, or discounted by his or her parents, the child develops negative complexes, which then produce emotional difficulties such as low self-esteem, self-hatred, or depression. Because these themes are universal human experiences, one finds them depicted universally in world literature. For example, all cultures have fairy tales about enchantment by a wicked witch or sorcerer, who turns a prince into a frog; the "enchantment" actually results from a negative mother or father complex. These "prince-turned-frog" stories are traditional ways of depicting the effects of serious devaluation in childhood; the person feels that he or she is worthless, irrespective of his or her actual value, for reasons that he or she may not be able to understand or articulate. Actually, the "evil spell" is in the unconscious. It is as if the accusing parent lives on inside the child's mind, criticizing and demeaning the child from within, in the form of a mother or father complex that says, "You are no good." As a result, as Jung[6] puts it, it becomes impossible to affirm "the whole of one's nature." These and other developmental factors, which are well described by psychoanalytic theory, are, however, only part of the story. They help us understand the human level of the complex, which is determined by painful or traumatic experiences with one's parents and the culture at large. In addition, the human level of development is gathered around an archetypal core (Fig. 1).

The archetype acts like a kind of magnetic file folder, into which are gathered all the experiences that relate to it. For example, all human beings have the experience of being mothered, and everything that goes into mothering constitutes the Mother archetype. Thus, from the time we are born, all our experiences of being cared for and nourished, whether by our actual mother or a mother substitute, gravitate around the Mother archetype. Over time, the child has more and more experiences with mothering figures, and this leads to an accumulation in the mind of images, ideas, memories, fantasies, and, most importantly, emotions that have to do with "mother." All these human experiences are inextricably intertwined with this archetypal core. In psychological shorthand, the result is called a "mother complex." The emotional coloring of a complex feels positive when we had good parenting, or it feels painfully negative if we were abused or rejected by a parent, or if a parent was overly intrusive or impinging on the child. Importantly, the suffering produced by such a complex contains a numinous, transpersonal element at its center, which is not the result of developmental factors. (I do not think the origin of this level can be explained; here we can only invoke notions of "destiny" or what James Hillman[7] refers to as "the soul's code.")

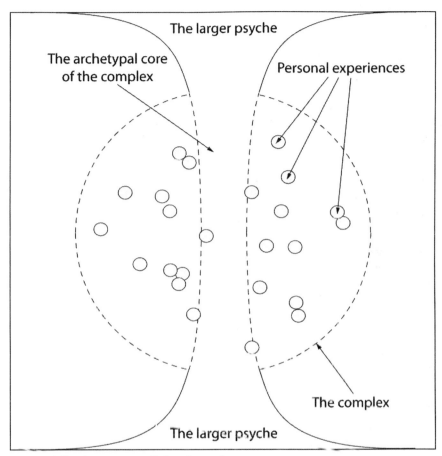

Fig. 1: The Structure of the Complex

The archetype at the center of the complex provides the *potential* to experience mothering or fathering; the family and local culture determine the manner in which these roles are carried out. Thus, the *content* of the archetype, the way it expresses itself, may vary tremendously. In any society, mothers and fathers are expected to fulfill a particular role, so that one's cultural conditioning determines the way in which the archetype is actually experienced. As a result, in traditional societies, a positive mother complex makes it possible for us to give to others and to ourselves what we need to grow, to feel safe and cared for. Similarly, a complex forms around the archetypal Father, which may also have a positive or negative emotional tone. For example, traditionally the role of the father was that of breadwinner, transmitter of the voice of cultural authority, disciplinarian, and so on. Having a positive father complex would make one competent to be a mentor and guide to others. Fortunately, these stereotypical roles are changing, so that today there is no reason why men and woman cannot fill each other's traditional roles.

Because the archetype has a numinous emotional charge, when we are children our parents seem especially awe-inspiring. To the small child, the parents actually evoke the power of the archetypal Mother or Father, which is partly why being a parent carries so much weight. As we mature, we see our parents in a much more human light, and we are less prone to confuse their attitudes with our ways of thinking about the divine. However, as I discuss further below, in some personalities the influence of parental projections onto a God-image is still heard. Thus, religious fundamentalists, who do not think of the divine in metaphorical or symbolic ways, occasionally insist that natural disasters are the result of divine punishment because God is literally "angry" in the way that a parent would be when a child is disobedient.[8]

COMPLEXES IN OUR RELATIONSHIPS

Because the complex has an archetypal core—that is, it is partly spiritually determined—work on our complexes must have a spiritual dimension. This work is necessary because negative complexes not only make us feel that we are bad, but they also radically affect our relationships. A complex acts like an unconscious template in the mind, imprinting upon our current relationships the pattern of early ones. Consequently, we often repeat patterns established in childhood, as, for instance, when we marry someone with a personality similar to that of a parent with whom we had a difficult relationship as we were growing up. A complex is in operation, for example, when a person whose parent was an alcoholic when he or she was growing up marries a series of alcoholics in succession, not consciously registering in each case that the spouse-to-be has a drinking problem. Under the unconscious power of the complex, an individual may feel drawn to only a certain type of person, considering only that type to be interesting and sexually attractive. In fact, the complex makes us look for someone who will allow us to behave in particular, automatic ways. We then go from one troubled relationship to another. A person who had an abusive parent might be drawn to a partner who is abusive in a similar way, unconsciously producing a replication of the childhood situation. We may induce our partner to behave like our difficult parent, or we may simply experience the partner in that way, whether or not that perception is justified. For example, a man whose mother was domineering and controlling may marry a woman who has those tendencies, or he may behave in a way that induces women to control him. He may find all women domineering, no matter what they are really like, because he sees them through the eyes of the complex. Similarly, a woman with a violent father might marry a man who mistreats her. Gripped by the father complex, she may bring out the worst in her husband, so that he does mistreat her, or she may experience him as abusive even when he does not intend to be. At other times, because we seek to be whole, we unconsciously look to a partner to supply those shadow aspects of ourselves that we cannot otherwise be in touch with, so that a person who is tightly controlled, obsessional, and austere is drawn into a relationship with a partner who is loose, playful, or even hysterical. Because they are unconscious, some parts of ourselves may be accessible only in the form of a relationship. Unconsciously but inevitably our outer and inner worlds reflect each other. According to Jung, we experience the unconscious not only as inner events such as dreams, but also as outer events and people with whom we become involved; who we are influences what happens to us, because we are driven by our complexes.

COMPLEXES AND OUR PREFERRED GOD-IMAGE

There is a close connection between our personality, our complexes, and our preferred form of spirituality. We are born with the archetypal potential to develop a God-image, and research has shown that the God-image that finally develops is powerfully affected by early experiences in our family of origin.[9] The child develops a subjective notion or mental representation of the divine that depends greatly on the type of parents the child experiences, on the religious practices of the family, and on the way the child sees his or her parents relate to each other. If parents are loving and protective, the child's image of God is likely to have these qualities. God is then imagined as offering comfort and soothing, a God-image that does not need change unless a life crisis demands that such an idealized image be re-evaluated. The development of basic trust in one's parents allows the development of trust in a loving God, while parents who inspire fear with threats of punishment contribute to a fearful God-image. All this develops in the first few years of life, so that the child already has a private God-image well before being exposed to formal religious education. When the child is introduced to the official God-image of a religious institution, the child must blend or reconcile this image with his or her private God-image. For example, a person with a very negative father complex might be drawn to—or react against—religious teachings that stress the austere, remote, punitive, angry aspects of divinity. This type of theology imagines the divine as a powerful, male sky-God with strict rules and regulations who is vengeful unless we are well-behaved. For a variety of reasons, a person who is initially drawn to such a theology may eventually revolt against his or her father complex and seek an entirely different God-image,[10] or a different religious tradition. This may happen when one stops projecting the characteristics of one's personal father onto one's God-image. It sometimes happens in the course of psychotherapy that prolonged exploration of one's relationship with one's father leads to a concomitant change in one's God-image. As the harshness of a father complex softens, the inner world changes accordingly, which allows one to be in the world in a different way, with a different attitude, and one's God-image changes accordingly. For example, early in her personal work, a woman with a very problematic father dreamed that:

> I had been severely cut into, and was lying in a hospital bed barely alive. Instead of being cared for, someone took me to a big open square, all stone with columned buildings all around. A large hook was placed into my back and I was suspended high above the square. I called out to God for help. At the end of a long road ahead of me was God—a huge old man, as big as a mountain, with white hair and beard. Instead of helping me, he began firing objects like softballs at me from a canon. I could not believe his cruelty; I was shattered by it.

Some years later, after much personal work on her father problem, she dreamed:

> I move into a new home in a charming area, homey and lovely in every way. In the house is a room with hundreds of sculptures of God-images from every known religious tradition, from all over the

82

world. The image that stood out to me and captured my heart immediately was a large, golden statue of the laughing Buddha sitting in the center of the room.

The dreamer's association to this figure was that he represents a spirituality of abundance, happiness, and open-heartedness, in contrast to the austerity of the tradition in which she was raised. In other words, not only might our God-image reflect the ways our parents actually behaved, at times we are drawn to particular God-images because we are searching for traits that were *not* present in our parents.

Ideally, as we mature, our God-image evolves, becoming less colored by parental projections and more universal. However, as John McDargh points out, even a sophisticated theologian "who had thought his notions of God had been properly and critically demythologized is amazed to discover in a moment of personal crisis that he was spontaneously evoking the God of his childhood bedtime prayer."[11] Apparently the emotional claim of our early God-image may remain dormant, in spite of the superimposition of later conceptual thought and intellectual development. Our relationship with this image remains very real and alive, although any life crisis provides the opportunity for a revision of one's God-image.

ARCHETYPES, COMPLEXES, AND OUR SPIRITUAL LIFE

Because the archetype carries out two simultaneous functions, our spirituality is closely bound to our psychological development. First, because the archetype is at the center of our complexes, the archetype is important in the overall structure of the psyche and affects our emotional health. At the same time, because of its numinosity, the archetype also affects our spiritual life. Consequently, our psychology and spirituality, the personal and the transpersonal, interpenetrate in the complex—here, psychology and spirituality become synonymous. Since the archetype is at the core of both our complexes and our numinous experiences, the same archetype may be at the root of our emotional suffering and also generate an authentic spiritual experience. Consequently, our spirituality is not an isolated process that can be relegated to weekend worship services. Neither can it be fully contained within a dogmatic system of thought. Our spirituality develops organically as we mature. Ideally this means that it contains less and less childhood residues.

There is often a direct connection between childhood experiences, our complexes, and our experience of the numinosum. For example, many of the children who are reported to have seen apparitions of the Virgin Mary (the Great Mother of the Western tradition) appear to have had a strongly developed mother complex. St. Bernadette, who saw the Virgin at Lourdes, France, in 1858, at the age of 14, was temporarily separated from her mother before the age of one, a severely traumatic event for any infant. Returning to the family at the age of two, she spent her later childhood taking care of her younger siblings. Because of her parents' extreme poverty, she was put to work, despite her childhood asthma, gathering firewood.[12] Since she was forced prematurely to work and look after the other children, it is very likely that she did not experience much mothering herself. Like Bernadette, the two children who saw the Virgin at La Salette, France, in 1846 also had extreme difficulties in their relationship with their mothers.[13] In 1917, at the age of 10, Lucia dos Santos saw the Virgin at Fatima. (In her case, we can infer the negative mother complex from Lucia's own retrospective account in her autobiography, published when she was much older, that her mother insisted that Lucia was a fake and was lying about the visions, and she abused the child frequently.) Lucia's visions were thought to be the work of the devil by some of her contemporaries, even though the nature of the vision was clear.[14] This illustrates the point that people who experience the numinosum are sometimes envied and attacked, and this is why they sometimes keep silent about their experience. (At other times, obviously, such individuals become celebrities. Even though the Catholic Church was initially cautiously skeptical about the visions of Bernadette, the public was eager to hear about them.)

The crucial point here, however, is that, although the Mother archetype played a large part in the lives of these children, their visionary experiences cannot be explained away as "only psychological," implying that they were not real. A materialistic or reductive explanation might suggest that the appearances of the Virgin were simply hallucinations, based on an intense need for a positive mother figure.[15] In fact, this particular manifestation of the divine correlates with the importance of the Mother archetype in these children's psychology, although the message that Mary gave the children was not particularly comforting or maternal.[16]

Our complexes influence the way in which the numinosum appears, but the presence of a powerful complex does not necessarily mean that a numinous experience is purely psychogenic and not an experience of the sacred. For the children of Lourdes, La Salette, and Fatima to understand what they were seeing, the visions had to be recognizable, so for them the Mother archetype had to appear in the form of the Virgin Mary. If the archetype had assumed a more abstract form, or an image from a different religious tradition—something entirely possible[17]—it might have been experienced as meaningless.

SPIRITUALITY AND PERSONALITY IN ST. FRANCIS OF ASSISI AND ST. PAUL[18]

The confluence of the psychological and the spiritual helps to explain why numinous experiences, and our preferred spiritual path, are so often related to personality factors and emotional conflict. In his youth, St. Francis of Assisi was rather spoiled and self-absorbed. He was the extravagant, vain, free-spending son of a wealthy merchant, who was very ambitious for him. Francis's parents treated him as if he were very special and destined for greatness, and this undoubtedly produced a core sense of his own importance. In his early 20s, Francis went through a painful period of reorganization of his values. He was taken prisoner while fighting in a local skirmish with a rival city, in which he experienced suffering that he had never seen before. He was kept locked up in a dungeon and released after a year, when he father was finally able to raise enough money to pay for his ransom. Two years later, he decided to pursue a military career in earnest. However, he found himself unable to continue, mainly on account of a numinous dream in which a voice told him that "it is better to choose the master than the servant," meaning that he should choose to serve God rather than a military commander. He turned around and headed back for home less than a day after he had set out. When Francis returned home he was made to feel that he had failed the socially accepted test of manhood of the time. Severely disillusioned and humiliated, he felt that he was a disappointment to his parents and the community. During a subsequent period of depression, he had a numinous visionary experience in which the figure of Christ on a crucifix said to him, "Go, Francis, and repair my house, which as you see is falling into ruin."

A radical change began. Whereas he had previously been an affluent dandy, Francis now became indifferent to his appearance and gave away money (much of it his father's) to the poor. Because of this, the townsfolk mocked him and his father was outraged. Their conflict was so severe that at one point his father resorted to chaining him in a dark closet in their house. Finally, Francis disavowed his father in public with the words: "Hitherto I have called you my father on earth; henceforth I desire to say only, 'Our Father who art in Heaven,'" thus renouncing his inheritance and embracing a life that was the polar opposite of his first 24 years. In the years that followed, he preached and lived a life of total poverty and asceticism, with no earthly possessions besides one coarse robe. He begged for his food and cared for lepers, whom he had previously found repulsive. Eventually, he founded a new religious order, thus achieving fame in a way that his father could never achieve, even with his wealth. Francis then had no need for military glory or social status. At the same time, by virtue of his ability to adhere to an extremely demanding way of life, he demonstrated great moral strength. In his childhood, Francis's parents had treated him lovingly, so he had a reservoir of love and self-esteem on which he could draw. A major part of his spirituality took the form of love for Christ and for suffering people, animals, and nature in general. However, in insisting upon an extremely ascetic way of life, which involved very little food, exposure to cold and minimal shelter, he expressed this love in a way that may appear harsh and painful to us today.

Francis had to use his spirituality to deal with several aspects of his emotional life. Some aspects of his spirituality seem to have developed in reaction to his father, while others seem to be a part of his innate or archetypal constitution. Sophie Jewett's biography of Francis, titled *God's Troubadour*,[19] records that as a child he loved to listen to stories of King Arthur and his knights, and dreamed of being a knight like Lancelot. He loved to sing songs of love and war, and throughout his life he composed and sang songs and poems. His father wanted Francis to be elevated to the nobility, and a military career offered this possibility. But such a life path did not really fit his temperament,[20] and he ultimately rejected it. He dealt with the problem of having to meet his father's expectations by radically renouncing his father's materialistic values. Indeed, his stress on poverty and self-denial would appear to be a reaction against his father's excessive materialism—perhaps even an overcompensation. He resisted his father's attempts to dominate him, and submitted instead to a heavenly father. In a public display of his break with his father, he went into the town square and stripped off the expensive clothes he was wearing (which had been paid for by his father)—a symbolic act by which he gave up all rights to the family inheritance. He also became indifferent to people's opinion of him, because he realized that wealth and military achievements were worthless from the point of view of his spirituality. He demonstrated a great deal of fortitude, but also perhaps a degree of self-doubt in that he wondered if he was pure enough for his heavenly father, even in the face of his complete self-denial and ascetic lifestyle. It is striking that he was able to care for animals and suffering people with great compassion, but he seems unable to have had compassion for himself, and especially for his badly abused body.

Given all this, however, no amount of psychological insight into the *origins* of his particular form of spirituality *invalidates* it. My intention is simply to show how his archetypal potentials, his personality traits, his development, and his emotional life interacted with each other.

While St. Francis struggled with, and reacted against, his father's materialistic approach to life, St. Paul struggled with his "lower," "carnal," or sinful nature—what he called "the flesh."[21] In his extensive writings we can find clear indications of his psychology and his personal God-image. He appears to have chosen celibacy as a personal spiritual path, and this preference was woven into his theology and spirituality in a way that profoundly influenced the development of Christianity. In fact, the systematic treatment of sin in Christian theology begins with St. Paul.

From his letters and the Book of Acts, we gather that Paul was a single-minded, zealous, passionate character. Before his conversion, Paul (then known as Saul) was a strict observer of Jewish law and, by his own account, "excelled his peers" in the Jewish faith (Gal. 1:14). His religious zeal for the "tradition of his fathers" expressed itself as intolerance of the followers of Christ, whom he persecuted "in a raging fury," (Acts 26:11) even dragging them off to prison (Acts 8:3). To our modern ears, his overly conscientious observance of the letter of the law comes across as rather compulsive. We now know that compulsive behavior often springs from uncontrollable anxiety, which religious rituals can sometimes serve to contain. However, Paul's zeal for the Law may have sprung from another source. There are indications in his letters[22] that he may have harbored doubts about the Jewish faith from the very beginning on account of his temperament and personality type,[23] doubts that he was not free to express and therefore was forced to repress. His conscientious observance may well have been a compensation for the unconscious feelings of guilt he might well have experienced over questioning the tradition of his fathers. This would also account for his persecution of the early Christians; in attacking them he was attacking the disowned part of himself (his positive shadow) that they represented, the part of himself that identified with them, the part that secretly rebelled against the established tradition. His conversion, following his spectacular experience on the road to Damascus, was a tremendous release, for he could now stop pretending to believe in the meaningless rituals he had once so faithfully performed (Rom. 7:6). He was finally able to be himself and live out his destiny.

The Gospel account of the life of Jesus may inspire different people in different ways. All mythic stories have multiple meanings. When an individual reads a particular myth, the meaning that seizes him or her is the one that resonates with the structures of his or her personality. Thus, when we read the life of Jesus today, we invest it with the meaning that best fits our own individual personality. If his teachings are important to us, we will hear them; otherwise, we will read into the story what we want it to say, based on what our complexes allow us to hear.

DOCTRINE AND COMPLEX—A CLOSE CONNECTION

Just as an individual's spirituality has an archetypal basis that is partly a function of his or her personality, so religious traditions themselves may be dominated by a set of complexes or emotionally based attitudes. The Church's strategy of setting itself up as the authority on the definition of "sin" gives the Church the power to set the limits of the problem for which it claims to have the solution—that is, it creates the very conditions that it says it has been appointed by God to heal; it makes people feel guilty or sinful and then offers to take away their guilt or sin.

Christianity bases its view of the sinfulness of man on the story of the "Fall" of Adam and Eve as told in the Book of Genesis. This myth reflects some of the punitive aspects of the Western God-image. According to Genesis, Adam and Eve disobeyed God in the Garden of Eden by eating the forbidden fruit. This act is believed to have been the cause of humanity's "fall" from innocence. Since St. Augustine formulated his theory of Original Sin in the fifth century C.E., the Catholic Church has taught that the whole human race shares in Adam and Eve's guilt (in a legal sense) and therefore deserves to be punished. (One can hear in this idea the anthropomorphic fantasy of the divine as strict judge). According to St. Augustine, all of humanity partakes of Adam's identity, and we must therefore partake in his punishment as well. For Augustine, Adam's punishment was lust, that is, the desire for the pleasures of sex. Before the Fall, Adam looked upon the naked Eve without lusting after her, since their union was a spiritual one, but after the Fall, he could not look at her without desiring her physically. Through the idea of Original Sin, or inherited legal guilt, and inherited punishment, Augustine was able to explain how all human beings experience "illicit" sexual desires: if Adam's punishment was lust, and all humans must share in Adam's punishment, then all humans must feel lust like Adam did. For Augustine, this is how lust came to be inherited, like guilt in the legal sense. But Augustine went even further; he claimed that because lust was a *punishment* for Adam's sin and inherited from Adam, humans were utterly incapable of controlling their sexual passions and could rely only on the irresistible grace of God for help in doing so.

In his *Confessions*,[24] Augustine tells us that his mother Monica (a devout Christian) warned him repeatedly as a teenager to be careful of women, especially married women, and to keep his distance from them. However, at the age of 16, he found that he could control his sexual desires no longer and gave into them against his mother's warnings. The inner conflict that resulted undoubtedly contributed to the formation of a powerful complex, which played a significant role in his adult attitude to sexuality following his conversion, and also colored his understanding of the story of Adam and Eve and his view of human nature. Thus, Augustine's complex in regard to sexuality led indirectly to the formulation of the doctrine of Original Sin and the idea of the "total depravity" of human nature. This in turn led to the establishment of the practice of Infant Baptism. Augustine argued that if every human being shared in Adam's guilt, then infants were born in a state of sin (having inherited Adam's guilt) and needed to be baptized as soon as possible after birth so that their souls might be saved, should they die in infancy.[25] Following Augustine's reasoning, the Catholic Church still practices infant baptism today. Another religious belief that emerged from

Augustine's formulation of Original Sin is the Catholic dogma of the Immaculate Conception,[26] the teaching that Mary, the mother of Jesus, was conceived without Original Sin. This teaching was a logical next-step from Original Sin: if Jesus was definitely without Original Sin, and Original Sin is inherited, then his mother had to be free of Original Sin too. Here, then, is a striking example of the close connection that can exist between religious doctrines and personal complexes. As a result of one man's sexual conflicts, a complex resulted that was magnified through the Catholic Church's authority to the point where it eventually became the complex of an entire religious tradition.

Augustine's thinking is very much in the tradition of St. Paul, who wrote about the potential for sexuality to draw a person away from spirituality.[27] He interpreted the story of Adam and Eve in such a way as to suggest indirectly that Eve bears greater responsibility for the Fall since she sinned first, and seduced Adam into sinning as well; but he also went on to say that as descendents of Eve, women can redeem her and themselves from this lapse by bearing children.[28] This sounds somewhat like Augustine's approval of sex only for the purposes of procreation.

A further example of the way in which a complex can lead to a doctrine that guides an entire tradition is seen in the Hebrew Bible's theme of the covenant. This doctrine arose as a reaction to centuries of persecution of the Israelites, who have been enslaved and subjugated throughout their history. They were slaves in Egypt, then, having entered the Promised Land, they were plagued by the Philistines. After a brief "golden age" during the reigns of Kings David and Solomon, the kingdom was split into two parts. The people of the northern kingdom were conquered and exiled by the Assyrians, and were eventually scattered and dispersed, never to return. Shortly afterwards, the people of the southern kingdom were conquered and taken into captivity by the Babylonians. Seventy years later, they returned to the Promised Land, only to be overrun by Alexander the Great. This was followed by intense persecution by Antiochus Epiphanes in the 2nd century B.C.E., whose merciless treatment of the Jews led to a bloody revolt by the Macabees. By the 1st century B.C.E., the Romans had occupied Palestine, and once again the Jews were under subjugation. Further persecution followed, culminating in the Nazi Holocaust, but long before this event, centuries of persecution had produced permanent scars on the Jewish psyche.

Constant persecution over the centuries led to the development of a collective victim complex, which cried out for some kind of explanation. The antidote came in the form of the doctrine of the covenant that God is said to have made with Abraham. This doctrine is now thought to be invention of pious scribes and priests in post-Exilic times, who wrote a "sacred" history of the Israelites and attribute it to Moses. Around the 4th or 3rd centuries B.C.E., the post-Exilic scribes portrayed a glorious past for the Israelites. They invented the idea that the Jews were God's chosen people, and that God had made a covenant with Abraham to bless Abraham's seed in perpetuity and give them the land of Canaan, provided that they remained faithful to him. This comforting doctrine helped the Jews through some difficult times under Antiochus Epiphanes, the Romans, and subsequent persecutions. It also gave rise to the idea of the Messiah, a great leader who would come in the future and bring the covenant to fulfillment. The tradition says that he will defeat the enemies of Israel, and thus make sure the Jews live in the land promised to them. He will rebuild the Temple, reinstitute sacrifices, and bring history to a climax in which an earthly kingdom will be established. The people's suffering was thereby given a salvific value, embodied in the idea of the Suffering Servant of Isaiah (53: 3-5), a man who is despised and rejected, "wounded for our transgressions" and "bruised for our iniquities," but "with his stripes we are healed" (v. 5). Eventually, he is to be rewarded with prosperity (v. 12). Isaiah gives the Israelites a way to accept their continuous suffering by seeing it as something they were bearing vicariously for the sins of heathen nations—"he [the Suffering Servant] bore the sins of many, and made intercession for the transgressors" (v. 12); thus the complex gave rise to the notion of vicarious suffering, later taken up by Christianity, which saw these passages as referring to Christ. The defensive nature of this collective fantasy is obvious—it rationalizes the suffering of the people. According to Orthodox Jews, the doctrine of the covenant explains why the nation had been so persecuted—they had failed to follow the laws of the Torah. The only solution seemed to be more and more zealous following of the law, so the tradition became increasingly legalistic.

One wonders at the synchronicity by which an unconscious victim fantasy combined with the notion of being chosen by God continued to attract persecution throughout history. It is well known that children who are persecuted in childhood may themselves grow up to abuse others, a process known as identification with the aggressor. Many psychologists see this process at work in some of Israel's current behavior.

Christianity continued the theme of vicarious suffering, but Christ modified the Suffering Servant archetype by saying "My kingdom is not of this world." Christians were then able to embrace persecution as conquerors rather than as victims. Even when they were persecuted, they remained psychologically free, because they had been freed by the suffering and death of Christ, who inaugurated a new covenant whose terms had more to do with spiritual well-being than material prosperity and being chosen over other nations. One reason why Christianity spread was that the notion of election was no longer based on being a descendant of Abraham: anyone could become a member, as long as he or she accepted Jesus and his gospel.

DREAM IMAGES, ARCHETYPAL PATTERNS, AND MYTHOLOGY

Because each complex contains an archetype at its core, there is always a spiritual background to our emotional life. If we do not view our psychology as separate from our spirituality, we will be able approach our emotional difficulties with a spiritual sensibility. For example, a young man who has an angry and frightening father and an absent mother finds that being in natural surroundings brings healing. Since childhood, he has found refuge in nature since it is the only place in which he feels safe. It is as if he has been nurtured by Mother Nature but has received little human mothering. For this man, the wilderness is highly numinous. The simple act of walking in natural surroundings has a spiritual significance that far exceeds the demands of his allegiance to the tradition in which he was raised. His dreams are full of imagery related to landscapes and animals, such as the following:

> I am walking in a spectacular desert. I come across a pool of water, from which I pull an unusual silver fish, about two feet long, with a huge head and vicious teeth. I intend to eat the fish, but a wise old aboriginal man tells me that the fish is sacred and should not be eaten.

The desert landscape corresponds to a psychological state of emotional and spiritual dryness, an aridity of the soul. In the middle of this he finds water, a source of life, and this suggests that his situation is not hopeless. He associated the fish's teeth to his fear of aggression, his own and that of his father, but could say nothing else about the fish except that it had a numinous quality. In this kind of situation, the meaning of the dream is not clear, and this puts us in something of a quandary. Yet, we want some understanding of the dream because we want to participate in the larger life or Consciousness from which the dream arises.

It helps to remember that the individual psyche is seamlessly continuous with the transpersonal psyche, which uses the language of symbol and image to express itself. One of the great reservoirs of such imagery is to be found in the mythologies and religions of the world. We can sometimes find a parallel to a personal experience within this storehouse, since what happens to the individual is often the playing out of a recurring archetypal pattern that has manifested itself many times before and has been recorded in the world's stories. Jung's method was to look for parallels to a mysterious personal dream image within these great symbolic systems, in order to allow the image to speak more clearly. It is then as if we are asking the world soul how it has used this image before, in the hope that the image has been used in a way that is relevant to us. This process of amplification often enables the dreamer to enter into the experience of the dream more fully, and also makes it possible for the dreamer to feel that he or she is part of a larger drama, and not isolated or disconnected from the rest of the world. For this purpose, only those mythic images that are emotionally resonant with the dreamer are important. It is not enough simply to find any match between a myth and a dream image.

The natural language of the psyche seems to be metaphor and symbol. In a dream, a fish often points to something in the psyche that can live in depths that are inaccessible to human beings. Our mythic heritage helps us discern what the fish is pointing to. In various fairy tales and legends, the fish represents something deeper than the world of appearances, or a life-force that suddenly emerges from these depths. The fish is also numinous, and this leads us to seek out its spiritual implications. In some religions and mythologies of pre-Christian antiquity, the fish was associated with the Great Mother. The shape of the fish reminded early people of the crescent moon—an association reinforced by the fish's silver color—and the moon was sacred to the goddess. Sometimes the fish was sacred to the goddess of love, perhaps because the shape or the scent of the fish reminded the ancients of female genitalia. Because the fish lays many eggs, and some fish are phallic in shape, in some cultures it was also a symbol of fertility. The fish was a sacred symbol to the Babylonians, Egyptians, Phoenicians, and Assyrians. For this reason, some early cultures forbade the eating of fish, as the aboriginal man does in the dream. Conversely, in many of the mystery religions of antiquity, fish was used in sacramental meals. Several centuries later, the early Christians adopted the fish as a symbol of Christ. For this dreamer, the most emotionally resonant aspects of this matrix of associations to the fish were the fish's phallic shape and its associations with the goddess. In combination, these features indicate the union of masculine and feminine sacred energies in the unconscious.

The fact that this man dreams of an animal rather than a person suggests that some of his difficulties are in an instinctual, not-yet-humanized form within his psyche. Evidently he is not yet ready to assimilate this situation, since he is told not to eat the fish, that is, incorporate it and make it a part of himself. This advice is given by an aboriginal elder, whom the dreamer associates with closeness to the spirit of the natural world. Aboriginal culture is wise about the land and in tune with its energies, and therefore has a connection to Mother Earth. The aboriginal man represents ancient masculine wisdom, which the dreamer never experienced in childhood. This numinous dream gives us an indication of the presence of an important complex in the dreamer, but it is also part of a healing process, in that it makes it possible for the dreamer to experience his situation metaphorically and imaginally, and it thus deepens his awareness of it. Until he had this dream, the dreamer had no idea why he had been so preoccupied with the natural world or why it is so numinous for him. It is typical for such a prominent archetypal orientation to act as a driving force within the personality.

In any given individual some archetypes, and the complexes that form around them, are more dominant than others. Consequently, the way we experience the numinosum is often related to our complexes. Complexes often reveal themselves in dreams, whose numinous imagery may depict the specific configuration of the archetype at the center of the complex. If the negative Mother archetype is dominant, we may see dream imagery such as this:

> I am floating down a river at night on a small canoe. It is very dark, but ahead I see a patch of light on the water. As I reach the light, I see that it is emanating from a gigantic female figure, who stands astride the river with a foot on each bank. She has many breasts. As my boat reaches the light, I cannot stay conscious. I fall off the boat and drown.

The dream is numinous because the archetypal Mother figure is so much larger than life. Her many breasts indicate her enormous capacity to nourish, a capacity that this woman's mother had in abundance. However, this mother was also overwhelmingly dominant in the dreamer's life, so that whenever the dreamer was in her mother's light, she would lose consciousness of her own sense of self—she would drown psychologically.

This dream represents the feminine aspects of the divine in a pre-Christian form.[30] In order to express the workings of this archetype within their own psychology, many people need a particular image of the Divine Mother, which the psyche may express in many forms. As depicted in all the world's mythologies, the goddess can be as ruthless and bloodthirsty as she can be loving and protective. She can be as sexual (and even promiscuous) as she can be chaste. Similarly, within the psyche of the individual, the goddess may manifest herself in a wide variety of ways, some of them very unexpected.

A woman physician about to enter a residency in psychiatry dreamed:

> I enter the room of a woman patient and find her lying on the floor next to her bed in the fetal position. She is weak and emaciated, and two thirds of her body is covered with bruises, where she has been beaten. I realize that she has spent all of her life in jail and has been severely abused. She also has a reputation for being dangerous, combative, and out of her head. I lift her frail body into my arms and turn her on her back so that I may listen to her heart. I lay her down gently. I can see the terror on her face and I have the sense that she is like a vicious animal and may attack me at any time. I ask her permission to listen to her heart, then gently lift her gown, revealing no more than is necessary to place the stethoscope, so that she will not feel invaded or that I do not respect her privacy. Her face and entire body soften with relief and she allows the examination. I come away with the awareness that she is very ill and that she will be my first psychiatric patient—someone I must see

through to the end. Her name is Mary, and I realize that she is, in
fact, the Blessed Virgin Mary.

Obviously, this is not a traditional manifestation of the Virgin Mary.
Nevertheless, the dream depicts the way in which she is configured in
this woman's psyche. The patient has been abused and beaten, and this
has made her dangerously violent. The dream portrays the way in which
an archetypal aspect of the dreamer's soul has been abused, presenting
an image of the archetypal core of the resulting complex, indicating how
intimately the human and the transpersonal levels are connected. The
dream suggests that the archetypal feminine can be redeemed by the
dreamer's care and love, and in the opinion of the dreamer it also depicts
the way in which the goddess has been treated by the culture, so that the
dreamer carries a burden larger than her own difficulties. Her work on
her own problem will help in the redemption of the larger culture.

Lest we think that traditional or mythic depictions of the archetypal
feminine belong to another era and another land, consider the following
dream of a young man who found it difficult to sustain relationships with
women as a result of a difficult relationship with his mother:

> I am tied to a stake at the base of a high gilded throne, on which sits
> a huge woman with large teeth and long, flowing hair. Blood flows
> like a river down the steps in front of her. It's a hazy, bloody scene.
> I cannot even talk as my energy drains—another woman is sucking
> blood from my neck and arm. I'm terrified but too weak and helpless
> to do anything.

Here the Goddess appears in a way reminiscent of the fierce and terrible
Kali of the Hindu pantheon, who requires bloody sacrifices.[31]
Traditionally, Kali is depicted with black skin, her fearful countenance
dripping with blood, circled by snakes and hung with skulls and human
heads—a long way from the gentle Virgin Mary, but nonetheless an
authentic image of the Terrible Mother in her destructive aspect. This
mythology expresses the spiritual truth that the feminine aspects of the
divine may give life or take it, by famine or disease, at the same time as
she is the source of love and blessing. She is not simply a mother. The
dreamer is being drained by a vampire like figure and is in servitude to a
female figure who demands blood sacrifice. This Kali image in the psyche
of a modern man depicts the archetypal configuration of his mother

complex. It was this kind of graphic imagery that led Jung to say that the experience of the archetype strikes at the core of one's being. A man who is so emotionally bound to the goddess is not likely to worship a male sky god. He needs a mythology other than that of the Judeo-Christian tradition, one that will resonate with the structure of his personality. We must also remember that a specific image such as this is valid only *temporarily*, arising in response to the state of his psychology at the time of his dream. At another period of his life, a different image or symbol of divinity may be called up.

Of course, the Father archetype, and the complexes that result from it, may also have an important influence on a person's spirituality, and this archetype too has its mythic counterparts. In the ancient Greek stories, several versions of the divine as negative father can be found. Ouranos tried to prevent his children from being born by pushing them back into their mother's womb and imprisoning them there. Cronus castrated his father (Ouranos) and freed his siblings, but eventually proved to be as tyrannical as his father—he swallowed his children as they were being born. His son Zeus, the great Father God of the Greeks, punished mortals severely if they disobeyed him, and would often withhold the necessities of life.

Here we should remember that what we call mythology is actually the sacred stories of other cultures, analogous to our Bible. Thus, a mythic image is a religious image from another cultural tradition, just as our Bible would be considered to contain our mythology by those outside our tradition. We see from such mythic stories why Freud and Jung found parallels for the study of psychopathology within mythology.

DIFFERENT TEMPERAMENTS, DIFFERENT SPIRITUALITIES

Many religious traditions have recognized that people with different temperaments need different spiritual practices.[32] The Hindu tradition has long recognized that one may approach the divine in various ways; one may use the path of the intellect, the path of devotion to God, the path of selfless service to others, or the path based on meditation, physical postures, and control of the mind. In the West, medieval Christian monks also recognized that one could use one's natural strengths and weaknesses to grow in the spiritual life. They appropriated the classical Greek idea of the four temperaments based on the four elements.[33] Until the beginning of scientific medicine in the 1700s, this theory was a mainstay in the understanding of both disease and personality. Since then, a number of other ways of classifying types of people have arisen. One of the most useful typological systems is that created by Jung[34] and the closely related Myers-Briggs Type Inventory.[35]

For Jung, a fundamental distinction is to be found in the differences between extraverts (E) and introverts (I). Extraverts are drawn to the outer world, and are good at dealing with it. For introverts, subjective impressions of the world, or the internal effects of the world, are more important than the outer world itself. Whereas extraverts welcome the world, introverts tend to be rather defensive about it and find the world intrusive. Private prayer or meditation comes more easily to the introvert, who enjoys doing things quietly and alone. The extravert, on the other hand, would find such activities more challenging, because he or she prefers external stimulation. Communal prayer or other group activities suit the extravert much better; such a person is much more likely to express his or her spirituality by means of service to the world in a way that may

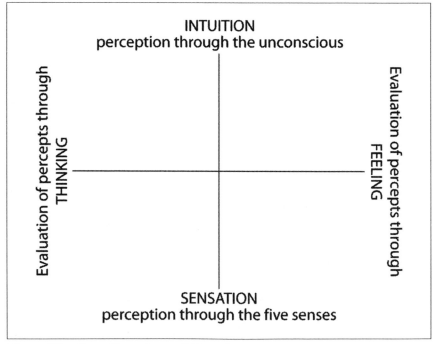

Fig. 2: The Four Functions of Consciousness

not be possible for the introvert. Many people fall somewhere on a spectrum between these extremes.

Jung also described four functions of consciousness involved in perceiving and evaluating the world around us (see Fig. 2). There are two principal ways of perceiving the world. One is the sensation function (S); it uses the five senses, which assure us of the reality of what is physically present. The other uses our intuition (N), which is a form of perception that taps into the unconscious. Intuition tells us what is possible in a given situation by means of a hunch about what may be round the corner rather than by means of what is directly perceptible. When intuition is dominant, we know something, but we do not know how or why we know it—the idea just arises. Having perceived an object and its possibilities, we then make a judgment about it. There are two fundamental ways of doing this as we evaluate our perceptions. One is the feeling function (F), which tells us whether we value something or not, whether we like it or dislike it, whether it is pleasant or unpleasant. Feeling has its own logic, the logic of the heart. Feeling promotes harmony between people and mutual appreciation. The other is the thinking function (T), which is analytical and values clarity. Thinking enables us to be logical about an object, name it, classify it, judge it to be true or false, and determine how it is related to other similar objects.

It is important to mention that in contemporary Western society, extraversion, sensation, and thinking are valued much more than introversion, intuition, and feeling. This fact has profoundly affected the form that spirituality takes in the West today. As a result, many Westerners who are introverted feel that their spirituality is out of place in Western society, because they find it difficult to cope with social demands to be extraverted. Their mode of being in the world is devalued, so they may feel that there is something wrong with them. By contrast, the East has traditionally valued introversion and intuition, which partly accounts for the type of spirituality one finds in the East.

Although everyone possesses all four functions, one of them is stronger than the other three in each individual personality, and this is known as the first, or *dominant*, function. The second function that the ego uses always lies on the *other* axis from the dominant function and is known as the *auxiliary* function. The third, or *tertiary*, function, the polar opposite of the auxiliary function, is less accessible to us than either the

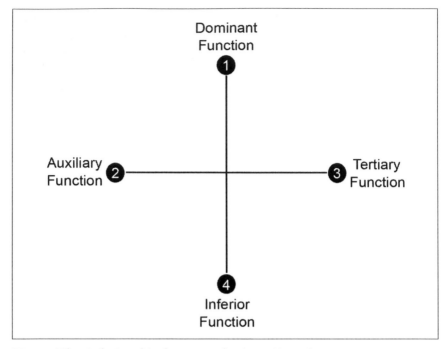

Fig. 3: The Relationship between the Four Functions

dominant or the auxiliary function, while the fourth, or *inferior*, function is the polar opposite of the dominant function and is the most unconscious and least accessible (see Fig. 3). Generally, we exercise the dominant functions and neglect the less accessible ones. However, beginning in mid-life, we usually start paying more attention to the neglected functions in an effort to become more well-rounded, and the less developed functions begin to strengthen.

Sensation types are realistic and practical; they prefer facts and details to speculation. When they are extraverted, they tend to be interested in the facts and details of the rituals, the bricks and mortar, and the finances of a religious organization. They enjoy sensory religious symbols, such as rosary beads, the sacraments, incense, statues, icons, and other tangibles. They tend to involve the physical body in prayer through the use of such practices as kneeling or hand gestures. The introverted sensation type values religious symbols only as pointers, and is concerned mainly with their subjective effects, such as stimulating the imagination to think about what the symbols mean for him or her personally. Thinking types are concerned with the philosophy behind their religious tradition. If extraverted, the religious thinker tries to relate his or her faith to what is going on in the world, to see how it fits with current science and social issues. The extraverted thinker may also be interested in the planning and administration of religious institutions. If introverted, the thinker is concerned with his or her personal reactions to the doctrines and truths of the tradition, and seeks to understand the tradition rationally. Good examples of this type of *religious* thinker are the medieval theologian St. Anselm of Canterbury, who said, "I believe that I may understand," and defined theology as "faith seeking understanding," and St. Thomas Aquinas, who believed that reason was the cornerstone of morality and that all human behavior had to meet this standard.

Introverted intuitives look for and find the divine internally as a discernible, if subtle, Presence. Spiritual teachers who stress the importance of Presence in spirituality tend to be introverted intuitives, and often do not realize that people with other types of personality may relate to the transcendent in other ways. They are at home in the spiritual world, which may seem more real or more important to them than the outer world. An introverted intuitive is often a contemplative or a visionary of some kind, often arriving at ideas without any direct evidence. Mystics in general were introverted intuitives. The 16th-century Spanish mystic, St. John of the Cross, and St. Teresa of Avila, are good examples. Ralph Waldo Emerson, the "patron saint" of the modern back-to-nature movement, was an introverted intuitive. Henry David Thoreau was most likely a member of this type as well (although some claim that he was extraverted). T. S. Eliot, who was deeply spiritual, and was greatly influenced by St. John of the Cross, was almost certainly an introverted intuitive. C. S. Lewis is yet another outstanding twentieth-century figure who is often classified in this category. Extraverted intuitives see the possibility of spiritual transformation of the outer world. They serve God in the world, and they guide others or look for spiritual guidance in this endeavor. St. Francis of Assisi is a good example of a man who sought communion with the divine through denial of the senses but who was adept in social matters and derived great joy in ministering to others and guiding them spiritually. A modern-day figure who fits this profile would be Mahatma Gandhi, the spiritual Father of Modern India.

Feeling types are very aware of their emotional life and care deeply about human concerns, values, and loyalties. Extraverted feeling types express their spiritual concerns readily. They prefer harmony around them, and tend to adjust their spirituality to the norms of their social group. Introverted feeling types are more difficult to understand, because they keep their feelings hidden and find it difficult to put them into words. They may keep their spirituality (which may be idiosyncratic) very secret, or express it on the basis of deep loyalty and inner conviction. Feeling types in general are particularly drawn to prayer that focuses on the love of God and to expressions of repentance and gratitude.

The first and second functions operate together as an archetypal coupling of perception and judgment that shape our experience of the world. People who function with a combination of thinking and intuition (NT or TN) are good at conceptual thought, the exchange of ideas, the discovery of organizing principles, and theories such as the theory of evolution. They enjoy systems of thought, research, analysis, clarity, justice, lawfulness, and ways to synthesize the big picture. In the Hindu tradition they would be followers of *jnana yoga*, the path of knowledge, a way to the divine that involves the intellect. The Buddha seems to have followed this path. When NTs are extraverted, they make good spokespeople, teachers, and builders of religious systems. They are typically drawn to systems such as Zen, often preferring austere surroundings and very simple ritual practices. Often, they have an impersonal God-image, a unitary perspective in which the divine is thought of as an undivided Totality or as pure Consciousness.

Those who function with a primary combination of feeling and sensation (SF or FS) are by temperament considerate and helpful people who combine practicality with kindness and compassion. They are concerned with preserving warmth among people, and their spirituality thrives on beautiful surroundings and ritual practices. Their approach to the divine is intensely worshipful; God is a lover, friend, or parent to whom they relate in love. In the Hindu tradition they would be followers of the path of *bhakti yoga.* For them, God is not pursued as an abstract idea. This kind of spirituality is exemplified by Ramakrishna, one of the great Indian saints of the 19th century. In Christianity, Martin Luther exemplifies the stress on feeling. Luther was well known for his hospitality and practical goodness, and his entire theology (starting with the doctrine of justification by faith) was based on the notion that God is a personal and loving God who gives salvation to humankind as a free gift out of his love for the human race.

The combination of sensation and thinking (ST or TS) produces a result-oriented realist who can be accurate, efficient, and detailed. Because such individuals are highly responsible, well-organized people who are not ruled by feelings, their spiritual journey involves action directed towards others, a path comparable to the path of *karma yoga* in Hinduism. As solid citizens who care about duty and fairness, they often choose a path of service to others or to organizations, mostly as administrators, stewards of the faith, or technicians, because they tend to be cool and detached. They like authority, rules, and structures that are clear, with concepts of right and wrong that they can live by; their approach to the divine is often legalistic. The most obvious example from the Bible is St. Paul, whose authority was widely accepted by his contemporaries and who is now generally regarded as the architect of the Christian Church. Another Biblical example is King Solomon, who chose wisdom (2 Chron. 1:10) rather than riches or fame or friends. A modern-day personality that fits this typology would be Martin Luther King, Jr., with his sense of civic duty, his commitment to desegregation, and his administrative and leadership qualities.

The combination of intuition and feeling (NF or FN) produces people who are humanitarian and visionary, insightful about human nature, empathic, concerned with relationships, enthusiastic, warm, and inspiring. They are idealists whose spirituality involves bringing meaning and value to their own lives by making life better for others because they care about them, often passionately so. Mother Teresa is an example of someone who made a virtue out of selfless action towards others, carried out for the sake of the divine. These types are in a minority in our society, and they often suffer because their values and gentle approach to life run counter to the more hardheaded, reality-oriented attitude of the dominant culture. NFs and FNs are better at imagining future possibilities than they are at dealing with the concrete details of the present. Jesus is perhaps the most outstanding example of this type.

While there is always the danger that typology will be used to pigeonhole people, if it is used carefully it can lead to an understanding of differences and so to greater tolerance and forgiveness of others. A typological analysis can also help one to understand oneself, to know that one's strengths and weaknesses are to a large extent innate and that one shares them with others of a similar type. The typological system also demonstrates that there is no single form of spiritual practice that applies universally to everyone, so the function of the community is to assist the individual in his or her search for the practice or practices that best suit his or her personality type.

As Jesus pointed out, spiritual reality (in his language, the "Kingdom of God") is present everywhere, even if we do not see it. The problem is how to get from here to there—how to bridge the gap between what seems to be just the daily grind (our ordinary, ego-dominated state of mind) and our awareness of the Presence of the Self. A study of typology makes it clear that such Presence expresses itself in different ways within different personalities. Depending on our temperament, we may experience it as Awareness, as the energy field of the body, or through relationships, dreams, synchronicity, or other types of numinous encounters, but it is always present. This is a life-changing spiritual insight that may produce sudden, radical illumination, or it may act as the seed and driver of continuing spiritual understanding that leads to the conviction of certain knowledge. The problem then becomes one of finding a way to put the ego in its proper perspective and of stabilizing our awareness of the reality of the Self. (This issue is discussed further in Chapter 7.)

ON SPIRITUAL HEALTH AND SPIRITUAL DISORDER

From the point of view of the spiritual approach to the psyche, mental health and disorder look very different from the way they are portrayed in the *Diagnostic and Statistical Manual of Mental Disorders* (*DSM*) of the American Psychiatric Association. This latter approach pays little attention to *spiritual* health and disorder.[36] In order to be spiritually healthy, we have first to acknowledge that we (and the planet) are not independent, competing entities. Depending on whether we are drawn to the path of unity or the path of devotion, we will then see ourselves either as being connected seamlessly within the consciousness of the Self, or as being in relation to an Other who is conscious of us. Once we begin to see ourselves in this way, our new awareness will have a profound effect on the development of our personality. We come to realize that if we are not as separate as we have been taught to believe we are, if consciousness is indivisible, nothing we do is without its effects on others. In fact, there are no others at the level of the Self—it is the same Self in all of us. In principle, this awareness could allow people who wish to avoid aggressive or ruthless competitiveness to do so. If we knew that we are a part of a totality, we would not inflict gratuitous cruelty on each other. We would understand that to care for any single individual is to care for the whole world. Our attitude to nature would change if we realized that the human race and the natural world are inseparable. However, in practice, this realization is confined to a relatively small number of people. To recommend compassionate behavior *without* the awareness of our oneness with all things is only to suggest an abstraction; *with* such awareness it becomes a living reality.

Given our essential unity, our contemporary Western cultural attitudes must be seen as spiritually unhealthy to the extent that they value individual achievement at the expense of the collective. If we are not separate entities, if there is no self without the other, then aggressively self-centered behavior is an artifact of the type of self that is encouraged by our culture. The fact that this behavior has persisted suggests not only that it reflects particular aspects of human nature, but also that it has had some evolutionary importance for the development of Western culture. One cannot find an ultimate cause of this development, since so many factors—historical, geographic, linguistic, religious, and population pressures—must have contributed to it. We may find its origins in our child-rearing practices, which are said to be much more abusive than those found in many tribal cultures [37] We may point to our cutthroat economic system, which justifies exploitation of people and the environment in the service of an expanding economy. Our formal education approaches tend to alienate us from the body and its environment, suppress some of our innate needs, and undermine self-esteem. Whatever the origins of our contemporary sense of self, its spirituality includes materialistic striving for success, status, possessions, and celebrity, whether or not this is consciously acknowledged.

Fortunately, there seems to be an inherent movement towards spiritual balance within human nature, a kind of instinctual pressure to get past our mundane preoccupations and realize our connection to the larger Reality of which we are a part. Sometimes we are driven to such realization out of sheer exhaustion from the meaningless round of daily routine. We may then take up a spiritual practice, but the last thing we need is another goal to feel guilty about because we cannot meet its demands. However, a degree of conceptual understanding of our situation is a useful starting place, because it sows a seed that may grow into personal spiritual realization. But this must be an organic process: until we are ready for a spiritual teaching, we run the risk of adopting it prematurely. There is no point, for example, in someone telling us to turn the other cheek if we are full of fear and rage or if we have been brought up to believe that we have to be ruthlessly competitive in order to survive. Meekness may or may not suit us, but it cannot be adopted artificially by those whose temperament is naturally assertive. In our society, the meek need a spirituality that enables them to cope with the pressures of an aggressive world without feeling somehow inferior and without pretending to be assertive.

We must become aware of the complexes—both cultural and personal—that cause our disturbances before we can mitigate their disturbing effects. We may then realize that our complexes contribute to the story that we think we are. Eventually, we realize that we can let go of our story, since it is only a conditioned point of view. Just as the human level of our complexes contribute to this conditioning, so does the archetypal core of each complex. That means that our illusions and stories are archetypal as well as personal in origin, so that in the end we must try to understand the archetypes that influence us. In the next chapter, I will discuss some of these influences.

PART TWO

Through Psyche's Lens:
A Depth Psychological Approach
to Spiritual Questions

CHAPTER FOUR

A Depth-Psychological View of Some Religious Ideas

INTRODUCTION

All religious traditions may exert a powerful hold on their adherents when they address important psychological needs. These needs express fundamental archetypal patterns in the psyche. This chapter considers the widespread religious notions of salvation and redemption, followed by a discussion of spirit and soul from a psychological point of view. Although most religious traditions express these archetypal ideas in some form or other, their underlying similarities are obscure because they are cloaked in different metaphysical assumptions, which are based on different sacred texts and different images of God. Nevertheless, if we look beneath these cultural overlays, we find important psychological factors in common, which we may clarify without resorting to any theological or metaphysical assumptions. In the process, we also discover more evidence of the close connection between religious beliefs and personality.

SALVATION AS A PSYCHOLOGICAL NEED

Jung pointed out that religions are psychotherapeutic systems in the sense that they help us deal with important human anxieties. One of the most profound of these arises from our sense that we need healing. We feel incomplete in some way, or we feel that there is something wrong with us as we are. This yearning for greater wholeness is addressed by the archetypal idea of salvation, which is found in many traditions in various guises. The word "salvation" comes from the Latin *salvus*, which means "safe," but it can also mean "whole, healthy." That is, when religions offer salvation, they try to heal us, or make us whole, by offering us something we lack. Different religions try to fill in the missing "something" in their own way, based on the notion that human beings and the world are not as they should be. Each tradition offers its own brand of salvation by telling us that some special good will happen to us if we believe and practice the right things. The nature of this benefit varies with the tradition, but typically the Western religions promise that if we follow their rules we will go to heaven, we will be especially close to God, we will be one of the elect, we will attain eternal life in the hereafter or be successful in this life, and so on. In the Eastern traditions, salvation takes the form of allowing us to get off the wheel of birth and rebirth.

We are susceptible to such promises because feelings of incompleteness or deficiency are inevitable, given that most of us do not grow up in a perfect childhood environment. When the development of our sense of self is disrupted by childhood difficulties, we are particularly prone to feelings such as painful emptiness, anxiety, and depression. These feelings tell us that we need something, which we search for in a variety of ways, of which religion is one. If we consider the origin of these problems in childhood, we see the essential needs that the promise of salvation is trying to fulfill.

Children have an innate sense of their value; they want to be treated as if they are important, as if they are what the psychoanalyst Heinz Kohut called "the gleam in mother's eye."[1] From the archetypal viewpoint, this is so because every child reflects or is a human embodiment of the archetype of the Divine Child, a child of God, a manifestation of the transpersonal Self. Every baby is born with a connection to this Inner Light. The Divine Child is an immediate, felt Presence within the child that provides a numinous sense of joy and a feeling that one deserves to be loved. Ideally, parents and caregivers respond to these feelings of intrinsic worth in a way that makes the child feel wanted, cared for, and loved. Given enough affirming responses to the child's sense that he or she is important, and enough meaningful responses to his or her feelings and to his or her essential Self, the child develops a strong sense of self. Should the child be responded to in a way that is dismissive, as if he or she does not matter, or as if his or her feelings are unimportant, the child feels "I cannot be worth much. I must be unlovable." The result is a painful sense of worthlessness, a fragile sense of self, and low self-esteem. There always seems to be something missing. The potential prince or princess feels like the frog of the fairy tale.

In Christian mythology, the image of the Divine Child is found in the story of the Magi bringing gifts to the baby Jesus—they realize who he is, and they are drawn to him.[2] This mythic theme is constantly re-lived when we see the sacred value of a child and treat the child accordingly. We are then witness to the divine essence of the child as well as to the child's humanity. Not only must we respond to the child's feelings and ordinary humanness for him or her to feel valued, but the child's essential, non-verbal sense of connection to divinity must be instinctively recognized by his or her caregivers, even if not at a conscious level. If the divine essence of the child is not mirrored, or worse, if the child's connection to that level is envied and hated, it may become submerged and be difficult to access. The child has been cast out of Paradise, and such an individual grows up with a chronic sense of yearning for something seemingly inaccessible. Religions arise in part in our attempt to reconnect with this lost element.

If one feels vulnerable and empty because of emotional deprivation in childhood, it may be hard to resist being told that, if we have faith, Jesus will take care of everything, or that we have become "a new creature in Christ" (2 Cor. 5:17). When being "saved" in this way does not make us feel better, the traditional explanation is that we remain corrupted by our sinful nature. The reality is that doctrine alone (without an experience of sacred reality) may not provide us with what we seek. We may try to follow the teachings of Jesus or the dictates of the Torah, but we still feel not quite right inside, not to mention our nagging doubts about the validity of what the traditions tell us. We may be drawn to religion partly because of the promises it makes, and because it offers consolation for our suffering. But faith alone may not make us feel better at any given moment; this is why churches have changed their manner of offering salvation in order to ensure large congregations. Many contemporary churches try to respond to everyday concerns as opposed to stressing otherworldly matters such as the fate of the soul. These churches recognize that many people go to "worship services" not so much to praise God or to listen to esoteric theology, but to belong to community, to experience intimacy, or to feel like part of a family. These are the real ways our incompleteness is soothed and we are comforted. Then, relationship is our real salvation, and not always relationship with the divine in the traditional sense but the divine experienced as community, as connection with others. Much of this crucial aspect of organized religion is described as "fellowship," which traditionally means sharing worship and faith. In fact, for many people fellowship is actually a way of dealing with a sense of emptiness because it gives them the feeling that they belong, or it is a way of shoring up a fragile sense of self by being with others who share their values.

Because of these psychological needs, rather than because they wish to worship according to a doctrine that appeals to them, people often change denominations until they find a church that suits them, without too much regard for the underlying theology of the institution. The experience of connection with others is far more important than details of doctrine, because relationship fills emptiness but doctrine does not. Such churchgoers may declare that salvation is based on faith in Jesus, but their actual salvation, and their actual experience of the sacred, arises from the numinous sense of relatedness provided by the church. Many of those who attend contemporary "megachurches" are more concerned about relationships with people than about abstract doctrinal models of the divine, which they are content to leave to professional theologians. Consequently, to meet various types of relational needs, a spectrum of churches is available, from those that stress how sinful we are to those that are warm and accepting of human failings to those that favor ecstatic movement and singing. We can always find what we are looking for, even when this turns Jesus' teachings or traditional theology on its head. We can even find a church that tells us we can use faith in God to intensify our search for more money—witness the "prosperity theology" of many evangelicals,[3] which must be making St. Francis of Assisi turn in his grave.

Under the rubric of saving their souls, many churchgoers really seek healing, albeit unconsciously, and indeed when we find a religious organization that meets both our spiritual and psychological needs, true healing may result. The pollster George Gallup predicts that the need for healing will be a major theme in the future of religions.[4] There is little doubt that faith benefits health, and interestingly, it does not matter what type of spiritual practice one uses. It seems that a connection to the Self, in whatever form one imagines it, acts as a kind of glue that helps to hold one together. However, if we are in a tradition that does not resonate with the way we experience the sacred, religion becomes just another strategy in our attempt to distract ourselves from our painful feelings of incompleteness. Religion is then just one more in the list of temporary fixes, which include drugs, alcohol, shopping, or entertainment. None of these are lasting solutions to painful feelings, because they are all based on external solutions to what is an internal problem. Even when religions help us emotionally, the cures that they offer depend on a set of beliefs and practices, or on a savior figure, which do not necessarily deal with the psychological problem at its own level. Consequently, should the traditional beliefs ever fail us, we may find nothing within ourselves to fall back on; this is why loss of faith in a tradition may be so painful.

Like religions, contemporary psychotherapy also tries to deal with the sense that we are incomplete in some way, that there is something we need that is missing, or that something about us needs fixing. By offering its own solution to our feelings of incompleteness, psychotherapy can be thought of as a secular form of salvation, so that religious systems and psychotherapy offer alternative approaches to the same problem. In fact, one contribution to the waning of the power of religion in the last one hundred years may be the concomitant rise of psychotherapy. Psychotherapy tries to deal with what is missing in our sense of self by attempting to ameliorate painful childhood feelings by understanding them in a new way, by reworking them within the therapeutic relationship, and by providing the emotional supplies that were not available in childhood. This process has the virtue of dealing with the origin of the problem at its own level, by dealing directly with the individual's sense of deficit and conflict. When a psychotherapist recognizes not only the personal level of the individual's difficulty but also the transcendent level of that person, psychotherapy cannot be considered a purely secular pursuit. Psychotherapy that acknowledges the presence of the Self is as much a spiritual practice as any traditional religious service.

The psychotherapeutic approach to our lack of wholeness tries to provide what is needed by means of a human relationship, and at the same time values our becoming more conscious. Our religious traditions have a different goal; they comfort us by promising to save that part of us that is immortal. Unfortunately however, in the long run, neither religion nor psychotherapy alone can make up for what is missing. Religions are not equipped to heal psychological wounds, because they offer broad-brush solutions to individual difficulties that require detailed understanding. In its turn, psychotherapy is limited because it uses approaches that are inevitably incomplete, since no psychological theory can encompass the totality of the human being. At best, a psychological theory can address only a part of us, and most theories ignore the spiritual dimension as if it were not the province of psychology. Psychotherapists, like the clergy, are limited human beings who can see their clients only through a particular lens. This means that psychotherapy, while helpful in alleviating a great deal of suffering, can never fully solve the problem of our not feeling whole. For this purpose, most of us need to blend our psychology and our spirituality seamlessly.

THE PSYCHOLOGICAL NEED FOR REDEMPTION

We find further important connections between belief in religious doctrine and personal psychology when we look at the theological concept of redemption from evil. A person is particularly vulnerable to theological insistence that he or she is sinful and therefore in need of redemption when he or she has developed a persistent sense of personal badness during childhood. Such a sense of badness may occur in many ways. For example, if we were rejected or abandoned in childhood, we may have decided that this happened because we were bad, and we must do everything possible to prevent this from happening again by behaving well, by saying and believing the right things. Children project their own reactions onto people who hurt them. For example, if a child feels anger at being abandoned by a parent, the child feels it is too dangerous to say, "I am angry with father/mother for leaving," so the child assumes that father or mother left because he or she was angry at something bad that the child did. The *feeling* of being rejected is converted into the conviction that the rejection was *deserved*. The child's experience of a rejecting parent thereby becomes a bad part of the child's self. The child's interior dialogue says: "My badness caused this rejection by mother, or abandonment by father.

If others get to know me, they too will reject me." It is safer for the child to say, "I am bad" than to admit that he or she has an abusive or unreliable parent; to admit this would be terrifying if that parent is all that is available to the child. Often, this sense of badness is intensified by parents and religious institutions which use guilt and shame to make a child conform to their wishes. Other parents project their own insecurity onto the world, making the child feel that only the chosen few—the true believers—are good, and the rest of the world is evil.

Such a deep-seated worry about personal badness can be reinforced by theologies that place great emphasis on human sinfulness. At the extreme, the (literal, not metaphorical) conviction that "God has withdrawn from me" is a well-known delusion of people suffering from severe depression, who feel pathologically guilty or sinful. Such depression, which may be triggered by an experience of abandonment or loss, is often an adult re-living of a childhood experience. As a result of a childhood separation that caused a child to feel that his or her badness has driven mother or father away, the child may allow himself or herself to feel only positively toward a loved one in the future. Thus, the depressive personality has trouble acknowledging his or her own feelings of ordinary hostility; such a person may stay with an abusive partner, believing that "if only I could be good enough, the mistreatment will stop. I must deserve it. Abuse is the price I must pay for relationship." Transferred onto a relationship with God, this means that we must experience God only as love, and if necessary suffer privation, because "I must deserve whatever bad treatment 'he' doles out to me—father knows best." The internal dialogue goes on to say something like: "Something in me drives God away; I try to be good, but I constantly fear my badness. I must repent constantly." At least in the Catholic tradition, this dynamic is fostered by an insistence on confession and ecclesiastically sanctioned absolution and the need to belong to an institution that promises restitution.

There are many other similar mechanisms. Sometimes the most emotionally sensitive child in a family, or the one who is least able to deny the elephant in the living room (Daddy's drinking, for example), is shamed and ridiculed for being "too sensitive." The child then blames himself or herself for being so "inadequate." Some children are constantly accused of being selfish for expressing quite ordinary needs that a parent is simply unable to cope with, for reasons that have more to do with the parent than with the child. Or perhaps parents set very high standards, so that the child feels he or she can never quite live up to them. This attitude produces guilt, the sense that one has done something wrong, and/or shame, the sense that one is defective because of what one has done. Such feelings make people vulnerable to traditional religious teachings that tell them they are intrinsically sinful. If one feels sinful, the idea of a redeemer becomes very important, an idea fostered by the New Testament association of redemption with the forgiveness of sin (e.g., Col. 1:14 or Tit. 2: 14).

To deal with the threat of evil, and relieve us of our anxiety about how we will be judged after death, religious systems promise reconciliation with God. Christianity offers the idea that Christ's self-sacrifice pays a price on behalf of humanity that makes it possible for us to be reconciled with God in spite of our sinful nature. The doctrine that we are intrinsically sinful is intensified by the fact that our culture induces feelings of guilt and shame in its child-rearing practices. Christianity allows that forgiveness of sin is possible if the divine is approached properly, but this doctrine does not deal with the psychological sources of our feeling of badness, which have deep roots in childhood. Consequently, such belief does not bring people permanent relief. This leads to an addictive cycle; a perpetual sense of badness is temporarily relieved by repentance, only to re-surface after a short time. Overall, therefore, by insisting that we are sinners, some traditions have created the very problem for which they claim to have the solution, and they have institutionalized a strictly temporary solution. As an alternative to this, we can deal with our sense of badness or incompleteness at the level of our psychology, if we first see its origins in childhood, in our relationships, and in our cultural attitudes. To do so is crucially important in the healing of self-hatred, from which many people suffer. Otherwise, one is in the paradoxical position of trying to love others while hating oneself.

SPIRIT AND SOUL IN TRADITIONAL RELIGIOUS THOUGHT

The concepts of spirit and soul are found in all spiritual traditions, and this suggests that they are archetypal ideas. If we look at the ways in which religions, mythology, and folklore have used the notion of soul and spirit, we can discern the psychological processes that these words are trying to convey.

The idea of "spirit" shows how the unconscious permeates our language. The meaning of the word has changed gradually over time. The Latin *spiritus* means "breath." For early peoples, spirit or breath seemed to be something in the person that keeps the body alive, since the body dies when breath ceases. Spirit was traditionally spoken of as the "breath" of God, the cause of life, as if it were a subtle vapor that animates the body. The contents of nature such as the sun, the moon, trees, or volcanoes, were also felt to be alive and purposive because of their spirit. The spirits or powers of nature were personified and worshipped as gods and goddesses. Sometimes, these were imagined as disembodied entities that inhabit an unseen dimension of reality, such as hell or heaven. Occasionally, mortals claim to see spirits; we call these apparitions angels or ghosts. In various religious traditions, disembodied spirits are thought to be powerful—there are invisible good and evil spiritual beings all around us. Good spirits fulfill our desires and bring luck and happiness; evil spirits or demons cause illness and other troubles.

In the Western monotheistic traditions, spirit gradually came to mean a kind of celestial power. The Bible tells us that in the latter days God will "pour out his spirit on all flesh" (Joel 2:28), which seems to mean that he will transfer some of his power or grace onto people. When people are "possessed" by the spirit, they lose themselves; that is, the everyday-reality ego is overwhelmed, and the individual becomes an instrument of the spirit. Often such a person is then in an altered state of consciousness. For example, one may become ecstatic and speak in tongues, a kind of heavenly language that Paul suggests is spoken by angels (1 Cor. 13:1). Or, people behave in other unusual ways. In the Bible, Samson had unusual strength, and King Saul became melancholic and violent, because of the power of the spirit. Bezaleel, the man who designed the Tabernacle and much of the holy temple, was able to do so because God filled him with his spirit, so that Bezaleel became especially skilled and a particularly good craftsman (Exod. 31:2 11). The prophets were thought to be able to speak on behalf of God because they were filled with his spirit. Jesus' enemies accused him of being possessed by an evil spirit. When Jesus left the earth, he said he would send the Holy Spirit to take his place until he returned. Initially, this seems to have implied that he granted the Apostles the power to work miracles in his name. St. Paul interpreted the idea of the Holy Spirit in several ways. By this term, he means the immanence of the divine presence, or sometimes our higher nature, through which we may commune with God. For Christianity, "spirit" has come to mean the indwelling power of God that guides people to the truth (see John 16:13) and bestows various gifts and virtues on them, such as wisdom and healing. The Christian tradition often contrasted the "spiritual" life with the life of the body, in the sense that the spiritual life was said to "rise above" purely material or economic concerns. Today, the recovery of the spiritual dimension of the body and matter in general has become a vital cultural task.

Today, when we use the word "spiritual" we usually refer to those aspects of life that are directed towards some kind of higher power, to the pursuit of meaning in life, or to ultimate values, such as love, goodness, holiness, and beauty. From the perspective of the ego, the idea of spirit splits the world into two realms, the physical realm, where mortal beings live, and an unseen realm, a realm of non-physical, immortal beings. It also splits the person into a combination of spirit and matter, as if these were radically different. This is the perspective of everyday consciousness, which experiences spirit and matter as somehow different, and perceives spirit to be more difficult to access than matter. For this reason, various religious traditions have developed disciplines and practices that are intended to help us to access this spiritual realm of being. Such practices seem to be necessary because we have the sense that we are suspended between two worlds and we feel compelled to try to unite them. Unfortunately, by maintaining the distinction, these attitudes sometimes perpetuate a spirit-matter dualism.

SPIRIT AS ARCHETYPE

For depth psychology, the term "spirit" is synonymous with the archetypal realm, which means the transpersonal principle of order and pattern in the psyche-body. We postulate the existence of this principle because when we look at mythic themes, religious ideas, dreams, complexes, human development, the functions of the body, and synchronistic events, we see regularities, as if there is an invisible harmony operating that is beyond our comprehension or control. Here it is important not to fall into the traditional difficulty of regarding spirit as somehow radically distinct from the body or the material world. Rather, we may think of matter and spirit as different expressions of the same

118

underlying Principle. Matter and spirit are experienced differently by the ego, but it is not clear that they are really different.

As discussed in Chapter 1, contact with the archetypal realm produces numinous experiences. In the body, we experience this dimension in the form of intense emotion. Emotions are crucial aspects of the structure of human personality, so much so that our sense of self is profoundly affected by the emotional transactions with caregivers from the moment we are born. Emotions are archetypal organizers of behavior, just as spiritual in their origin as any exotic image or symbol. Because an archetypal repertoire of emotions is present at birth, the baby can immediately signal its needs to caregivers—the baby uses emotions to communicate, and we are designed to understand them instinctively.

The ways in which we learn to deal with our emotions in childhood have a major effect on the development of personality. Much depends on whether the child's caregivers help the child to deal with painful feelings. Damage occurs if the child is rejected because of his or her feelings, if these feelings are dismissed, or if the child is forbidden to express them. In such traumatic situations with caregivers, the child experiences the negative aspect of the mother or father archetype, and this results in the formation of complexes with a painful emotional tone. When a complex becomes activated, its emotional coloring dominates our consciousness. If we have not been helped early on to cope with strong emotions, or if the emotions are overwhelming, we collapse into anxiety or depression. If the emotion is within the limits of our capacity to bear, it acts as a signal that what is happening is important. In other words, one way that spirit incarnates or comes into human life is by means of our complexes, whether pleasant or painful.

Since spirit (as an archetypal process) may express itself in the form of complexes, spirit forms some of the deep structures of the personality and thus profoundly influences the development of the individual. This means that the transpersonal dimension is not somewhere else; it is inextricably a part of us. As Jesus is reported to have said, in the Gospel of Thomas, the Kingdom (of God) is both inside us and outside us; the Kingdom is "spread out upon the earth and men do not see it."[5] They do not see it because they do not recognize the form it takes. For contemplative (or spiritually-oriented) psychology, the "Kingdom" to which Jesus refers is the larger field of the transpersonal psyche. Depending on how we look at it, either we are immersed in this field as separate personalities (the dualistic viewpoint), or we simply are a manifestation of that Consciousness (a unitary viewpoint). In either case, there is no need to speak of spirit as if it were somewhere else, an attitude that has given rise to the idea that we must "transcend" this material world. Too often, attempts at transcendence merely lead to denial and avoidance of the world. Rather than "transcending" the world in the sense of valuing spirit over matter, on a more ordinary level we can understand transcendence to mean that we are less caught up in the ego's concerns, we are aware of our continuity with the larger dimension of Consciousness, and we see the working of spirit everywhere and in everyone. There is a great freedom in this perspective, and this is why, in the East, people are said to be "liberated" when they have a stable sense of transcendent levels of Consciousness.

SOUL IN TRADITIONAL THOUGHT AND IN
DEPTH PSYCHOLOGY

When traditional religions talk of soul, they mean a kind of immortal, non-material, animating force that keeps the body alive—actually a way of talking about spirit in the body. The soul is the closest thing to God within the person. According to traditional accounts, the soul enters the fetus at some moment—the exact time is a matter of debate—and it leaves the body at death. The soul is said to have been created by God, and it will return to God or to heaven after death, unless the person was a sinner, in which case the soul will go to hell.

In the English New Testament, the word "soul" is a translation of the Greek "*psuché*," and for many depth psychologists "soul" is truly synonymous with the English word "psyche," which is derived directly from the Greek "*psuché*."[6] The psychologist cannot make any metaphysical claims about the psyche, and so has to leave open the question of whether the word "soul' as used in theology refers to consciousness or to some other principle. Perhaps to avoid the accusation of dabbling in metaphysics, some depth psychologists have built on the work of Evangelos Christou. In his *Logos of the Soul*,[7] Christou suggested that what we call body, mind, and soul are different orders of reality, each with its own perspective. The body's reality is built of sense perceptions and emotions, whereas the mind's reality consists of ideas and concepts, which are different from physical facts. But our psychological life is more than just a combination of body sensations and concepts, so Christou distinguishes a unique third order of reality, the reality of the soul. Just as a physical object is not the same thing as our sensory data about it, so there is a difference between our sensory data and meaningful psychological experience of both the physical object and the sensory data. We use the organs of the body and the functions of the mind *in order* to live, but the soul is about *how* we live, about what it is like for us to live, and about what really matters to us. The soul is about meaning in life, and so it is just as real to us as body and mind. "Mind" is the name we give to our ability to have ideas; "soul" is the name we give to our ability to fantasize about these ideas and to elaborate them in our imagination. The soul is thus what makes it possible for us to have far more than a mere conceptual understanding of the original experience. The soul is concerned with what we *do* with our mental and physical states, with what they mean to us subjectively, with our feeling reaction to them, and with their integration into our lives. This is why we cannot interpret the actions of another person from the outside, reduced to a series of learned behaviors—the soul is essentially subjective.[8]

We call an experience "soulful" when we mean that it seems deeply significant. Here we are trying to describe what we experience when spirit embodies, or becomes conscious within, a discrete personality. The embodiment of spirit affects us powerfully, producing both strong feelings and vivid imagery in the body-mind. Unless mind and body are split, an experience of soul involves the simultaneous experience of image and emotion, which are inseparable. For example, if a complex were to become activated so that we feel enraged, we would normally have angry images in the mind and the body would become tense and aroused. But, if we have split the mind off from the body (or vice-versa), either we feel only the bodily arousal with no mental imagery, or we have violent fantasies without being consciously in touch with any bodily feelings of rage. In either case, we have only a partial experience of soul, which includes body and mind as a unit.[9]

Jung thought of the soul as a set of psychological functions. For him, soul is the maker of symbols and images, for example, the images in our dreams. The unconscious could not become conscious without some kind of translator or bridge, so he used the term soul to refer to the psyche's linking function. When we dream, the soul acts as a receiver for spirit. Spirit is cast into images and emotions that are felt in the body and in our awareness. This process allows the ego-Self axis—that is, the human capacity to be in dialogue with the Self.

In traditional Jungian thought, unknown dream figures of the opposite sex to the dreamer are spoken of as "soul figures." Jung believed that a female figure in a man's dream, or a male figure in a woman's dream, represent parts of the psyche that are particularly unconscious. He thought that these parts are more unknown to us, or more other, than those represented by same-sex dream figures. This observation was made during a time when the roles and behavior of men and women were markedly differentiated and heavily circumscribed by culture, and there was little freedom outside these stereotypes about how men and women were supposed to behave. What remains important today is that we use the term soul as a way of describing the embodiment of spirit, or as the process of linking the human and the transpersonal levels of consciousness.

In the development of the child, it is crucially important for the embodiment of spirit to take place as soulful experience. During development, the Self incarnates into a personal self—that is, the baby is born with a set of archetypal potentials that are the psychological analogues of the DNA in the seed of a plant, acting as a blueprint for the developing personality. These potentials embody themselves as they are lived out in the world. However, for the child's archetypal potentials to incarnate, the child needs help in dealing with the intensity of the emotions that are part of these potentials. As we saw above, ideally the child's caregivers help him or her to deal with these intense emotions, so that they do not overwhelm the child. But sometimes the child's parents do not offer the child the help it needs and the child is unable to bear the feelings. Then the emotions have to be split off or put into cold storage, isolated from the rest of the personality, because they feel too dangerous or too threatening to the relationship with a parent. As a result, some aspect(s) of the child's archetypal potential cannot become embodied. It is then as if a piece of the soul is lost, or remains in suspended animation, and contributes to the sense of "something missing" described above.

Sometimes the child's spiritual potentials simply never have a chance to incarnate because the environment does not provide an opportunity for them to do so. A person with the potential to become a great musician may never be given music lessons or encouraged to learn to play a musical instrument. A potentially great poet or artist may be forced by his or her parents to "do something practical." In such cases, some of the person's spiritual potentials cannot become embodied. Such a person remains spiritually impoverished, until a mid-life depression makes him or her realize that he or she has an unlived life, that part of his or her soul needs to be reclaimed or retrieved. Part of the task of psychotherapy is to assist in the incarnation of these unrealized potentials.[10]

Finally, for many depth psychologists, what seems to be an individual soul participates in, or is a part of, the soul of the world; what I call "my" soul is continuous with what has been known since antiquity as the *anima mundi* (or, "world soul"). From the psyche-centered perspective, soul, spirit, and body reveal different processes of Consciousness. We now turn to one of the great mysteries that Consciousness produces: our experience of evil.

CHAPTER FIVE

A Depth Psychology of Evil

INTRODUCTION

The problem of evil is an important challenge to any form of spirituality. I believe that the major contribution of the depth-psychological approach is it clarifies what motivates evil behavior and provides help in coping with it.

Our news media, literature, and movies are constantly filled with accounts of evil, a fact that suggests that evil is somehow fascinating to us. This fascination is no accident. We are particularly interested in people and events when they correspond to something that is emotionally important to us, or when they resonate with some aspect of ourselves. Events and behaviors that do not resonate with anything in us tend to be uninteresting. If evil were not interesting, its coverage by the media would not improve ratings, and so it would remain largely unreported. The hard truth is that we are fascinated by evil because it provides a window onto certain aspects of the human soul. Our cultural images of the extremes of good and evil, such as those of Mother Teresa and Hitler, have a powerful effect on us. Both are numinous.

The problem of evil has become particularly pressing because our technology has developed to the point where we can destroy ourselves in huge numbers. We can also inflict damage to the earth to such an extent that we could destroy all life. The need for an effective response to evil has therefore become even more urgent; yet world events suggest that traditional religious teachings about evil have had little effect, despite the fact that so many people pay lip service to them. The monotheistic traditions have responded to evil with moral teachings, threats of punishment, spiritual exercises to prevent it, strictures for the guilty, and compassion for its victims.[1] However, as we will see, the traditional theistic views about evil present some intractable difficulties.

Do We Know the Essential Nature of Good and Evil?

Part of our difficulty is that good and evil[2] are notoriously difficult to define in absolute terms. When the Inquisitors burned "witches" in the belief this was necessary to save the witches' souls, were these men evil or just ignorant, fearful, superstitious, and unconscious? If we judge them to be evil, what criteria are we using to make this judgment? How are they different from dangerous wild animals, poisonous snakes, or earthquakes? We do not consider these aspects of nature to be morally evil; although they cause fear and pain, they are simply acting according to their nature, so evil cannot simply be our name for whatever causes suffering. One criterion is to say that a human being is evil when he or she is, or should be, conscious of the damage he or she is doing, and has the capacity to refrain from behaving in a harmful way but does not. This would make at least some evil acts secondary to either unconsciousness, lack of self-control, or ignorance, and therefore not always a primary quality. (It also raises the question of freedom of choice, which I will address later.) Thus, deliberate selfishness and greed are roots of evil behavior, but selfishness and greed themselves have their own causes, and this in turn makes them secondary to something else, rather than absolute qualities in their own right. Sometimes evil is the result of malignant narcissism, that is, an inflated sense of one's own importance with no capacity for empathy towards others. This too would make evil not a primary quality in its own right but secondary to developmental factors; as we will see, the childhood origins of such narcissism are becoming increasingly clear to depth psychology.

Another difficulty arises from the possibility that, at the transcendent level of reality, what we call good and evil are simply two aspects of a unitary phenomenon. From this unitary (or *monistic*) point of view, there is no need to label qualities such as cruelty or compassion as evil or good, since these are categories that apply only within the ego. When we divide life in this way, we create a tension of opposites or a fragmentation within a reality that is actually an indivisible whole. From this perspective, evil behavior towards others is understood to arise because we do not understand the indivisible nature of reality, its wholeness. In unitary reality, we are not separate from others, so whatever we do to others we do to ourselves. However, we experience reality in a way that separates people from each other and divides reality into distinct pieces. Accordingly, psychological approaches are intrinsically dualistic. They can deal with good and evil only as human experiences rather than as cosmic principles. Therefore, rather than becoming tangled in the question of whether evil is absolute or relative, psychology must use the word "evil" as a shorthand term to mean behavior that we perceive to be evil. Our experience of raw evil is real, but in the end, the problem of evil is a *koan*[3]: it cannot be solved conceptually.

In what follows, the depth-psychological attempt to *understand* evil must not be seen as an attempt to *justify* evil, or to make it any less evil. Some people are suspicious of any psychological approach to evil; they fear that such approaches run the risk of excusing evil or denying its reality, perhaps even dishonoring its victims. I take a different view, which is that the better we can understand evil, the more effectively we can respond to it. The psychological approach does not absolve us of the responsibility to do something about evil. Rather, it helps us to find an individual response to the problem. An approach that works for one individual may not necessarily work for others; consequently, the depth-psychological perspective on evil cannot begin with an absolute moral philosophy based on the notion that there exists a "will of God" that applies equally to everyone. To base our approach on God's will would be to raise the question of which interpretation of God's will is correct. Embroiled in such disputes, we would rapidly depart from the province of psychology, which is ultimately concerned not with arguments about absolutes, but with human experience. Thus, depth psychology must begin with the individual's personal experience of evil and attempt to understand this experience in terms of its origins in the person's life and its effects on the personality.[4]

The essential nature of good and evil is a metaphysical matter. Are good and evil absolutely independent of each other, or are these qualities meaningful only in relation to each other, two sides of the same coin? If the latter is the case, then we cannot logically have one without the other. This leads to a further question: Are there degrees of good and evil such that they shade into one another? Whatever our answer, it is clear that at least some of what we call good and evil is not absolute, but is based on personal preferences and cultural attitudes. Human concepts of good and evil have changed over time and vary from culture to culture. In contemporary Western society, we might all agree that evil includes the domination or exploitation of others, behavior that is anti-life, anti-love, and anti-relationship, and the exercise of cruelty and destructiveness for its own sake. We believe that it is evil to inflict suffering consciously on another sentient being for our own purposes, especially if we take pleasure in doing so. We believe that it is evil to behave in a way that deliberately denies the humanity of another person or deprives that person of his or her rights as a human being. However, we have to bear in mind that these are *our* categories, and that other cultures might—and often do—see the world in quite different terms. A personal judgment that something is radically evil does not necessarily imply that it is evil in an absolute sense. Although there are cases in which we feel it safe to make an unqualified judgment of radical evil— the Holocaust, for example—the majority of situations are much less clear-cut. Our Western cultural concepts of good and evil are loaded with Judeo-Christian assumptions, and our focus is often directed towards less serious problems, such as those involving sexuality, while little attention is paid to the more damaging aspects of our culture, such as gratuitous violence, hidden racism, and blind patriotism.

THE WESTERN MONOTHEISTIC APPROACH TO EVIL

In accounting for the existence of evil, the monotheistic religions are severely limited by their presuppositions and theological positions. They describe the divine as being both all-good and all-powerful at the same time; this makes it difficult for them to provide a satisfactory explanation for the presence of evil and a satisfactory approach to dealing with it. Given that there has always been evil and suffering in the world, either God is not all-good or he is not all-powerful, since evil continues unchecked. If he really is omnipotent, he should be able to prevent evil; but if he does not do so, how then can he be said to be all-good? If God cannot prevent evil, or if he can but chooses not to do so, we cannot really turn to him for help and expect to be helped. Perhaps he allows evil and suffering to come upon us just to see how we will handle it, and he may lend us a hand from time to time if he so chooses—but this makes him partly complicit in evil and once again not a suitable or reliable source of help. It would not be easy to go into a concentration camp or a children's cancer ward and solemnly proclaim the total goodness of God. In the face of this kind of cruel reality, some theologians do not even attempt any kind of justification of God. Instead, they claim that God's ways are unfathomable, and all we can do is trust his wisdom and mercy. However, our experience of God's wisdom is that it does not always seem like wisdom to us, and our experience of his mercy is that it is not always extended to us when we are in need of it. So our minds are not so easily pacified—especially if we ourselves have been victims of evil and have borne unimaginable suffering and grief. We cannot help asking, "Why evil?" and "Why me?"

THEODICY: THE JUSTIFICATION OF GOD

Some theologians do try to explain evil, taking the position that it is logically compatible with the goodness of God. The attempt to justify God in the face of evil, or at least to understand the necessity of evil in the context of the goodness of God, is called theodicy. Many theodicies have been offered through history, some more desperate than others. I present a brief review of some of them here so as to point out their shortcomings from a psychological viewpoint.

A typical theodicy is one in which the world as a whole is seen as good, even though individual parts within it may appear to be evil to our limited human minds, which cannot see the bigger picture. In psychological terms, however, while our minds may well be limited, they are all we have in our struggle to come to terms with our experience of evil. We have no other way of looking at life but from the human perspective. While the appeal to a "bigger picture" may be good theology, it is certainly not good psychology; those parts of the bigger picture that we cannot see or experience cannot form the basis of a psychological approach to evil. It is of no help to a victim of evil, for example, to be told that in the bigger picture his or her suffering is really not evil but good, and it only *appears* to be evil from his or her limited perspective. To the suffering person, his or her subjective experience of that suffering is all that matters. To maintain that what we experience as evil is actually in the service of a higher good is not much use either if we cannot know what that higher good is. Christ's suffering was meaningful to him because he saw the higher good that it could accomplish, but most of us who suffer are not in such a position. If we were at a very elevated level of consciousness, we might, like Christ, be able to see the higher good that our suffering is accomplishing, but few of us are at that level. And when we are suffering, we are not inclined to believe that our suffering is doing anyone any good, and even less inclined to take someone else's word for it.

Many theologians define evil in terms of sin, and they define sin as going against the will of God. But there is little agreement among the world's religions on what exactly God's will is. The layperson suspects that all too often "God's will" is really the will of those in power dressed up as God's will to gain legitimacy and authority. Even if we were certain about what God's will is for us, the evidence that suffering is a punishment for sin is weak. When harm is done to babies, or animals, or the environment, for example, one has to ask what sin they have committed to deserve the evil done to them.[5] It seems clear to our contemporary sense of justice that the evil that befalls people may have little or no relation to their behavior. To the modern mind, the Biblical God comes across as arbitrary and unfair. I have also heard fundamentalist preachers declare that evil and suffering are in the world as a warning to us to behave properly; they are intended to wake us up spiritually. This, however, is an appeal to fear rather than to love, and it suggests that God is somehow trying to coerce us into being good. The modern mind reacts instinctively against such indirect forms of coercion.

Some theologians maintain that God does not cause evil; he merely permits it. This, too, does not satisfy the modern mind, for it sounds very much like the theologians are trying to get God off the hook. For the victim of evil, this theological distinction is just so much hair-splitting, for it makes little *practical* difference to the suffering whether God causes evil or merely permits it. Knowing that God simply allowed the suffering to happen does not make the pain any easier to bear. And even if God's only connection to evil is that he sanctions it, the *innocent* victim of evil still wants to know why God permits his or her suffering when it is completely undeserved. A further argument in accounting for the existence of evil is that if we are to offer willing, uncoerced obedience to God, then we must also be free to disobey him, and this immediately opens up the possibility of doing evil. Free will and morality would be logically impossible if evil had no place in the universe. This is indeed a philosophical problem—one for which there are no obvious psychological answers. Freedom does indeed come at a price, a price that not everyone might be psychologically ready to pay. Most people would see the "freedom vs. evil" problem as a trade-off: How much freedom do I have to give up in order to avoid pain? How much pain do I have to bear in order to have freedom? Most reasonable people would be willing to put up with some suffering in exchange for freedom. However, the trade-off appears to have reached a tipping point, where human suffering now appears to be out of all proportion to any benefits that might be gained in having freedom of choice. The imbalance is becoming psychologically impossible to endure, especially for the Western psyche, where tolerance for pain has become relatively low. Finally, it is argued that humans need challenges in order to grow morally and spiritually, and dealing with pain and suffering provides us with just such a challenge, hence the old adage, "Adversity builds character." In psychological terms, adversity, like anxiety, can have a positive effect when it is experienced in limited amounts. Low levels of anxiety can actually trigger alertness and spur a person on to action, but when the anxiety level crosses a certain threshold, it can have a crippling effect. Adversity and suffering appear to have reached a similar threshold in the Western psyche.

There have been attempts to modify the traditional God-image so as to make it more compatible with our modern experience of the divine. A school of thought known as process theology[6] suggests that God has two natures: abstract and concrete. In his abstract nature (or transcendent aspect), God is timeless and perfect, while in his concrete nature (or immanent aspect), he is not all-powerful, not changeless, and not all-knowing, and not the ultimate source in the universe. He is one factor among many that operate in the world, and is as much in the process of evolving as the universe is, since he contains the universe. God does not bring about events in the world unilaterally or by force; divine power is only the power to persuade. Creative power exists as a principle separate from God, and he does not have sole access this power. Events in the world have a creative power of their own that interact with the power of God. Some basic principles of the universe are inherent in the nature of things, and even God cannot change them. One of these fixed principles is that love cannot operate through force, and God's love therefore requires him to allow people to make evil choices if they wish. God does not bear full responsibility for the evil in the world because he is not all-powerful and is not the sole creative power in the universe. Furthermore, God cannot prevent evil because to do so he would have to use force, and this is incompatible with his love. In fact, it is not God's purpose to prevent evil at all. Since we are in God and God is in us, he suffers evil with us. Evil arises from conflicting interests, and God works lovingly to try to bring all of these conflicting interests into harmony.

Deeply influenced by the ideas of process theology, Rabbi Harold Kushner wrote *When Bad Things Happen to Good People*[7] as a way of coming to terms with his young son's death from the incurable disease progeria. Kushner differentiates between natural evil and human evil. Natural evil includes natural disasters, the spread of disease, and other random events; such evil does not happen for any particular reason. The laws of nature and randomness do not distinguish between good people and bad people, so good people get diseases and die in earthquakes and accidents along with bad people. In such cases of *unavoidable* suffering, it is less important to ask why good people have to suffer than to ask what they will do with their suffering. Human evil arises from the fact that God cannot use force to stop humans from doing cruel things to other people. Some of our suffering we bring on ourselves, and this is *avoidable* suffering. God can help us to avoid such suffering. When we face our suffering with courage and dignity, God is manifested in us.

These attempts to reshape our God-image are a step in the right direction. They suggest that the human race is struggling towards a new form of spirituality that will speak to our experience of the divine as it occurs in our time. Ultimately, our way of relating to evil is tied directly to our personal God-image, and each one of us will have to work out that God-image for himself or herself.

THE APPROACH OF SACRED TEXTS

For the psychologist, the appeal to the authority of a sacred text in addressing the problem of evil poses the question of how to decide which one to trust. The Judeo-Christian tradition, for example, claims that the Bible is the ultimate authority on good and evil. However, the Bible appears to approve of behavior that in contemporary terms would be considered clearly evil. The wholesale slaughter[8] by the Israelites of various tribes living in the so-called Promised Land would today almost certainly be described as ethnic cleansing. Thus, each religious tradition deals with evil in terms of its own history and its fundamental beliefs. In the Bible, evil and suffering on the one hand, and happiness and success on the other, are attributed to disobedience and submission to the will of God respectively. Misfortunes, natural disasters, defeat in war—these are all the result of the Father God's displeasure at his chosen people's disobedience; "as a man disciplines his son, so the Lord your God disciplines you" (Deut. 8:5). Morality comes from God, and suffering is the punishment for breaking his rules. But the punishment is for our own good, "for the Lord reproves [censures] him whom he loves, as a father the son in whom he delights" (Prov. 3:12). All that is necessary is for us to turn from our evil ways. Although we do not understand God's ways, we are largely responsible for what happens to us, since we can choose how we behave. This is a God-image with a keen sense of justice, but also full of mercy and willing to forgive if approached through the right channels.

However, this tidy system of rewards and punishments is called into question as it becomes obvious that good behavior does not always bring rewards. The Hebrew prophets Jeremiah[9] and Habakkuk take up the theme of the prosperity of the wicked. Habakkuk protests to God that evil and oppression seem to go unpunished: "[T]he law is slacked / and justice never goes forth. / For the wicked surround the righteous, / so justice goes forth perverted" (Hab. 1:4). God even tells Habakkuk that things will get worse, because the Chaldeans, a "bitter and hasty nation, who ... seize habitations not their own" are about to invade the land—at God's instigation; Habakkuk understands this as a chastisement of his people. Nevertheless, Habakkuk protests that God allows his people to suffer unjustly: "[W]hy dost thou look on faithless men, / and art silent when the wicked swallows up / the man more righteous than he?" (Hab. 1:13). However God does not answer Habakkuk, but simply says that eventually the wicked will fail and be punished.

Habakkuk is relatively easily satisfied, but not so the Biblical Job. He suffers appallingly as a result of a wager between God and Satan. God allows Satan to torment Job in an experiment proposed by Satan. Job is confused by his suffering; he cannot understand what is happening in terms of anything he has done. Job's friends assume that his suffering must be a punishment, because this is the standard explanation for suffering, but Job maintains that his guilt in not enough to warrant the severity of what has happened. He wants to understand what has happened, and he needs God to listen to him. Perhaps God has some other purpose. Doubts about the fairness of God creep into our mind as we are convinced by the obvious sincerity of Job's protests. Job is not interested in his friends' opinions; he wants to hear from God himself. Finally God admits that suffering is not just a punishment for bad behavior, but a human being simply cannot understand the ways of God—they just have to be accepted. God knows best, after all, but he cannot explain his ways to his children. Job passes the test, and God wins his bet. At the end, the book implies that the evil that Job suffered is made good when what he lost is restored to him, except that the book glosses over the fact that his children are still dead. This gloss is typical of traditional theodicies. The assumption that one day God will make everything all right ignores the fact that so much horror has happened that whatever God does, some things will never be all right. Even if one bright day in the future we see that Auschwitz was "necessary" for some divine purpose, it will still not be acceptable at the human level.[10] For us, the indictment stands, unless divine omnipotence is able to cancel it out.

The later book of Ecclesiastes is more deeply skeptical and pessimistic than the Book of Job. The author is grappling with the same problem with which we are still concerned; he admits that he is trying to understand the "unhappy business that God has given to the sons of men to be busy with" (Eccl. 1:13). The theme of the book is that much of human striving is pointless, people are oppressed by the powerful with no recourse, and much evil is the result of vanity and dissatisfaction. Evil women are a particular problem. Since we cannot understand God's will, we should resign ourselves to it and seek wisdom.

In later Judaism, the rabbis attributed sin to an evil inclination within human beings, the remedy for which was strict adherence to the law. They realized that the suffering of the apparently innocent and the success of the clearly wicked posed a problem. Therefore, to balance the books, any reward or punishment that was not obvious in an individual's life would accrue to his or her descendants (Ex. 20:5-6). This solution was necessary as a consolation for the persecution of the Jewish people. In spite of all their suffering and exile, the Jews found it inconceivable that God could be anything but scrupulously fair. Rather than blame God for their misfortunes, they accepted their suffering as a punishment for their own bad behavior. When the rabbis attempted to explain why the innocent suffer and the wicked prosper, they fell back on the idea of trusting in divine providence. The rabbis frowned on any questioning of God's justice, since to them challenging the wisdom of God was the ultimate act of hubris on the part of a creature towards its Creator (Is. 45:9-10). The attitude of resigning of oneself to the will of God can be seen in Aaron's reaction to the death of his two sons by fire from heaven; the Bible says simply, "Aaron was silent" (Lev. 10:3).

Because of their firm commitment to monotheism, the Jews could not accept the possibility that evil was located in another supernatural power; evil must somehow be part of God. Thus, in the writings of the prophets one finds statements such as: "I am the Lord, and there is none else, there is no God beside me .... I form the light, and create darkness: I make peace, and create evil" (Isa. 45:5-7). This idea is much more acceptable in Judaism than it is in Christianity, where evil is restricted to the creaturely realm. Later, the medieval rabbis (such as Moses Maimonides and Abraham Ibn Daud[11]) took a position similar to that of the Church Fathers in regard to good and evil· God does not create evil—this would be inconsistent with his nature—but evil arises in the absence of good. The rabbis also invoked the free will argument: we must have evil in the world in order to be able to exercise choice and to choose good freely. Yet another justification for evil was that it is our challenge—without it we cannot develop spiritually. However, these attempts to make evil less of a problem are not completely convincing, and the existence of evil has remained a major problem for traditional Judaism. For many Jews, the Holocaust has made it necessary to rethink radically the God-image of their religious tradition.

In fact, the Holocaust can be used as a criterion by which all theories of evil may be tested. All earlier rationalizations about why God allows evil pale into irrelevance under the enormity of this event, and in fact any attempt to rationalize it is a dishonor to its victims. In our anguish in the face of evil on such a scale, some of us will demand an explanation from God, while others will maintain a mute, heavy-hearted acceptance—the silence of Aaron. Since there can be no denying that God bears ultimate responsibility for not doing anything to stop the carnage, religious thinking has no other option but to fall back on the idea of the mysteriousness of God's ways.[12] For many people, the Holocaust demolishes once and for all the traditional image of God as all-good. The problem of evil is insoluble as long as this fantasy of God is maintained.

The Christian God-image has proved to be no more helpful to our understanding of evil than the Jewish one. Like the writers of the New Testament, St. Augustine[13] attempted to explain the existence of evil by tracing it to the disobedience of Adam, since this was how evil was supposed to have come into the world. Augustine believed that evil emerges in the absence of goodness and in the context of human failings. The modern theologian John Hick, in his *Evil and the God of Love*,[14] approaches the problem in the same way as the second-century Bishop Irenaeus. The world's hardships are the arena in which humans may struggle for the good, so that they may ultimately choose God freely; the world is the "vale [valley] of soul making": evil and suffering are the fertile soil in which the soul can grow towards God. However, this notion raises its own problems. How can *physical* experiences in the *material* world affect the soul, which is supposed to be a *non*-material essence? If it is only the ego that suffers and makes moral choices, then what is the nature of the interaction between the ego and the soul? It is true that exposure to suffering and evil sometimes brings out the best in people, things such as courage and self-sacrifice, but suffering also equally often brings out the worst in people. Much of evil and suffering is anything but morally uplifting in its effects: we don't, for example, see why it is good for thousands of innocent African children to be starving or dying of AIDS. Besides, if suffering is good for the soul and was intended by God for human spiritual development, then all medical practice must be banned, since it sets itself squarely against the will of God in its efforts to ease pain and cure illness.

Simone Weil argues that "the sense of human misery is a precondition of justice and love."[15] In a similar vein, Jane Mary Trau, in *The Co-Existence of God and Evil*,[16] revisits the traditional idea that evil may produce a greater good. If evil is necessary for soul making (a greater good), then the world we live in (the "vale of soul-making") with all its multiple sources of suffering must be the way God intended it to be. This theory is based on the principle that the end (i.e., the spiritual development of human beings) justifies the means (evil and suffering). The life of Jesus is a prime example of the notion that suffering is necessary for spiritual attainment. The point of the passion and death of Christ is not merely that God does not relieve us of our suffering, but rather that God is present to us within it—this is the significance of the image of Christ crucified. Furthermore, Christ's resurrection offers hope for the eventual triumph of good over evil. For Christian theologians, at least, behind this kind of justification of evil is the image of the suffering of Jesus, which they see as clearly for a greater good. If he could suffer with equanimity and faith, so can we, and there must then be some higher purpose to our suffering as well. Without suffering, we would not have the opportunity to practice forbearance and compassion. The reward of patient endurance of suffering in this world is eternal life in the next.

Does this theory justify the pain and suffering of children and animals, or people who have never even heard of Jesus? What about evil that happens for absolutely no good reason, with no apparent "greater good"? According to this view, our spiritual development is more important than our happiness, and we can develop spiritually only if we suffer. While it is true that spirituality may be strengthened by suffering, since some people do turn to God in their distress, this theory does not answer the question of *why* suffering is necessary for spiritual development. Additionally, it does not take into account the fact that evil and suffering may also lead to more evil, to bitterness, rage at life, and the destruction of relationships. Since some people develop spiritually through love, joy, and gratitude, it is clear that suffering is not the only means of spiritual development.

Using Auschwitz as a yardstick to measure this view of suffering, we might ask: How does it help a child on his or her way to the gas chamber to know that this horrifying experience is necessary for his or her soul making, or that it will help his or her spiritual development? Is this explanation of any help to us today, as we think about that child more than half a century after the event? The explanation is simply too remote from current human experience. St. Paul's assurance that God has "made foolish the wisdom of the world" (1 Cor. 1:20) is not of much help either, since it just takes us back to the Father knows best argument, a kind of justification of God by faith. The believing Christian can participate in the story of Jesus by accepting Christ's crucifixion as his or her means of salvation, but this makes suffering a prerequisite for having a relationship with God.[17] A God-image that involves pain and human sacrifice speaks of a God who is angry and needs to be appeased. Is there really no other way to have a relationship with God than through appeasement? Does such a God speak to our needs today?

Humans have always sought scapegoats to carry their darkness. We victimize the people who represent to us the bad things that we deny in ourselves, and we attack those we envy because they have the good that we desire but feel is beyond our reach. Scapegoating and projection make it possible for us to maintain our illusion of innocence. Hitler was able to use these mechanisms to convince the German people that they were superior, while Jews, gypsies, homosexuals, Slavs, and others were a scourge. The Jews particularly have been susceptible to projected unconscious envy because of their self-proclaimed status as God's "chosen" people. Christianity uses similar processes in making Jesus bear the sins of the entire human race and portraying his death as a sacrifice that redeems the world.[18] We have always been preoccupied with our own evil, and we have always needed a scapegoat to purge ourselves of our sense of guilt. We need not even have *done* anything evil to feel guilty; Freud observed that we may feel guilty about our murderous thoughts, as if the very thought were the equivalent of the action itself, in much the same way that Jesus said it was.[19] We engage in all kinds of superstitious practices or religious rituals to ward off the evil that we fear. Sometimes these practices actually alleviate our anxiety temporarily and thus give us a sense that our religious faith is "working."

Christian mythology is often presented as containing the ultimate example of self-sacrificing love, but its violent shadow side is almost always ignored. The Christian story has had both positive and negative consequences in history because its underlying God-image is ambiguous. The constant Christian emphasis on the goodness of God serves as a mask for the dark aspects of the God-image portrayed in the mythology. We tend to pick out of a mythological system those aspects that fit our own psychology. Oppressed people may identify with Jesus' suffering and see him as a liberator, but when there are sadomasochistic tendencies within a personality, the cruel aspects of Christian mythology can just as easily give rise to oppression. Throughout the history of Christianity, for example, women have generally been relegated to a subordinate role. This pattern continues even today in the denying of ordination to women in some Christian denominations, as well as in the 1998 assertion by the Southern Baptist Convention that a woman should "submit herself graciously" to her husband's leadership.[20] The ambivalence of the mythology is also reflected in the fact that while Biblical ideas were at the heart of the Civil Rights Movement and contributed to the ending of racial segregation in the United States, they have also been used to justify slavery and racial discrimination against Blacks.[21] And just as some Christians once believed that their racist attitudes were in line with the Word of God, so some today still believe that their homophobia has Biblical justification. To prove their point, they quote St. Paul: "Or do you not know that the unrighteous will not inherit the kingdom of God? Do not be deceived: neither fornicators, nor idolaters, nor adulterers, nor effeminate, nor homosexuals ... will inherit the kingdom of God" (1 Cor. 6:9-10). This kind of thinking owes much of its power to the darker side of the Christian message.

The God-image that underlies traditional theodicies raises other problems as well. For one, it speaks of God in human terms, portraying him as a Being who behaves a certain way, as if God were somehow a Very Big Person. In his *An Introduction to the Philosophy of Religion*,[22] Brian Davies points out that all the traditional arguments for the existence of God assume that God is a moral agent, the way humans are—an individual being among other beings who can have effects outside of himself. But this way of thinking about God actually diminishes his status as God by reducing him to something contained in the universe. If he is truly God, then nothing can be outside of him since he contains everything, including the universe—he is Being itself, not *a* being. If this is so, then he cannot be thought of as a moral agent who has duties and obligations and makes moral choices that affect others (such as humans). In depth psychology, this problem does not arise, since the divine is not

139

seen as an entity, but rather as an organizing principle. Jung spoke of God as the Self, as the Totality of Consciousness. If the divine is the totality of consciousness, then we must admit that God manifests himself *also* through evil, as a dark power, like the Yahweh of early Hebraic thought. Like the Hebrew prophets, the depth-psychological approach acknowledges that the Self, the God-image that we experience, has both a light side and a dark side. Christian theologians, however, usually reject this position because it does not fit with their image of an all-good God of love, and because it rejects the notion of a *personal* God. There is also the fear that allowing for a dark side to the divine could lead to such occult practices as witchcraft, black magic, and Satan worship.

However, dark divinity has a more common, more familiar face. Are not the rape of the environment, corporate greed, the exploitation of the powerless, and the pursuit of war in the name of democracy evidence that identification with the dark side of the Self is actually a popular, if unconscious, form of religious practice? Of course, traditional theologians might argue that this sort of evil behavior is of either human or demonic origin, but certainly not divine. Still, we are left with nagging problems. If the evil in the world is of demonic origin, then the demonic would appear to be on an equal footing with the divine, since God seems to be powerless to prevent bad things from happening—or, at the very least, he chooses not to intervene. On the other hand, if we regard evil as a purely human phenomenon, then we cannot account for its numinous, gripping power. In any case, for the depth psychologist there is no powerful psychological manifestation that is *purely* human. What we call the "human" psyche is permeated with transpersonal elements; those complexes that make us treat others badly have an archetypal core, even when they arise from human experiences.

PSYCHOLOGICAL APPROACHES TO EVIL

Some people have a personality that is structured predominantly by hateful and destructive complexes, so evil characterizes their behavior all the time. Others are plagued by periodic outbreaks that temporarily overwhelm their usual personality. When a negative complex grips us, for a moment we feel possessed, and we do things that we later regret, saying, "I wonder what came over me." We have the sense that we are out of control, because the ego really is not in control; for that moment in which we are overcome, the complex dominates the mind. Whether or not the devil is an objective entity, from a psychological point of view what mythology calls the devil is a destructive complex within the personality that creates havoc when it breaks loose. In the case of people we call wicked, this sector of the personality is always active, but even in the average person it may take only the right combination of circumstances to evoke the shadow sector of the personality.

In Nazi Germany, the government murdered millions of people by recruiting the latent shadow of an entire country, a shadow that Hitler personified. Given that there were social, historical, religious,[23] and economic forces also operating to allow the Holocaust to happen, the psychologist's contribution is to discuss the mental mechanisms that facilitated the rise of the Nazis. In recent years, a debate has arisen about how many Germans were actually involved in the mass murder of the Jews. Whatever the exact number, there clearly were many who were actively involved, or who collaborated willingly, and this raises the question of what psychological processes made it possible for some Germans to resist the blandishments of the Nazis, but not others.

Many Germans were swept away by Hitler's oratory. In part, this happened because of the process of idealization, an extremely powerful— if infantile—psychological mechanism. During times of uncertainty and anxiety, certain people desperately need soothing and a sense of direction from a strong figure. When these needs are not met in childhood, an intense desire for them remains in adulthood, and when a charismatic figure who seems to offer the right answers comes along, he or she is immediately idealized, or seen as more than human, sometimes even god-like, and his or her flaws go unnoticed or are excused. Hitler's oratory induced many in his audience to identify with him, because he could play upon their chaotic feelings, even while giving those feelings focus and structure. There was a resonance between what Hitler was saying, the way people felt, and what they needed to hear to make them feel strong again after their defeat in the First World War. In the course of his speeches, Hitler would appear to be transformed from an insecure, fragile figure into an all-powerful superman, and this provided the Germans with a striking visual analogy of themselves as a nation being transformed from a humiliated, defeated, disunited people into a powerful and feared superpower.

Some Germans had to numb themselves psychologically or with alcohol in order to do the killings, but there were many who indulged in the brutality simply because they enjoyed it. Among the latter group were latent sadists and sociopaths; Hitler's brand of nationalism merely gave them a socially acceptable outlet for their pathology, and they were able to rise to positions of power that they would never have attained under ordinary circumstances. Still others were brainwashed by the regime's propaganda[24] into accepting an ideology that classified people into two highly polarized black-and-white categories: those with us and those against us; the chosen and the rejects, the saved and the damned, the all-good and the irredeemably evil. This kind of thinking is not confined to Nazism alone; there are many examples of it in our own social and intellectual world. Psychologically, it is based on the infantile defense mechanism known as splitting. Experiences in an infant's mind are organized according to whether the baby's needs are satisfied or not; this helps to regulate and stabilize the infant's anxiety. Reality is split into all-good or all-bad, and caregivers are perceived in these all-or-nothing terms, either as persecutors or as totally loving. In healthy development, these extremes are gradually integrated into a more realistic perception of others and an acceptance of the fact that people have a range of qualities, both positive and negative. In abnormal or primitive personalities however, such as those of the Nazi leadership, the splitting persists, and this makes it possible for them to see certain people, such as Jews, gypsies, and Slavs, as aliens or as not fully human. Within the framework of this ideological conviction, the Nazis had no difficulty splitting off the humanity of their victims, and they could thus commit genocide without conscious guilt. The Jews were ready-made targets for the projection of the country's misfortunes, given the generations of government and Church-sponsored anti-Semitism that had prevailed in Europe up to that point. In the presence of pathological splitting, they became convenient scapegoats for the country's social ills.

To understand the behavior of those Germans who were not as psychologically primitive as the Nazis but who nevertheless participated in the murderous Nazi agenda, we have to turn to the extreme effectiveness and persuasiveness of the Nazi propaganda machine. The Nazis were able to co-opt for their own purposes the existing authoritarian bureaucracy, with its emphasis on duty, obedience, and respect for authority. All of this, combined with the use of terror, was enough to indoctrinate all but the most independent-minded people in Nazi ideology. Once the authorities had declared a certain group to be less than human, the mass murder of members of this group was tacitly given official sanction and could be carried out with a clear conscience in the service of nationalism, ideology, and loyalty.

The effectiveness of Nazi propaganda was enhanced by the dark brand of spirituality that Hitler also offered the German people. Primitive idealization is actually a search for a divinity. Underneath the need to idealize a heroic figure lies the need to project the Self, to experience a divine figure. Hitler intensified the spiritual dynamics at work by means of his romantic appeal to race, blood, folk-values, and pagan imagery, thus tapping into the mythic or archetypal levels of the national psyche. He also used the power of ritual—huge rallies and marches, and a quasi-religious attitude towards the leader—to overwhelm the consciousness of his followers.[25]

The seeds Hitler sowed flourished in a cultural soil that was authoritarian, ethnocentric, rigid, and militaristic. Some historians have suggested that such traits are particularly German, implying that a Holocaust could happen only in Germany. Rudolf Hoess, the head of the Auschwitz death camp, insisted that he was simply a citizen who was doing his duty. It might be thought that such servile obedience to authority is a uniquely German characteristic. However, subsequent world events, world history, and modern psychological research have shown that the potential for mass murder and for destructive obedience to authority is present in many societies, and that this potential can be realized quite easily, given the right set of social conditions.

In 1963, Professor Stanley Milgram conducted an experiment at Yale University to test this claim.[26] The experiment was designed to study how willingly people would obey orders, even when it looked like they were doing serious harm to others. Milgram simulated a teaching and learning situation in which he told students that he wanted to test whether punishment affected the speed at which people learned. Each volunteer "teacher" in the experiment was told that as part of the teaching method he or she was allowed to administer painful electric shocks, if necessary, to the "learner," a mild-mannered individual with a "heart condition," who was in reality an actor collaborating with Milgram. The teachers were told that the shocks could be given if the learner failed to memorize pairs of words and that they could increase the intensity of the shocks to dangerous levels. The learner, strapped to a chair with fake electrodes taped to his body, actually felt no pain, but responded as if the shocks were real. The teachers increased the intensity of the pretended shocks enough to make the learner scream in agony, and finally appear to become comatose. The teachers were given the option of refusing to participate at any time during the experiment, and about a third of them did so when the shocks started causing the learner obvious distress. However, with the encouragement of the investigator, those who did not quit the experiment voluntarily kept administering the shocks to the point where they would have caused serious damage had they been real. Sadly, this experiment showed that even if one is raised in a democratic environment, one cannot always be counted on to resist the promptings of authority figures to behave in a brutal and inhumane manner. Given the right circumstances, the need to conform to the dictates of authority may override the dictates of an individual's personal values. Milgram concluded that his experiment shows that some people will do what they are told without being restrained by their conscience. A more disturbing implication is that some people simply enjoy inflicting pain, and will indulge this pleasure without restraint when given the opportunity to do so in a socially acceptable form.

Professor Philip Zimbardo carried out an equally disturbing experiment[27] at Stanford University in the summer of 1971. He paid student volunteers to participate in a two-week-long prison-simulation experiment. Six days after the experiment began, it had to be terminated and the mock prison had to be closed down because the simulation had turned dangerously close to reality. The participants began behaving as if they were real prisoners and real guards—they quickly lost sight of the boundary between reality and make-believe. Although the participants were given the freedom to leave the experiment at any time, none exercised this right. The "prisoners" became pathologically dependent and betrayed their cellmates for favors such as an extra blanket. The "guards" vilified, cursed, and derided the "prisoners" in a most sadistic manner. Like Milgram's experiment, Zimbardo's experiment demonstrated that given the right social forces, ordinary people can and will behave in a shockingly abusive manner—not just because they are told to do so, but because their innate cruelty is given an outlet.[28]

The students in these experiments were not raised under a highly authoritarian government, with leaders who exercised total power, nor were they exposed to the kind of official brutality that prevailed under the Nazis. We therefore have to ask what it is in human nature that made the students behave way they did. We cannot be content with projecting our own darkness onto the Nazis, the Chinese police in Tiananmen Square, or Saddam Hussein and his henchmen. The regimes that these people represent offer ready-made "hooks" for this projection because they personify evil. But unless we are in denial, we sense that we are all susceptible to certain types of evil, and we are often concerned that evil could dominate us the way it has dominated so many other people.

THE PROBLEM OF PROJECTION

Each of us has his or her own way of dealing with our sense of our darkness, even though traditional religions have a great deal to say about good and bad behavior and require us to comply with the moral standards they set. These dictates are not difficult to follow if they coincide with our personality. But most of us have to struggle with our impulses and desires when we attempt to adhere to the standards of traditional morality. We may have to suppress them—that is, we consciously use our willpower to inhibit our less acceptable impulses, albeit at the cost of a vague feeling of guilt, which must constantly be assuaged. In order to comply with what is considered socially acceptable, we have to repress our desires, with the result that we prevent ourselves from even becoming aware of the negative impulse. While this enables us to keep our guilt out of consciousness, we then often project our badness onto others. When we find a scapegoat to carry our darkness, we are able to put on a moralistic and self-righteous front. The result is racial, ethnic, or gender prejudice, or some other kind of intolerance. The projection of one's own unconscious darkness onto others is at the root of wars, witch-burnings, genocide, pogroms, Crusades, and the many massacres of heretics that pepper the history of Christianity. Alternatively, instead of projecting the shadow, we may simply dismiss it as unimportant; that is, we may be aware of it, but we do not admit its emotional significance. In the long run, these splitting mechanisms do not work; the shadow, that part of the personality that we would like to repudiate, leaks out, even from the saintliest of containers.

The use of splitting and projection onto others to maintain a sense of personal righteousness means that some aspect of our self has to be sacrificed as opposed to being faced consciously and worked through. When the shadow is denied, we may see a persona of goodness, a façade that hides the shadow but does not deal with it. It is dangerous to maintain such a radical split between good and evil. Some preachers of traditional Judeo-Christian morality are so identified with goodness and the official values of the tradition that they are completely unconscious of their own shadow. But the denied aspects of the personality do not go away, and they may grow all the darker for being ignored. The shadow contents of the personality make periodic demands on the person. When the shadow breaks through, as it inevitably does in the form of sexual or financial misbehavior, those who once appeared to be paragons of virtue are often plunged into despair, because they are no longer able to use their preaching at others as a way of concealing their own difficulties.

The Unconscious Underpinnings of Evil Behavior

Preaching, teaching, prayer, confession, and other traditional methods of dealing with the personal shadow are only partially successful because they focus exclusively on conscious attitudes. In the last one hundred years, depth psychology has discovered that there are powerful unconscious motivations for evil behavior. This discovery is important, because it is easier to deal with evil that we understand than with behavior that seems incomprehensible. The more clearly we understand what is driving evil behavior, the better able we will be to help people to deal with it, and the less likely we will be simply to tell people not to do it. One of the insights of depth psychology is that the same behavior carried out by different people may have quite different unconscious sources. We cannot understand behavior without a grasp of these underpinnings. Therefore, in a depth-psychological approach to spirituality, it is not sufficient simply to label certain behavior as "sinful" without trying to understand its origins. Universal prescriptions for good behavior may be of little value in the individual case; it is not always helpful to tell people that they must grapple with their impulses and improve the flaws in their character; good advice alone may not be enough to deal with powerful complexes. We cannot get rid of the unconscious simply by making rules, so there is not much point in merely defining the "seven deadly sins" and declaring them forbidden. (Our legal system also recognizes that there are powerful emotional forces within the personality that may diminish the possibility of self-control.)

Human evil is at times more tragic than blameworthy. Sometimes people behave in evil ways in an attempt to master the evil that was inflicted on them. We often see destructive behavior resulting from childhood deprivation so severe that the person is unable to resist the forces that drive him or her to evil. A good example is one of my patients, a middle-aged man, whom I will refer to as Sol. At first glance, it looks as if he lives a fairly average life. He has a professional practice, a wife and children, and on the surface there seems to be nothing unusual about him. However, he is unusually sensitive to abandonment, since he was often abandoned as a child. These episodes of abandonment were intensely painful and traumatic for him, with the result that as an adult he has become "allergic" to abandonment—even the slightest hint of it is enough to bring on in him an overwhelming emotional reaction of anxiety and depression. An argument with his wife or the feeling that she is abandoning him is all it takes to make him start falling apart. To hold himself together, he feels absolutely compelled to visit a prostitute, and he has to tie her up in order to have sex with her. Afterwards he feels ashamed, guilty, and horrified at his behavior, and he determines never to do this again. But each time he feels abandoned, the same complex takes over; he acts as if he is in an altered state of consciousness, as if he is not in his right mind. When in the grip of the complex, he has to find a woman whom he can hate and control completely. He ties her up so that she cannot leave him, so that he can act out his childhood trauma but give it a different ending. Rather than saying that this man is "possessed by the devil," we can say that a negative complex is activated, and his abandonment depression and separation anxiety are so intense that he has to find a way to relieve them by means of an enactment. It is of no help to tell him that his behavior is bad; he knows that, and he is appalled by it, but he is powerless to stop it.

Sol's compulsion to act out his abandonment problem points to the existence of sectors in the personality that have values and goals that are radically opposed to our usual view of ourselves. These parts of us are frightening because they act like loose cannons within the personality.

When they break loose they make us behave in horrifying ways and create havoc. These "demonic" sectors of the personality are where we store our childhood traumas, where we keep our unlived life and our most painful needs. The internal "devil" is often that part of ourselves that turned to evil because it felt abused, or that part that was corrupted by the evil to which we were exposed.

The demands of these shadowy parts of the personality are very important. When they cause distress, we pay attention to them; distress gives us an opportunity to deal with them consciously. Sometimes these neglected parts seek revenge on those who hurt us, but sometimes they cry out for redemption or healing, so that we cannot simply equate the shadow with evil, as if the shadow were always an entirely malevolent force. Just as the mythology of Satan depicts him as a rebel against God, so the dark or satanic side of our personality rebels against the rest of us and will not let us rest until we pay attention to it. Rebellion seems to be necessary for human growth, just as the behavior of Judas (said to have been inspired by Satan) was essential for the story of Jesus to unfold as it did. For Sol, "evil" emerges autonomously from a particular sector of his personality; it is not the conscious choice of his usual self. We sometimes make a "pact with the devil" in the sense that we behave badly in order to deal with pain, to get what we desperately need, to maintain self-esteem, or sometimes just to survive. The resulting behavior looks demonic, but it may be driven by uncontrollable desperation.

For early peoples, and still for some religious fundamentalists, the sense that there is an independent force within the personality that can take over from time to time is projected outwards onto the external environment. This process of projection gives rise to the idea of Satan as an entity that affects us from outside ourselves. However, whether or not there is actually an entity such as Satan, the idea of such an entity might be useful in bringing home to us the transpersonal nature of evil. Like all complexes, the destructive aspects of the personality have an archetypal or transpersonal dimension to them, so they are a force to be reckoned with, not underestimated. In the Bible, the transpersonal nature of the core of the complex is made explicit in the story of King Saul and David. Envious of David's popularity, Saul throws a spear at David because "an evil spirit from God rushed upon Saul" (1 Sam. 18:10). Today, the "evil spirit" would be described as a complex that suddenly took possession of Saul. Such rage attacks occur when we cannot contain ourselves because of the emotional intensity of the complex. The complex, in this case envious fury, overwhelms the entire personality. Saul's rage has an archetypal component, so it is a mixture of personal and transpersonal elements. If there is any "blame" at all, it rests on both elements, but blame in the legal sense is of little value for the psychotherapist. Speaking therapeutically, the solution is to become as conscious as possible of the presence of the complex and to try to integrate or soften it. In the case of rage, for instance, integration might eventually lead to healthy self-assertion, or the ability to fight for an important cause in a controlled manner.

In religious terms, the devil is spoken of as a kind of being or entity who opposes the power of goodness. He is said to tempt us, and may even take over entirely if we are not on our guard. From a psychological point of view, this is a characterization of the struggle we experience with two opposing types of forces within us. Our conscience, and feelings such as remorse, compassion, and regret, struggle against our more negative impulses. Perhaps this is why so much mythology and theology, including that of the New Testament, views our world as an arena in which God and the devil fight for possession of the human soul. The devil tempts Jesus by offering him authority over the kingdoms of the earth if he will worship him (Luke 4:5). It is difficult to know whether the Biblical writers were speaking literally or metaphorically when they refer to the devil as the "ruler of this world" (John 14:30) and the "God of this age" (2 Cor. 4:4) or say that "the whole world is in the power of the evil one" (1 John 5:19). Christian theologians have continued to speak of the devil as an external, autonomous power, although they insist that this power ultimately derives from God, who alone has absolute authority. In psychology, we cannot make such a rigid distinction; within the personality are light and dark complexes, each of which contains an archetypal core, an incarnated aspect of the Self. The part of us that is the most emotionally powerful is the one that tends to dominate behavior at any given moment.

Depth psychology tries to understand *in depth* why people behave in an evil manner. "In depth" means that we take into account the unconscious underpinnings of the behavior and not just its surface manifestations. Judeo-Christian morality, which stresses the need for our

149

conscious will to behave well, was an important developmental step in the evolution of our cultural standards, but it does not take into account our unconscious sources of motivation. Today, it is not sufficient simply to insist that our evil will be redeemed by a savior who offers himself up as a vicarious sacrifice, or that we will be saved by rituals of expiation, such as confession, or that will power alone is sufficient. It is naïve to insist on "self-control" and "personal responsibility" in the presence of powerful emotional forces that cancel out any such possibility. At the same time, we must face the fact that some people simply enjoy hurting or torturing others. To understand how these traits originate within a personality, we must look into the innate endowment of the individual, at his or her developmental process, and into his or her cultural background. Then, to assist the victims of evil, we must try not only to heal the trauma but also to reduce its effects on the personality, since evil may have a corrupting influence. Although we cannot say whether or not there is objective or metaphysical evil outside of individual behavior, it is clear that there are psychological processes that make people do evil things, and such behavior can be influenced by psychotherapeutic intervention.

I should note here that sometimes it seems that the fates conspire against us even when we do not consciously desire evil. This occurs when outer events coincide with a particular psychological predisposition. One reading of the story of Oedipus is that evil behavior, in this case Oedipus's act of killing his biological father, Laius, occurs as a result of a synchronistic event: Oedipus and Laius happen to arrive at the same moment at a crossroads. Because neither is willing to give way to the other, they come to blows. Ironically, in killing Laius, Oedipus commits the very act that he is in the process of trying to avoid by fleeing from his adoptive parents' home. His evil act is determined not so much by an evil disposition or faulty development, but by fate.

EMPATHIC UNDERSTANDING OF EVIL BEHAVIOR

Behavior that we consider to be evil can often be understood (which is not to say excused) by a process of empathy with the individual concerned. Here the word "empathy" is used in the technical sense in which the psychoanalyst Heinz Kohut described it. For him, empathy is not the quality of being kind or forgiving—it is, rather, a means of obtaining information about what is going on in the inner world of another person. Empathy requires a psychological merger, an emotional resonance, with the other person. We open ourselves up to being influenced by the feelings of the other by trying to see the world through his or her eyes, by imagining what it is like to be, or to be inside, him or her. Empathy brings understanding, and understanding is a crucial factor in dealing with problematic behavior.[29]

THE DEVELOPMENTAL ORIGINS OF EVIL BEHAVIOR

Human beings are born with the potential to experience the tension between love and hate, between cruelty and concern for others. Our childhood environment influences the balance of these feelings. For example, we know that most people who abuse children grew up in highly disturbed families and were themselves the victims of some combination of sexual, physical, and emotional abuse. By contrast, the person who was abused in childhood but struggles and suffers with the past, instead of inflicting similar trauma on someone else, is helping to reduce the toxicity of the evil that was done to him or her. If the victim of abuse uses what happened to help others, or if forgiveness is ultimately possible, that evil may actually be redeemed. Unfortunately, it is not always clear why some abused children grow up to be abusers but others become helpers. Perhaps one difference lies in the way in which the abuse was experienced. Some people manage to retain a sense of personal integrity in spite of being abused, while others seem to become corrupted by the abuse. It seems that in many cases a loving childhood connection to at least one caring person may make all the difference.

Some psychologists, such as Alice Miller,[30] believe that all cruelty to others is revenge for cruelty to oneself. This is a typical psychoanalytic explanation for the behavior of people such as Adolf Hitler. Such cruelty is thought to be the result of similar brutality that the individual suffered in his or her early life. The theory is that when we have been the victim of cruelty or brutality in childhood, we feel a horror and terror that we never want to experience again. Accordingly, we may try to get rid of the dread by making someone else feel it. This strategy forces some other person to deal with these unbearable feelings even as it allows us to avoid enduring them ourselves—we have turned passive into active. We may also kill or torture others because they unconsciously represent to us a part of ourselves that we hate, or that part of us that was tortured in childhood.

By identifying with the victimizer, we can escape from our feelings of vulnerability and the torment of helpless subjugation as victims. By abusing another person we unconsciously maintain contact with the part of ourselves that was victimized, and we give some form to the nameless dread that we would otherwise fall into. From this point of view, evil behavior can be understood as stemming from our need to ward off the terror we feel at the prospect of being a helpless victim yet again—evil behavior keeps dread in check. Furthermore, if in childhood some attempt at establishing a connection with another person led to pain and terror, then all relationships with others are seen as potentially dangerous. Cruelty allows a perverse form of connection with others in a way that ensures that we are not in any danger of being hurt again.

Even if these dynamics shed some light on the problem, are there some people whose evil is out of all proportion to what happened to them in childhood? Adolf Hitler is said to have been beaten daily by his alcoholic father, and this presumably filled him with the hate and rage that he later inflicted on others. (Some biographers dispute or ignore this aspect of his early life.) We also know that Hitler's mother had lost two children to diphtheria and a third just after birth, before Adolf was born. We can imagine the grief of such a mother, and perhaps also her reluctance to bond deeply with another child. (Some biographers portray her as overindulgent.) Do these circumstances make what he did "understandable"? Or was his behavior disproportionately evil, needing some additional level of explanation?[31] Are there some people who behave in an evil way regardless of the type of childhood they had? Is there such a thing as a "bad seed," a kind of Rosemary's baby, a child of the devil, whose childhood environment is irrelevant? On the surface, it seems that some children with apparently awful backgrounds grow up into well-behaved adults, while children from seemingly good backgrounds may end up acting in evil ways. We are therefore tempted to write off some evil behavior as genetic, using the "acorn" theory of development, which suggests that such children are born with a unique destiny to live out. However, judgments about the quality of a child's background are often superficial, since they do not take into account the possibility of forms of emotional trauma and abuse that are not obvious. Subtle forms of abuse that occur in early infancy are not apparent to the average observer. They can be detected only by careful observation.

The psychoanalyst Ronald Fairbairn[32] believed that the psychotherapist is the successor to the exorcist, because in our times the casting out of inner demons is really about trying to heal the damage caused by early experiences with abusive caregivers. Consider the hateful individual, the type of person that we experience as nasty and destructive. Fairbairn suggested that if a child feels that its mother rejects its love for her, or if the child feels that its love is actually harmful to its mother, the child may conclude that love is destructive. Loving relationships are then felt to be dangerous to oneself as well as to others. The child must therefore neither love nor be loved. It may then turn to hating instead, since this brings at least some degree of satisfaction. Fairbairn describes this as a kind of pact with the devil, which says, "Evil, be thou my good." It seems to be generally true that if we abandon a child to chaos and helplessness, the child may well take up evil as the only available resource to organize its sense of self and stave off a constant sense of hopeless emptiness.

Some psychologists believe that it is incorrect to assume that there is such a thing as an intrinsically evil child, since the destructive, hateful, and envious areas of the child's mind develop mainly in response to the way the child is treated. Using ordinary empathy, we can imagine that if a baby is treated hatefully, or is continually left alone, afraid and hungry, it will eventually feel enraged and persecuted. The only way the baby can signal its overwhelming distress is by crying or screaming, but if no one responds, the baby eventually despairs. In time, the abandoned, helpless, terrified baby falls into a state of formless dread, like falling into the darkness of a bottomless pit. We can understand empathically that if these experiences are repeated often enough, they can lead to a core sense of chronic depression and impotent rage. As these sectors of the child's mind form, if nothing else, at least the infant's hatred, rage, and envy will organize the dreadful chaos and give him or her something to hold on to. It would be naïve to assume that such early trauma leaves no marks within the developing personality. Hatred, rage, and destructiveness become incorporated into the structure of the self, and in a character such as Hitler it is inevitable that they will be evacuated onto others, because they are simply too unbearable to contain. In such primitively organized personalities, the badness of the self and the badness of the world are not really differentiated. Only a state of continuous war makes sense. People who dismiss the importance of psychological approaches to events such as the Holocaust simply do not understand the power of primitive emotional states. The psychotherapist is filled daily with the unbearable feelings of patients—feelings that have been evacuated because they are so intolerable. The patient often induces such feelings in the therapist in an attempt to get help for those feelings and to make sure that the therapist knows how distressed he or she really feels.

Some theorists blame the parents; others point the finger at the child's innate aggression. Depth psychologists such as Melanie Klein[33] believe that the baby's fear of malevolent persecutors actually results from the projection of the baby's own innate rage and destructiveness onto its caregivers. However, if the caregivers are in fact malevolent, the baby may not be projecting at all. Typically, hateful people were themselves hated and persecuted in childhood by cruel or indifferent parents, or parents who did not want the child. As we enter empathically into the inner world of such a person, we discover that a person who is full of hatred is actually rather fragile, and the hatred carries out a set of very important functions. A hate-filled person needs his or her hatred because it is such an intense feeling that it strengthens his or her sense of self; such people use their hatred to hold themselves together and to make themselves feel alive, so that they know they exist. Alternatively, they may use their hate to clarify the boundaries between themselves and other people, boundaries that otherwise might feel frighteningly fluid. Some hateful people feel afraid of others because they have been exposed to unpredictable danger in childhood. By provoking others with their nastiness, they can at least exert a little control over interpersonal relations and feel less vulnerable to unexpected attack—attacking first rather than waiting to be attacked removes the uncomfortable element of uncertainty. If hateful people see themselves as completely bad and others as completely good, then they feel worse than ever about themselves, but if they can, through their own hateful behavior, provoke others into retaliating, then they can feel better about themselves, since they are not the only ones who have behaved badly. Part of the difficulty also lies in the fact that unpleasant events seem to occur synchronistically with higher than normal frequency in the lives of hateful people, because the outer and inner worlds tend to reflect each other.

Some people find that when they focus on their hatred, they do not feel the deep level of despair that would otherwise overwhelm them. Hatred is an emotion strong enough to hold people together when they feel afraid and powerless. Hatred provides a sense of identity when it becomes part of the history and lore of a group of people, as we saw in the Catholic-Protestant conflict in Northern Ireland and we see currently in the ongoing Arab-Israeli conflict in Palestine or Sunni-Shiite conflict in Iraq. Hatred is one way of making sense of difficult life situations; it energizes the self, and this feels a lot better than feeling hopeless and helpless. Because it can strengthen the sense of self, chronic hatred becomes addictive and so takes on a life of its own. Then, whatever increases hatred is felt to strengthen the self, and whatever decreases hatred is perceived as a threat to the self. In other words, people use hatred to provide some sense of psychological equilibrium; this is why hatred is so difficult to get rid of, and also why preaching against hate is often ineffective. When evil behavior is being used to maintain emotional balance, no amount of moral teaching will change the behavior.

MORALITY AND CONSCIENCE

The fact that we can provide an explanation for a particular negative behavior does not justify that behavior. Nor does our ability to understand evil behavior address the question of whether society should punish the evildoer or not. One of the criticisms of depth psychology is that it tends to remove personal responsibility from the individual and place it on parents or society. Indeed, it is possible for depth psychologists to overstate the connection between wickedness and childhood emotional conflict. It would be more realistic simply to claim that depth psychology offers a partial explanation for evil behavior, to the extent that it clarifies what goes on in the mind of the perpetrator—partial because social, cultural, and personal factors also play a part.

It is true that depth psychologists have tended to replace the concept of sin with ideas of mental aberration or illness. This happens because, at least for the psychotherapist, evil is a therapeutic problem and cannot be dismissed as purely a matter of morality. Conversely, morality cannot be understood as purely a matter of mental health—it is possible for a person to show no signs of mental illness when judged by the diagnostic criteria of mainstream psychiatry, yet still commit evil acts, just as an emotionally fragile person may still make socially acceptable moral choices. We would need a radical revision of our diagnostic manuals to make immorality itself a mental disorder, and there would be little agreement about its definition.

That is, in terms of the standard definitions of emotional disorder, evil and mental health are not necessarily mutually exclusive, although it is clear that when a person's emotional health improves, he or she is better able to integrate potentially damaging impulses.

The question of whether evil behavior should be called sinful or sick illustrates the difficulty with defining mental health and evil in absolute terms. Nor, for that matter, is it easy to define morality in absolute terms, although we do know something about its origins. There are several depth-psychological perspectives on this issue, the earliest of which is that of Freud. He believed that our unconscious consists largely of instinctual aggressive and sexual drives, which would clash with social standards if we were to express them freely. In childhood, we form standards for our behavior based on the demands of our parents and society. Freud developed the idea of the "superego," an agency of the mind that acts as an internal judge or conscience and makes us adhere to our moral code. If we do not live up to the standards of the superego, or if we transgress our ideals, we feel guilt because of the nagging voice of the superego. The problem with this view is that it sees morality as something superficial, only "skin deep"; a person may behave in a way that outwardly seems moral, even though what he or she does is actually driven by guilt, by the desire to maintain self-esteem, or just by the need to appear acceptable. Fanatics of all stripes routinely insist that their behavior is based on moral concerns.

Jung, on the other hand, believed that it is a mistake to assume, as Freud did, that the unconscious is solely a source of potential conflict with society. The unconscious also has its own built in, archetypal morality, and moral feelings may thus arise spontaneously as part of the deep structures of the psyche. Rather than thinking of conscience as forming only in response to family and societal pressure, Jung claimed that the potential for developing a conscience is an innate psychological function. What used to be called the "voice of God" could, in Jung's view, be called the moral function of the Self. Jung believed that a moral order is part of the "ineradicable substrate" of the soul; otherwise, the human race as we know it would not have emerged. For him, behavior can be called truly ethical only when conscience is subjected to conscious scrutiny. Whatever our conscious pretensions, our real morality may remain unconscious, and may then reveal itself in the behavior of dream figures who behave in ways that would horrify the waking personality. Piaget,[34] the famous developmental psychologist, also believed that morality is an innate potential that unfolds gradually. Lawrence Kohlberg[35] refined this idea by demonstrating that there are various stages of moral development. He showed that there is an important link between moral capacity and the strength of the self, understood as the capacity to withstand temptation, restrain impulses, defer immediate gratification, and focus attention. This is partly why threatening a child with hellfire and damnation fails to instill genuine Judeo-Christian morality; simply conditioning children to behave properly is less effective than nurturing the development of a healthy sense of self and the capacity for discrimination.

We cannot take the moral authority of conscience for granted, since what conscience permits individuals to do depends very much on the prevailing social norms. As Hannah Arendt has pointed out, in Hitler's Germany, what people on the outside considered evil became quite socially acceptable;[36] Eichmann's conscience spoke with a respectable voice.[37] We think we know evil and morality when we see them, but our judgments are subjective and influenced by our culture and our worldview. The Church's persecution of so-called heretics and the behavior of people in Nazi Germany both show us that if we simply do what our religious tradition or our culture and the laws of the state tell us is right, we may still be doing evil. In such a situation, an individual may feel compelled to behave in a way that conflicts with the conventional morality of his or her culture. The voice of the Self may contradict the voice of conscience and call for us to swim against the collective tide. The experience of totalitarian states demonstrates that for the individual the voice of the Self is a more reliable guide to good and evil than the conventional morality of a Freudian superego. We each have to respond to this call in our own way.

Part of the problem lies in the eye of the beholder. It hardly bears repeating the truism that one man's freedom fighter is another man's terrorist. Massacres committed in the name of God are legion. Some people regard abortion as evil under any circumstances, while others believe that in some cases an abortion may be the socially and psychologically responsible thing to do. But we do have some generally agreed upon social criteria that make us think that certain actions are more evil than others. Premeditated, deliberate harm to others, coldly and carefully planned, is considered more reprehensible than harm that is impulsive or carried out in a fit of rage. Yet questions remain when we try to assign degrees of guilt. Is the person who kills many people really more evil than the person who kills only one? Does it make a difference if the victim is unknown to the killer? Is the evil worse if the killer feels no guilt or remorse for the killing? Is the killing of civilians in wartime justified, or is this true only if the war is just—and who decides whether the war is just or not? There is a level at which morality becomes a personal matter, unless we are content simply to make a list of sins and require people to avoid them, but this is often merely a means of projecting our shadow. However, if we are trying to help people who are consciously struggling with their shadow, it is not of much use to make absolute moral judgments. Unless the individual is a psychopath (a special case, which will be discussed below), he or she already has some sense of right and wrong. We must ask: what *makes* someone vain, greedy, envious, hateful, violent, promiscuous, or lazy? Without a definitive answer to this question, our reaction is likely to be hit-and-miss, or we may retaliate in a way that may itself be evil, or we may simply project our own shadow and condemn it in the other. It is easy to tell someone to stop what he or she is doing because it is immoral or sinful, but it is much harder to understand such behavior empathically.

Shirley overeats and is accused by her minister of the "sin" of gluttony. The minister wants her to ask God for forgiveness and give up this behavior. However, this piece of moral advice is not helpful, because it is based on a false premise. The minister assumes that Shirley overeats because she enjoys food and she is self-indulgent and lacking in self-control. From his point of view, her problem is that she is too close to the pleasures of the body, which should be forsaken in favor of more spiritual pursuits. However, this particular woman had been cruelly emotionally abused in childhood. No one had ever responded to her feelings, except to criticize her and tell her how inadequate she was. She now feels worthless, bad, and ashamed of herself. She eats as a way of dealing with her feelings of painful emptiness and depression, feelings that food temporarily assuages. She eats to calm down and to try to cheer herself up. Rather than enjoying her body, she hates it. Rather than enjoying food, she hates it because of its power over her. Shirley's "gluttony" is not a *moral* problem; she is inconsolable rather than bad. To be told that she is sinful, a moral failure, only adds to these feelings. Her church has not been of much help to her.

Jim is obsessed with making money. He works constantly, rarely relaxes, never takes vacations, complains about the price of everything, has difficulty spending any money, and is intensely critical of himself and of others. In his business he is known to be mercenary and ruthlessly competitive, willing to succeed at the expense of others, and a harsh employer. His wife and friends tell him he is hard and greedy, something he already knows—but he cannot stop his behavior. Jim grew up in a very poor family, always on the edge of survival, always cold and poorly dressed. There was little opportunity for him to develop self-esteem because he could never satisfy his critical father, and no one ever responded positively to his childhood achievements. He saw his parents constantly anxious about paying bills, unable to afford everyday necessities, and he was made to feel guilty about normal childhood needs. His parents' poverty led to frequent arguments and the deterioration of their health, and both died young, worn out with overwork, bitterness, and worry. Jim is terrified that he will suffer a similar fate. At an early age he vowed to himself that he would not go through what his parents had to deal with; he was determined to have lots of money. Jim is therefore driven by the constant need to prove himself, coupled with a terror of being poor; this insecurity haunts him so much that no matter how much money he actually has, he never feels safe. The world feels precarious, life feels uncertain, and money seems to offer at least some kind of safety net. His greed is not primarily a *moral* problem; a moment's empathy reveals that he is more frightened than bad. Unless we are prepared to tar all such behavior with the same brush, and simply dismiss it as sinful, regardless of its origins, we have to carry out a careful process of discrimination.[38]

THE QUESTION OF RESPONSIBILITY

If a person behaves in an evil manner as a result of childhood abuse and deprivation, to what extent do these problems diminish that person's responsibility for his behavior? How blameworthy is such a person? Our legal system accepts that people who are mentally disturbed should not be punished if they lack the ability to make moral choices or to understand the nature of their act. For example, a psychotic person who hears voices telling him to commit a crime is considered to be more ill than bad. The notion of diminished responsibility becomes a gray area in the case of people who are not clearly insane but who nevertheless cannot control

159

their actions because of a severe personality disorder. Yet, the question of intention and control is always crucial to a discussion of evil. Could the offender have avoided doing what he or she did?

The problem is that some people are powerless to choose not to do evil because they have no free choice in their behavior. The inevitability of their evil does not diminish the evil, but it does cry out for an explanation. As we saw in the cases of Sol, Shirley, and Jim, abandonment depression, painful inner emptiness, or intense anxiety can take away free choice. These emotional difficulties may lead to behavior that is hurtful and evil even if the person does not intend to behave in an evil manner. There are gray areas, where the origin of evil and the degree of free choice are not clear, but the real problem is that there are people who seem to have free choice but nevertheless choose evil and enjoy inflicting it on others. Professor Berel Lang, in *Act and Idea in the Nazi Genocide*,[39] believes that evil consists not simply in knowing that what we are doing is evil, but in doing it *because* we know that it is evil, even by our own standards. Can we understand such behavior?

The empathic approach is pushed to its limits in the case of the psychopathic individual, whose behavior seems to offer an example of pure evil. We consider psychopaths to be both emotionally disturbed and immoral at the same time. These are the people whom we understand the least, with whom we can least identify, and who frighten us the most because it is extremely difficult for ordinary people to enter empathically into their inner world. The predatory psychopath has a callous disregard for other people and wants to dominate and manipulate others. Such a person will kill, rape, or manipulate with no guilt, shame, remorse, or pangs of conscience. The only thing that is important is power over others—there cannot be any meaningful emotional connection with another person. The psychopath lies so that he or she can control and feel contempt for the weakness of the other person. Psychopaths kill those who are good and loving because their envy makes them devalue and destroy what they cannot have, namely, their victim's quality of goodness. Some sadistic psychopaths derive pleasure from seeing others suffer. They make careful plans for the abduction of their victims, and often ritualize the process, taking the gagged and bound victim to a pre-selected spot, for example, before starting the torture. During the torture the sadist remains emotionally detached. Such people are malignantly narcissistic—

they feel entitled to exploit other people, as if no one else matters but themselves. It is not surprising that nineteenth-century psychiatrists described this as a condition of "moral insanity."

The antisocial type of personality is not found only among criminals. Nor are all psychopaths violent and aggressive. Some are highly intelligent and superficially charming and persuasive, and are extremely clever at avoiding any direct confrontation with the law. Because they have no qualms about using people and are determined to win at all costs, they may be quite successful in business, politics, or any profession that involves the exercise of power and authority.

The childhood of the typical violent psychopath is chaotically abusive, usually with extremely harsh discipline. There is no consistency or love, or family protection from the abuse. Often the child's mother is depressed and his father is explosively sadistic. Usually, one of the parents is alcoholic. The family atmosphere is unstable and unpredictably frightening, so that there is no sense of personal power or safety; this may be one reason why personal power becomes so important to the psychopath. The child is treated hatefully, and feels hatred towards his or her tormentors. Sadistic behavior develops as a means of self-protection. The psychopath cannot acknowledge ordinary emotions, partly because emotions make him or her feel weak and vulnerable and partly because he or she has little capacity for the expression of feelings. Instead of using words to communicate feelings, the psychopath uses words to manipulate and control others; this is what he or she experienced in his or her family of origin. In some cases the parents cared only about the use of power, and conveyed the message, often unconsciously, that the child had the right to dominate others. In such a dangerous family, one's own power is all that is left. Weakness is terrifying; power, aggression, and sadistic cruelty are all that the psychopath has at his or her command to stabilize the self and maintain self-esteem. The psychopath cannot take in love, nor is he or she capable of loving, never having experienced it and therefore knowing nothing about it. With this background, the psychopath cannot make normal attachments to other people, nor identify with loving and caring caregivers. In addition to these environmental factors, there is now a growing body of evidence that psychopaths have neurological deficits in those areas of the brain that mediate emotional expression.

Most psychotherapists considered the psychopath to be untreatable. Where treatment is undertaken, success is rare, usually at the hands of a few specialists. Therefore, even if we understand the origins of psychopathic behavior, society's only protection against the psychopath is incarceration. This is not a case where to understand all is to forgive all, yet there is an unpleasant truth in the way we deal with psychopaths. When we hate and devalue psychopaths, we take on the quality of their inner world. Just as they treat others as objects rather than as people, so we treat them as less than human, and in this way we become a little like them. We call for some kind of punishment or say that justice must be done, but at this point our moral judgments become fuzzy. Is it really necessary for us to get rid of what we cannot tolerate? Do we have to fall victim to the same kind of rage and hatred that possesses the psychopath? Or should we try to redeem whatever good there is in them that we can? Psychopaths raise moral issues even as they show total disregard for morality.

THE SHADOW

For the average person, morality has to do with one's struggle with the shadow, where the word "shadow" is used to refer to parts of oneself that range from manifestly evil to simply unpleasant, shameful, or unacceptable. The shadow is a kind of sub-personality that emerges when we are drunk, when we are possessed by a negative complex, or when we find ourselves in extreme situations, such as war. In dreams, the shadow is seen as a figure behaving in ways that our conscious mind would repudiate. The shadow is featured quite frequently in literature, as it is, for example, in Robert Louis Stevenson's story of Dr. Jekyll and Mr. Hyde, where Hyde, the killer, represents the shadow of the healer, Dr. Jekyll. (The idea for this novel first came to Stevenson in a nightmare.) In Charles Dickens' novel *A Christmas Carol,* Scrooge's shadow appears as the ghost of his dead partner, Bob Marley, who protests to Scrooge about his miserly behavior. However, the shadow is not necessarily evil; it may also contain positive qualities. A person with low self-esteem, for example, may not be in touch with, or may be unable to own, his or her good qualities and talents. In this case, it is these positive qualities that constitute this person's shadow. The habitual criminal's shadow is his or her impulse to be law-abiding; the shadow of the brutal individual is his or her sensitivity, which feels like vulnerability and is, accordingly, disowned.

It is not difficult to uncover the contents of one's shadow. We simply have to ask a spouse or close friend what he or she finds most difficult to deal with in us. Or, since we tend to project our shadow onto others, we can make a list of all the people we do not like and what it is about them that we dislike. The shadow may also torment us internally. If we were envied in childhood and the envious figure has been internalized, there may be something in our own mind that envies our own success. It is then as if something in us says, "How dare you succeed—I hate you for that." One's own envy may be projected and experienced as a fear of attack by others, so that we are afraid to be too prominent or too creative. Many cultures believe in the "evil eye," which is, in fact, a social manifestation of the inner fear that we can be harmed by other people's envy.

We tend to hide the shadow behind a persona of social adaptation and pleasantness; thus, confrontation with the shadow is embarrassing, but it is crucial for self-knowledge. The standoff between the persona and the shadow is an example of the tension of opposites within the personality: the shadow tends to want exactly what the persona says we should not have. Consequently, the discovery of one's shadow is unpleasant, and leads to moral conflict. Consciousness of the shadow makes us less internally divided, but at the same time we must not simply give in to it, especially if it is deadly. A surgeon I worked with was universally liked for his compassion and caring, but his dreams contained mercenary soldiers, men ready to kill for money. He had managed to sublimate his rage by means of his professional work, but he was plagued by continual anxiety, because this shadow material was never too far from consciousness. Sublimation of this kind channels the shadow into socially acceptable forms but does not necessarily integrate it or master it. When this is possible, we convert rage into healthy assertiveness, vulnerability into empathy for others, or arrogant grandiosity into healthy self-esteem. People who have integrated the effects of childhood abuse develop an amazing capacity for forgiveness. Humor, the capacity to laugh gently at oneself, is a mature ways of dealing with one's shadow. If all else fails, we simply have to endure the shadow or come to terms with it. The problem with coming to terms with one's shadow is that containing one's personal evil requires the ability to contain painful feelings and to resist the impulse to evacuate these feelings onto someone else. This is a difficult task for emotionally fragile people: their fragility makes the pain unbearable. This means that our capacity to control how we behave under severe emotional stress is diminished by a fragile sense of self. Cultural containers for distress, such as religion, art, poetry, or music, may be helpful for some people. Others need to participate in support groups, such as Alcoholics Anonymous, to contain their distress, which would otherwise be acted out harmfully. It is not enough to say that evil causes suffering; suffering also causes evil. Emotional fragility may lead to many evils, including the need to control, hurt, and dominate others.

The work of integrating the shadow is made more difficult by the fact that our personal shadow also contains the shadow aspects of the culture in which we live—its violence, prejudices, and indifference to social injustice, for example. If only by our silence, we participate in the evil that goes on around us. In a reciprocal manner, consciousness of one's personal shadow contributes to the well-being of the community, because when we take responsibility for our own shadow, it becomes less dangerous to others, and less infectious. We are less likely to dehumanize and reject other people when we can accept our own shadow without projecting it. We are more likely to project our shadow if we view ourselves as only good, if we find it unbearable to acknowledge personal faults. We must then project our faults onto others in order to preserve what goodness we have inside ourselves.

The work of becoming conscious of the shadow is the depth-psychological alternative to dealing with it by giving good spiritual advice, or by suppressing or repressing it. The religious traditions have always encouraged self-examination and the scrutiny of one's conscience. But without any awareness of the *unconscious*, there is a built-in limit to how much can be achieved by even the most rigorous introspection. Rather than rejecting the dark side of the personality and insisting that it needs redemption through religious belief or ritual, depth psychology maintains that the shadow contains the seeds of a new consciousness. It is no accident that the name Lucifer means "light-bearer"; the shadow contains those parts of us that need to be brought into the light. It is more reasonable to try to integrate the shadow consciously and reconcile it with the rest of the personality than it is to insist on an absolute split between good and evil.

For the psyche-centered approach to evil, the problem is not that we are hopelessly embedded in sin, but that we are unconscious of our shadow and unable to contain it without acting out. Herein lays a major difference between a spiritual approach to the psyche and the Christian tradition. For Christianity, evil is overcome once and for all by Christ's self-sacrifice on our behalf, since divine love conquers evil, as witnessed by the Resurrection. Unfortunately, a psyche-centered spirituality has no such certainty to offer. Rather than relying on an external savior, the depth-psychological approach to redemption from evil involves the development of consciousness, the capacity to contain painful feelings without acting them out, and help gained from relationships with others and with the Self. These two approaches are not incompatible; for a person who is a Christian and is at the same time interested in integrating his or her shadow, they can be combined.

Shadow problems such as hatred, envy, and rage can often be traced to a painful clash between who we were in childhood, what we brought to the family, and the way our innate endowment was treated by our caregivers. This endowment is an incarnated fragment of the Self, which provides a set of potentials at birth. These potentials include talents and assets as well as handicaps and liabilities. As we develop, we further incarnate these potentials by forming complexes that may be positive or painful, damaging or healing to ourselves and to others. Painful and traumatic childhood experiences favor the incarnation of the dark potentials of the Self, such as violence and hatred.

THE DARK SIDE OF THE SELF

For Jung, the Self, the God-image in the psyche or our experience of the divine (as distinct from the divine itself), is a symbol of totality, so it must contain the potential for both good and evil. Here we find a major difference between the traditional Christian God-image and the psyche-centered view. Jung believed that the power of evil is more than simply human. The evil that we experience is of gigantic proportions, and if we say that evil is only human, we do not give its power the credit it deserves. We could argue that occurrences such as the Holocaust or the bombing of Hiroshima were purely the result of human behavior and had nothing to do with the divine, but Jung felt that occurrences of such magnitude are far too terrible to be of purely human origin. We cannot afford to have a concept of evil that is too small. Theologians may tell us that God is only good, but this is an assertion for which the evidence is mixed. From a psychological point of view, our *experience* of God matters more than our *doctrine* of God. Of what use is it to be told that God is only good when we are overwhelmed by the horrors going on around us? The discrepancy between belief and experience is too great. Our daily—and historical—experience (as distinct from doctrine) suggests that the Self has a dark side to it. When the traditional God-image contradicts everyday reality so dramatically, it isn't any wonder that people are taking it less and less seriously. Horrors such as Auschwitz and Hiroshima simply do not fit into the traditional understanding of a benevolent God.[40]

When he discussed these ideas, Jung was misunderstood within religious circles because he used terms such as "God," "Yahweh," and "Satan" in their psychological sense rather than as theological concepts. Psychologically speaking, these words personify archetypal processes that have been given names. They behave like autonomous forces in the psyche, forces to which we must relate. Their absolute nature is not a subject of study for the psychologist, who is concerned only with how we experience them. If there is a deity that transcends the psyche, psychological concepts would not apply to it. Jung himself referred to this realm as the Unspeakable—when we try to speak of it, we speak about our images of it, not about the Reality itself. For the psychologist, "God" only refers to the way we experience God, and Jung was concerned that we not project human qualities, such as good and evil, onto a *transcendent* divinity that is beyond human experience. To do so would be meaningless. The ineffable is ineffable, so that for Jung not even the great religious traditions can say what the divine really is—they can tell us only how they speak of the divine. This is why Jung always speaks of the Self as an image of the divine. We cannot say that the Self is God or that God is the Self—according to Jung, we can say only that there is a consistent "psychological relationship between them."[41] Jung therefore makes no claims about the ontological nature of the divine itself.

Jung's concept of the dark side of the Self caused a good deal of controversy and led to accusations that he was not really a Christian. His proposition was nothing new, however; many ancient mythologies feature gods with both light and dark qualities. Some of the ancient Greek deities behaved quite atrociously from time to time, and the Hindu tradition recognizes divinities such as Kali, who has a very dark aspect. The ancient

Egyptian pantheon included the evil god Set, and ancient Norse mythology describes Loki, a god of malicious trickery and wickedness. Early Goddess-worshipping cultures also thought of the divine as being capable of both good and evil. Manichaeism held a doctrine of two opposing transpersonal principles, light and darkness, locked permanently in an eternal cosmic battle. Zoroastrianism, too, believed in the existence of light and dark spiritual principles. Even the Old Testament tolerates some darkness in its God-image; it is only in the New Testament (with the exception of the Book of Revelation) that we find an attempt to remove every trace of darkness from the Godhead and present God as nothing but pure light, especially in the Gospel of John. However, it is difficult to avoid noticing the dark side of the Christian God-image when one reads of avenging angels bringing plagues on unbelievers, as described in the Book of Revelation (chs. 15-16).

Many stories in the Bible reveal the dark side of the Biblical God-image. The story of Job indicates clearly that the evil that befell him had a transpersonal origin. God is described as hardening Pharaoh's heart so that he (God) can display his powers by bringing the plagues down on the Egyptians and making an example of them (Ex. 10:1-2). This description makes God sound distinctly sadistic— clearly a very human projection. Furthermore, the idea that God hardened Pharaoh's heart poses a confusing contradiction since it implies that Pharaoh could not exercise his free will. God therefore appears to be unfair in punishing Pharaoh for doing something that he himself made him do. The parents of the first born children killed by the Angel of Death in the tenth plague certainly experienced the dark side of the Old Testament God, who affirmed his power to kill at will when he declared, "I kill and I make alive;/ I wound and I heal ..." (Deut. 32:39).

In fact, the Old Testament God caused a good deal of suffering. The prophet Isaiah, speaking on God's behalf, says, "I make weal [well being] and I create woe" (Isa. 45:7), and the prophet Amos says that God causes the evil that befalls cities (Amos 3:6). Poor Jeremiah, one of the great Old Testament prophets, feels deceived and made into a laughingstock by God (Jer. 20:7). While there are several statements elsewhere in the Bible about God's involvement in evil and suffering (e.g., Lam. 3:38; Ps. 13:1 2), one of the most painful passages to read is Psalm 88: "You have put me in the depths of the Pit ... I suffer your terrors; I am desperate" (vs. 6, 15). The ambivalence of the Old Testament God-image—sometimes merciful, sometimes violent—is reflected in the experience of these writers.

When Jesus cried, "Why have you forsaken me?" just before dying on the cross, he was quoting from Psalm 22. His cry is typical of people who face the stark fact that God seems to sanction their suffering by withdrawing from them. The Old Testament writers often express their frustration at God's treatment of them, but they protest without loss of faith. This approach seems preferable to denying flatly that God has anything to do with evil, since an honest examination of history makes the claim dubious. Jung is therefore by no means alone when he insists that there is a dark side to our God-image. He points out that if we wish to remain truly monotheistic, *both* good *and* evil must be contained in our image of God.[42] Jung's position rests on the argument that our image of the divine must contain everything, including qualities that to us seem diametrically opposed to each other, such as good and evil. In psychological terms, Christianity is, in fact, dualistic because it splits off the dark side of its God-image and projects it onto the devil. Unless we indulge in a process of psychological splitting, it is impossible to keep identifying our experience of God with only the highest good, given all the terrible things that have happened—and continue to happen—to us as a race. Furthermore, to say that God, at the level of transcendence, is "beyond" human categories of good and evil, as some Christian thinkers do, is to sidestep the issue, since the very concept of God's goodness then becomes meaningless. In the light of all the evidence, it is remarkable that the idea that God is love has persisted for so long. Perhaps God's love is indescribably different from human love, but in that case we will not actually experience it as love, so it becomes psychologically irrelevant as *love*. The reality is that regardless of what the exact nature of the divine itself might be, we *experience* the divine as a mixture of opposing qualities. If the Self has its own shadow, then this must be integrated into a whole Self-image; for a *psychological* spirituality, the divine darkness can no longer be split off and lodged in the figure of Satan.

This kind of splitting into all-good and all-bad is characteristic of very young babies, who are unable to recognize that the mother who is, sometimes, the source of gratification and the mother who is, at other times, the source of frustration are, in fact, the same person. Such splitting can persist into adulthood in people who have unmanageable emotional difficulties; they experience the world in black-and-white terms. However, splitting is a primitive (and infantile) mental process. As the infant matures it begins to recognize that there are many shades of gray, and this is true for our God-image no less than for ourselves. Acknowledging shades of gray is difficult because it involves acknowledging our own shadow, to say nothing of the shadow of the Self. I would suggest that some human beings create the notion of an all-good God because they find the alternative terrifying. I suspect the idea of a dark side to the Self may never be acceptable to committed monotheists because it represents too much of a threat to the continuation of the monotheistic tradition, since this tradition typically derives its morality from God, and if there is only one true God, he has to be absolutely moral and therefore absolutely good, and can have no part in evil.

However, my own experience of the Self, and that of many of the individuals I have worked with psychotherapeutically, leads me to believe that what I experience as good and evil are products of the same Intelligence. I trust this Intelligence, even though I do not pretend to understand it, and I acknowledge that at times it appears to behave in ways that *feel* monstrous, even as I acknowledge that there is no point in my judging it. Like Job, then, I experience the darkness of the divine, and I am not afraid to admit that I experience it as a mixture of qualities, a mixture that includes love, but also relentless pain, madness, horror, and chaos.

Why is this so hard for some people to admit? Perhaps we idealize the divine and project onto it the kind of perfection that we imagine an idealized figure to have. Idealization springs from the normal childhood need to have someone we can admire, someone who is all knowing and all powerful, who can protect us when we are afraid or lost. Our parents are usually the ones who fill this childhood need in its earliest form, but they are eventually displaced from their pedestal as we begin to realize that they are not as grand as we thought they were—they too have human frailties. But, the need for a perfect protector seems to persist, and our God-image is a convenient place to lodge this need. Unlike Freud, however, I do not argue that this means there is no God, only that our image or fantasy of God has been colored by these childhood needs.

Some contemporary theologians do acknowledge that the presence of radical evil and suffering in the world force us to the notion that there is a dark side to the divine. The alternative is to think of God as limited in power, unable to prevent the catastrophic from happening. This view of God is even more unacceptable than the view that God is all-good, since such a God would not qualify for the title. In view of this, some theologians have given up the claim that God is absolute goodness. Robert McClelland[43] uses the metaphor of God as a "loving enemy" who wants us to face ourselves and learn that we live by His grace. A similar attitude is taken by the well-known writer and former atheist turned Christian apologist, C. S. Lewis. In his *A Grief Observed*[44] (on which the movie *Shadowlands* was based), he initially accuses God of being a Cosmic Sadist. He describes how at first he could feel only anger at God when his wife dies of cancer. As the disease progresses, his hopes are repeatedly crushed as she shows signs of recovering, only to take a turn for the worse. It suddenly comes home to Lewis that the worst spiritual crisis that can result from such suffering and grief is not the loss of faith but the realization that this is what God is really like—a torturer. In struggling with these feelings, Lewis achieves a new perspective on his situation as he comes to realize the element of selfishness in his grief. In the end, he arrives at the position that lived and embraced suffering is what raises humans above the level of animals and makes them divine. The feminist theologian Judith Plaskow[45] is another writer who thinks that the frightening and destructive aspects of the divine must be acknowledged, along with images of the divine as mother and womb of life. Her argument is that destruction and creation exist side by side in the universe and are closely interrelated. She claims that women often experience God as unpredictable, ambiguous, and irrational. Martin Luther suggested that God is by nature hidden, but is revealed to humanity in the crucified Christ, whose strength lies precisely in his abject weakness. For him, God is revealed in suffering. Perhaps this was his polite way of referring to the dark side of God.

For the psychologist, the dark side of the Self is embodied in human beings in the form of our negative complexes and our shadow, which are not purely personal, since they have a transpersonal core. This means that some behavior that we call evil originates in the objective psyche, or the Self, since the dark side of human nature has its archetypal origins in the Self, not just in the behavior of Adam and Eve. Thus, in people such as Hitler, we see a merging of human evil with archetypal evil—such people incarnate the dark side of the Self to an unusual degree. Because the personal shadow also contains an element of the transpersonal shadow, we have the potential to become vehicles for the incarnation of awesome powers of evil. The archetype, what Jung called the "organ of God" in the psyche, is destructive when it forms the core of destructive complexes such as those of Sol, Shirley, Jim, and King Saul in the Bible. In their negative form, the archetypes belong to the dark side of the Self, or the archetypal shadow, which, in a pure form, would be radical evil, expressed in the Christian mythic tradition as the Antichrist. However, in psychological terms there is no sharp rift between light and darkness, since the unconscious contains both, as well as every level of illumination in between. What we perceive as the opposition between good and evil emerges only as our experience is filtered through consciousness, and this is what creates the illusion that both good and evil are "out there"—outside of ourselves.

We cannot get rid of the dark side of the personality by piously splitting it off from consciousness. We have to accept that the dark aspect of the Self is incarnated in us and makes demands on us as it manifests itself through the personality. This leads to the terrible paradox that when we struggle with evil we struggle with the Self. Here we find another radical difference between depth psychology and traditional conceptions of sin. The theological conception of sin sees it as an offense against God. But the depth psychologist struggles with the problem that our negative complexes are partially *derived* from the Self, so that our evil is due to our living out the dark side of the Self. We must then ask the Self for help in dealing with the Self, just as Job appeals to God for help in dealing with God. Fortunately, even as we experience the negative side of the Self, the positive side is also available as a potential that can be realized.

Jung believed that as our consciousness extends into the unconscious, we discover more and more about the Self, and our Self-image changes accordingly. Jung describes this process as the "transformation of God."[46] In an attempt at a psychological theodicy of sorts, Jung suggests that the Self causes emotional pain in order to press for this new consciousness. Jung believed that the process of making more of the Self conscious in the individual has a reciprocal effect on the transpersonal Self; in traditional language, we might say (as the process theologians do) that just as God affects humanity, so humanity affects God. In the language of myth, just as Job was affected by the Almighty, so the Almighty was affected by Job.

This idea is helpful if we adopt the ego's dualistic perspective and separate the human from the divine. It helps us to realize that our conscious work on our shadow has an effect beyond our own immediate experience. If the darkness of the Self is fixed and unchanging, then the prospects for humanity are grim, and the idea is terrifying. But if the dark side of the Self can be transformed within human consciousness, then we are not helpless victims, and there is hope for the future. We are like Job, whose traumatic experience and determination to discover the root of his suffering led to a new image of the Self. Our work of making the Self conscious affects the way in which the Self expresses itself. Perhaps human freedom is really about being able to choose which aspects of the Self will be transformed within our personality. Some have expressed the concern that Jung's idea of the dark side of the Self indirectly legitimizes evil: if evil exists in the Self, then I can justify its existence in me. However, when we consider that Jung spoke of the *transformation* of the Self, it becomes clear that there is no question of legitimizing evil. Evil might be seen as the splitting off of the dark side, or the state in which we (and the Self) are unconscious of the shadow. If the ultimate goal of all human endeavor is to achieve the good, then achieving the good would be defined as the task of becoming aware of the shadow and thus increasing consciousness. In achieving the good, the Self is transformed as its dark side is integrated into its consciousness. In the ongoing process of integration, transformation, and expansion of consciousness, evil is gradually overcome.

What does the process of becoming aware of the shadow look like in practice? During the course of her work on her shadow problem of "gluttony," Shirley begins to feels less empty and better able to hold herself together without overeating. She realizes that her childhood problems were the result of unconscious parenting inflicted on all the children in her family by several generations of unhappy mothers, who were devalued because they were women. The effects of this societal tragedy were magnified as they filtered down from one generation to the next. Shirley is determined not to continue the cycle of passing this family burden on to future generations; she stops hating her body, and finally values her femininity and that of her daughters. The family complex stops with her. Eventually, she becomes a psychotherapist, specializing in treating eating disorders. Out of the consciousness forced upon her by her own wounds, she can help others. The evil that was inflicted on her is redeemed by her conscious work on her own shadow, which enables her to understand and have compassion for others in a similar plight.

Sol discovers that he has been using sex as a means of mastering the pain of his abandonment depression. He discovers his rage and hatred for his mother for abandoning him as a child, and for her subtly erotic relationship with him. As his sense of self becomes more solid, he gradually becomes able to tolerate separations without acting out and without sexualizing his difficulty. He is eventually able to express his pain in words, and is even able to forgive his mother and re-establish a degree of relationship with her as he begins to realize that her behavior was the result of her own misery.

Jim discovers that he no longer has to compete with his father and obsessively prove to everyone that he can support his family. He realizes that he feels responsible for some of his parents' misery only because he was made to feel a burden to them. He discovers that he treats his employees in the same harsh way he was treated as a child. He finally discovers that he can be a worthwhile person and a good provider to his family without working endlessly, driven by his childhood sense of inadequacy. His greedy shadow softens as he discovers that he can give to others with no loss to himself. Concern for the poor becomes more possible for him.

These individuals worked on their shadow problems using depth-psychological methods. By contrast, traditional religions offer repentance, confession, and the grace of God as the antidotes to the shadow. Christianity tells us that Jesus will carry the burden of our sins if we believe in him. Jung, however, reinterprets the message of Jesus to mean that we must live out our own destiny as Jesus lived out his. In Jung's mythology, the divine penetrates the human psyche with darkness as well as light, and our task is to struggle with the tension produced by these two sides of the Self pulling in opposite directions. Rather than take on such a painful and difficult task, many people choose one of the traditional solutions to evil: let God take care of it in his own time. However, while working on elements of the dark side of the Self is indeed burdensome, it is more true to our experience than the strategy of depending on the mercy of a God who is absolute goodness. We have waited too long for swords to turn into plowshares; they will not do so on their own. Our swords can turn into plowshares only when we have uncovered our psychological need for swords.

In its approach to evil, depth psychology relies on the conscious differentiation of the shadow, the attempt to understand its origins in childhood, and the idea that the Self may demand that we struggle with evil for the sake of the new consciousness that this struggle will bring. We then try to transform what we can and contain what we cannot. Sometimes, however, we come across evil that can neither be redeemed nor be contained, a force represented in folklore and mythology as a vampire or the Medusa; the only way to deal with such evil is to destroy it.

The notion that an encounter with evil leads to an increase in consciousness is part of the depth-psychological myth.[47] From the depth-psychological viewpoint, the problem of evil is a problem of consciousness rather than a problem of morality. In his *Vision of the Last Judgment*, William Blake said it well: "Men are admitted into Heaven not because they have curbed and governed their Passions or have no Passions, but because they have Cultivated their Understandings."[48] The ultimate solution to evil is to be found in an understanding of the nature of reality, that is, that all human beings are expressions of the divine and not separate objects to be manipulated.

If we accept the Judeo-Christian God-image of an all-good God and the anthropomorphic notion that this all-good God created the world, then the problem of evil becomes insoluble. Using the same anthropomorphic thinking, it must be concluded that since every created thing reflects its creator, and the created world contains evil, this evil is a reflection of the all-good Creator God. It is remarkable that the Judeo-Christian tradition is the only religious tradition that feels compelled to justify its God through theodicies, and the very fact that such a justification is felt to be necessary calls into question the morality of the tradition's God. It also raises the problem of how moral human beings are supposed to relate to a seemingly immoral God. In the next chapter, I discuss the way in which Job struggled with this dilemma.

CHAPTER SIX

The Dark Side of the Self and the Trials of Job: Transformation of the God-Image

INTRODUCTION

When analyzing Job's experience, the depth psychologist reads the Book of Job as a mythic text. That is, although we cannot comment on the book's literal or historical accuracy, it clearly speaks to people symbolically, spiritually, psychologically, and metaphorically. This attitude offends those committed Jews and Christians who think that other people's sacred texts can be called myth, but the Bible is the Truth. However, the discipline of psychology is in no position to comment on this claim. For the psychologist, the best we can say is that any book that has been accepted for millennia as sacred or divinely inspired must be emotionally important. A story like that of Job is important for what it tells us about people's beliefs and for the kind of God-image it depicts.

Our images of God can be derived from various sources, such as personal experience, tradition, culture and family, and the testimony of sacred texts such as the Bible. These texts are widely thought to describe the human encounter with the divine, and many people accept them as authentic accounts of divine revelation. Yet, it is important to remember that even if the origin of the Bible is in the divine realm, this source has to be filtered through human levels of the psyche in order to be written down. We therefore cannot say that Biblical language and perceptions completely reflect the transcendent realm, which is surely beyond human conception. That is why Jung believed that the statements in the Holy Scriptures are best thought of as utterances of the soul,[1] meaning that religious statements are psychologically important facts as well as statements about our God-image. In this view, the authors of the Bible are not necessarily describing the divine itself; rather, they are writing about their God-image, influenced by pre-existing beliefs.

By human standards, the image of the divine portrayed in the Bible is not entirely that of an all-good Being. It is, rather, of a deity who sometimes behaves morally, but sometimes seems to us to be unjust, angry, arbitrary, vengeful, and bloodthirsty. It is usually argued that we should not apply human standards to the divine, since we cannot understand the mysteries of God. Yet this argument is inconsistent if at the same time we insist on God's goodness, since we are also judging that quality by human standards. In fact, as psychologists, we are not trying to understand the divine mysteries themselves; rather, we are trying to understand how they affect human beings. Sometimes they affect us painfully, as is reflected in the story of Job, a typical example of the experience of the dark side of our God-image.

Like all mythic material, Job's story has eternal significance. Thus, when traditional explanations of his experience are no longer satisfying, we try to find new explanations. Job's question—why do the wicked prosper, while good people suffer?—has always been a part of the spiritual quest. I would like to look at this story on two levels, the personal and the archetypal. On the personal level, I suggest that the Book of Job depicts the experience of a man going through a catastrophic emotional crisis, which is resolved only when he arrives at a new understanding of the divine. Here I would ask the reader to bear in mind that we cannot apply contemporary psychological categories to people such as Job, who lived so long ago; for this reason, I speak of Job's experience *as if* he were a contemporary individual. This makes it possible for us to use the story as a vehicle for illustrating some common psychological dynamics found in people going through severe difficulties. In the absence of any conversation with the man Job himself, the best I can do is try to understand his feelings based on the text, exercising empathic imagination (with a dash of theory). On the archetypal (as opposed to the personal) level, I will explore some of insights that the book has to offer into the problems raised by the traditional Judeo-Christian God-image, as identified by Jung in his *Answer to Job*.

The Book of Job

The Book of Job is one of the later works of the Hebrew Bible.[2] Scholars typically date the book to the fourth century B.C.E., but the authors were probably influenced by folk memories and oral traditions that stretched back into the distant past.[3] Biblical scholars believe that the Book of Job is a composite work with more than one author. The text has come down to us through repeated oral and written transmissions, with a good deal of pious editing that attempted to soften the tragedy, so that by now there must be many deviations from the original text. Another difficulty is that there is more than one way of translating the original Hebrew material, and alternative readings of the same text can be dramatically different.[4] Biblical scholars and philologists continue to debate these issues. What matters to us is that the book has stood the test of time as the crystallization of many voices over many years. The projections onto the story that we use to explain God's behavior tell us something about our own God-image. We can discuss only the God-image portrayed in the text, because we can have no idea to what extent the image corresponds to the divine reality.

The story is that Satan has questioned Job's faithfulness by asking God if Job's goodness and piety might be merely the result of God's having blessed Job with riches and success. God agrees to let Satan test this theory by making Job suffer. The wager produces an immediate problem for the reader, as described by Jack Miles in *God: A Biography*. Miles points out that if God is this kind of gambler, whatever seems to come from God may actually come from Satan. Then we have no way of knowing whether any of God's other actions actually came from God himself; perhaps the Ten Commandments were the result of a wager with Satan! In Miles's words, "[N]othing God might henceforth do or say would deserve to be taken at face value."[5] This question haunts the whole book.[6]

Evil and suffering quickly follow the conversation between God and Satan. From the human perspective, the marauders who murder Job's servants and steal his animals are undoubtedly morally evil. The lightning that destroys his men and his sheep, and the storm winds that kill his seven children by collapsing their house, are forms of "natural" evil. The story tells us that Satan is behind all these disasters. Depending on how one reads the text, Satan either acts with God's tacit permission or at least the two of them negotiate the withdrawal of divine protection from Job.

Job's Reaction to his Losses

The irony in the story is that it is God who behaves in a faithless manner, not Job. Remaining faithful to God, Job seems to accept the news of his severe losses with what looks like resignation and acceptance of the will of God. First we see Job the patient. He worships God, grieves, and says: "Naked I came from my mother's womb, and naked I shall return; the Lord gave, and the Lord has taken away; blessed be the name of the Lord" (1:21). Satan then insists that Job would not be so good if he were to become physically ill. God allows this experiment also, and Job is afflicted with "loathsome sores from the sole of his foot to the crown of his head" (2:7). At this point his wife, who has lost her children and her home for no apparent reason, bitterly urges: "Do you still hold fast your integrity? Curse God, and die" (2:9).[7] But Job simply points out that if they have accepted good things from God, they should also accept evil.

Job's Dialogue with his Friends

Soon, Job's friends arrive to try to help him. They hardly recognize him because he is in such a terrible condition. They are so stunned at his plight that they cannot speak to him for seven days, but simply sit and grieve with him. Their silence mirrors the inchoate nature of his feelings. It is a testimony to the power of his friends' silent empathy with his grief that only at the end of this period of mourning do Job's real feelings erupt. It is as if his feelings have been so strongly disavowed that he needs his friends' attunement to his distress before he can finally put his feelings into words. (Because Job is portrayed as having two opposite attitudes to his suffering, some scholars have suggested that Job the Patient and Job the Impatient are actually two different characters rolled into one. In psychological terms, however, they can be seen as two aspects of the same Job, representing his "mixed feelings" toward his suffering.) I suspect that without the presence of his friends Job would have remained stuck in his grief and would have been unable to give vent to it. Job needed his friends to *provoke* him into becoming aware of his real feelings. Suddenly, there is an eruption of the rage that Job has been repressing. Job curses his own existence: "Let the day perish wherein I was born, / and the night which said, 'A man child is conceived'" (3:3). He protests bitterly against having been born, and questions whether there was any point in bringing him into life, since now he wishes only that he would die: "Why is light given to him that is in misery, / and life to the bitter in soul, / who long for death but it comes not" (3:20-21). No wonder he breaks out in boils trying to keep all this inside him; while he was being so patient and accepting at the conscious level, his body was expressing his unconscious feelings.

At this point, Job's friend Eliphaz suggests that if Job appeals to God, things will work out in the end, because Job is good and only the wicked end up badly. According to Eliphaz, what has happened to Job is actually good for him. If he repents and makes restitution, he will be better off than he was before. Eliphaz has had a dream (4:13) in which a spirit tells him that no man can be righteous and pure before God, since God is critical even of his own angels. In other words, for Eliphaz, Job cannot win against this God-image, no matter how he behaves. Like many people who are committed to a tradition, Eliphaz wants to generalize from his own beliefs and his own experience to everyone else. From our point of view, Eliphaz's dream is not necessarily relevant to Job.

Job realizes that his friend gives him this advice because he is afraid of the calamity that has befallen him, and that Eliphaz is trying to make sense of it. But Job does not want anyone to talk him out of his despair. When we are in despair, brave words and common sense miss the depth of how we feel; if they were any use, we would not be truly in despair. Job insists on his own truth; he knows he does not deserve what has happened, no matter what Eliphaz says. Job insists on not restraining his anguish: "I will complain in the bitterness of my soul" (6:11). He reproaches God: "What is man that thou dost make so much of him ... and test him every moment?" (7:17). He complains that even if he has sinned, "what do I do to thee, thou watcher of men?" Job is no threat to God, so why has God made him a target, and why can God not forgive him? Here we also hear a painful need for a connection to God, and a worry about the state of the relationship, as Job cries: "Why have I become a burden to thee?" Job reminds God that he must be quick if he wants the connection, because otherwise "now I shall lie in the earth; / thou wilt seek me, but I shall not be" (7:20-21).

Job's questions are understandable, but his friends find this outburst too painful to bear. It threatens everything they believe in, everything they have been taught. They are torn between their caring for Job and the way his speech threatens their religious beliefs. In the end, their wish to preserve their God-image proves stronger. They lose patience with Job, and they insist that he must have done something wrong to have incurred all this suffering. They present the traditional ideas that suffering must be a punishment for sin, or that Job is being disciplined.

Job insists that he is innocent, or that even if he has sinned these punishments are disproportionate. He complains bitterly that God is unfair. His friend Bildad maintains that God does not pervert judgment, but Job disagrees with this collective wisdom: "Though I am innocent, my own mouth would condemn me: / though I am blameless, he would prove me perverse" (9:20). God is indifferent: "It is all one; therefore I say, / he destroys both the blameless and the wicked" (9:22). No matter how pure Job were to become, Yahweh would still "plunge me into a pit" (9:31). In a beautiful reminder of his creation, Job reminds God that: "Thy hands fashioned and made me; / and now thou dost turn about and destroy me. / Remember that thou hast made me of clay; / and wilt thou turn me to dust again? / Didst thou not pour me out like milk and curdle me like cheese?" (10:8-12). In other words, why make this amazing creature and then destroy it for no reason? Job's friends cannot tolerate this accusation of their God. Zophar insists that Job is guiltier than he realizes. He again urges Job to repent, and points out the enormous power of God.

To this, Job responds with sarcasm. He already knows about the power of God, and does not need his friends to tell him about it. What he wants is the chance to argue his case before God. But because of their anxiety and their need to preserve their beliefs, his friends are now so lacking in emotional resonance with Job, so lacking in empathy with his feelings, that their connection to him is finally disrupted. Job becomes enraged at his friends: "As for you, you whitewash with lies; / worthless physicians are you all" (13:4). He tells his friends that it is dangerous for them to try to blindly vindicate God by lying, because if they give false testimony in his forthcoming trial, God will judge them severely. Job now takes his life in his hands and insists on presenting his case before God, even if

180

God kills him in the process. He asks God to let him know what his sins have been, and he demands to know why God bothers to torture such a worthless, short lived, insignificant creature. Why not leave him in peace?

In turn, Job's friends become angry with him. Eliphaz reveals his real fear; if Job is right, then religion is undermined. Job *must* be sinful—their whole belief system rests on this being the cause of his suffering, and Job has questioned this fundamental premise. Sarcastic in his turn, Eliphaz asks: "Are you the first man that was born? ... Have you listened in the council of God?" (15:7-8). "What do you know that we do not know? / What do you know that is not clear to us? (15:9). Perhaps remembering his dream, Eliphaz re-affirms human impurity and sinfulness, and asserts that the fate of the wicked is painful in the end. Job is not impressed. He's heard all this before, and he would say the same thing if he were in their shoes and they in his. As far as Job can see, God persecutes him "although there is no violence in my hands, / and my prayer is pure" (16:17). But his friends are unable to understand his protests, so convinced are they of the traditional arguments. Bildad accuses Job of treating them like stupid cattle. He accuses Job of wanting special treatment, perhaps revealing some envy of Job, and goes on to repeat the traditional story about the terrible fate of sinners. This lack of understanding tortures Job further. *God* is the problem, not him, and they are adding to his pain. Suddenly, in the midst of his despair, Job breaks out into an extraordinary confession of faith that seems to come out of nowhere:[8] "For I know that my Redeemer lives, / and at last he will stand upon the earth; / and after my skin has been thus destroyed, / then from my flesh I shall see God, / whom I shall see on my side, / and my eyes shall behold, and not another" (19:25-27). Here Job actually tells God what he wants, which may be why God appears to him at the end of the story.

Meanwhile, Zophar feels insulted because Job has accused his friends of making things worse. Zophar has a great emotional investment in maintaining the traditional view about the cause of suffering. He loses his temper with Job, accuses him of pride, and repeats Bildad's point. Job tries to be patient with them, and says that it would really help if they would only listen carefully. In great sorrow, Job then points out some hard truths. Contrary to what his friends have said, wicked people become powerful and prosperous, and die happy. The wicked man does not care if his wickedness affects his children. Many good things happen to bad people, even though they reject God. Don't his friends realize that the wicked are not condemned or punished? In the face of all this: "How then will you comfort me with empty nothings?/There is nothing left of your answers but falsehood" (21:34).

When Eliphaz hears Job's account of how the wicked prosper, he interprets this to mean that Job's prosperity must have been due to wickedness. Eliphaz then outrageously lists all of the faults that he imagines Job must have in order to explain what has happened. He accuses Job of cheating, and of greed, and of indifference to the needy, as if Job believes that God cannot see his actions. Eliphaz again recommends repentance, a suggestion Job ignores. Because he is convinced of his innocence, Job desperately wants a hearing so that God can judge him fairly, but he wonders how he can talk the whole thing over with God when he does not know how to find God. Job is also terrified because God is so persistently indifferent to human suffering. Why does God seem indifferent to the deeds of the wicked, or not care about the suffering of the poor? "From out of the city the dying groan, / and the soul of the wounded cries for help; / yet God pays no attention to their prayer" (24:12). Thanks to his own suffering, Job seems to have become very conscious of the plight of the poor: "They lie all night naked, without clothing; / hungry, they carry the sheaves ..." (24:10). This seems to be an indictment of God as the one responsible for social injustice. Who, Job demands, is going to prove that what I say about God's indifference is not so? At this point, Bildad, who seems to have grasped nothing of what Job has just said, makes another irrelevant speech about how human beings are just worms and maggots compared to the power of God. At this, with withering sarcasm, Job thanks his friends for their "help" and "advice." He swears that as long as he has breath in his body he will not speak falsely by admitting that they are right: "... [T]ill I die I will not put away my integrity from me" (27:5). (The writer implies that God's integrity is on trial here, rather than Job's.)

Sadly now, Job mourns the losses of his previous lifestyle. He grieves the loss of his belief that God watches over him, the loss of his children, the loss of being universally respected by important people, and the loss of the feeling that he is blessed because of his good works (ch. 29). Some of his grief occurs because he sees his fallen status as a sign that he has lost his connection to God, but this part of the story also gives us a clue to an unacknowledged problem—at least it would if this were a modern-day Job. Job says that he used to glory in his superior social position; he was so affluent that he was able to wash his steps with milk. When things were going well, Job was apparently rather self-satisfied, and felt special and full of his own importance. For this reason, some commentators have suggested that, before tragedy struck, Job had been rather complacent, even smug, and not quite as good as he portrayed himself to be—an important echo of Satan's original accusation. Although Job was charitable when he was wealthy, he seemed to think of his wealth as an entitlement. This is another reason why his reversal of fortune comes as such a shock to him.

Job complains that he is now so reduced that he is mocked by the meanest of people: "... [T]hey do not hesitate to spit at the sight of me ... they have cast off restraint in my presence" (30:10-11). "God has cast me into the mire, / and I have become like dust and ashes. / I cry to thee and thou dost not answer me; / I stand and thou dost not heed me" (30:19-20). This is not fair, Job says to God. I helped people in distress, but "when I looked for good, evil came; / and when I waited for light, darkness came" (30:26). Job also realizes that the same God made both him and his servants: "Did not he who made me in the womb make him? / And did not one fashion us in the womb?" (31:5). Now, however, unlike in the past, when his acts of charity merely emphasized his wealth, Job has *real* empathy for the downtrodden because he has experienced their plight for himself. Perhaps the point here is that only those who suffer themselves can really understand suffering. Because poverty and suffering predispose the sufferer to question religious beliefs, it is no accident that new spiritual movements begin among oppressed peoples. Job had no reason to question his God-image before his suffering began.

Job bitterly remonstrates with God: What was the point of all my virtue if misery is not just for sinners? Isn't God keeping a proper record? Not only is this a tacit agreement with his friends' theological views, but here we see what might be a guilty conscience in Job. Job tells God that *if* he has been vain or deceitful, or lusted after other women, or failed to respect the needs of his servants, or failed to care for the poor and needy, or sought riches, or secretly worshipped pagan gods, or wished evil on his enemies, or turned away strangers, or been unfair in business—then let him be punished. He's ready to account for everything he has done;

but, he asks, where is my indictment, so that I can justify myself? At least consciously, Job is convinced that he has done none of these things. He demands of God: "Let me be weighed in a just balance" (31:6).

At this point a rather self-important young man called Elihu dominates the conversation, angry because the three friends have not convinced Job that he is wrong. He stresses the limitations of human consciousness and points out that God speaks to us by means of dreams, which act as a warning against pride. This recalls the fact that Job had earlier complained about frightening dreams: "… [T]hou dost scare me with dreams and terrify me with visions" (7:14). It is sometimes the case that an impending tragedy announces itself by means of frightening dreams.

The voices of Job's friends could be regarded either as aspects of Job's personality, inner voices with which he has to contend, or as actual people. In either case, their God-image seems to be built on guilt and retribution, very much a legalistic model of the human relationship to God. Job's demand for justice is typically Hebraic, and thus not surprising, but justice is not the only thing Job wants. Without being able to consciously articulate what he wants, I believe that Job is searching for a different kind of relationship with the divine, one that is not based purely on sacrifice and obedience. I sense that he is resisting the imposition of a pre-existing God-image, which is also our contemporary situation.

GOD'S REPLY FROM THE WHIRLWIND

When the personal level is silenced, the transpersonal can emerge: it is God's turn to speak. The fact that God answers at all is very important, since it acknowledges that a relationship is present. God responds to Job out of a whirlwind. The numinosum can take so many different forms that the specific manner in which it appears to Job must have something to do with Job's personal psychology. This is an *image* of the Self; the whirlwind is not simply "God" in the transcendent sense of the word, but an immanent experience of the numinosum that is relevant to Job's personal psychology. The very idea that this is a wind has to be transmitted through the psyche for Job to have recognized it as such. God also *speaks* to Job, and we cannot have language without the personal levels of the psyche being involved. Job's experience of the divine is therefore mediated or colored by his associations to winds of this type; whirlwinds mean something to him. This particular Self-image suggests that Job's God is a storm God, the same God that killed his children by blowing their house down in a windstorm. This is the God-image that has always held him in fear, the image to whom he has sacrificed in vain to protect his children from being punished. If we look at the content of what God actually says from the whirlwind, we will obtain an even clearer picture of Job's God-image. What follows is not a description of the Unknowable itself; it is an experience of the numinosum colored by projections that arise within the structures of Job's (actually the writer's) personality.

The response that Yahweh gives to Job out of the whirlwind is a poetic outpouring about how powerful God is compared to Job. God compares his power with Job's smallness, thus reiterating what Job's friends have been saying all along. Usually this comparison is said to be simply ironic, an attempt to humble Job and cut him down to size. But I think that there is more than a little rage and sarcasm in God's response, a perspective that is very important in understanding Job's God-image. I will emphasize the sarcasm by simply emphasizing the word "you" in the text. God says: "I will question you, and you shall declare to me. / Where were *you* when I laid the foundation of the earth? / Tell me if you have understanding. / Who determined its measurements—surely *you* know!" (38:3-5). "Have *you* commanded the morning since your days began, and caused the dawn to know its place .... Have *you* entered into the springs of the sea, or walked in the recesses of the deep? Have the gates of death been revealed to *you* ... declare, if you know all this .... *You* know, for you were born then, and the number of your days is great!" (38:12-21). After these unanswerable questions there follows a long list of God's creations, which of course Job cannot match: the control of the seas, the coming of the dawn, the snow and hail, thunder, lightning and rain, the movement of the stars, and the ways of animals and birds. Strikingly absent from this list of divine achievements is any mention of humanity. In other words, for such an insignificant creature as a man to question the Lord of the Universe is ridiculous. Essentially, God says to Job, "Just who do you think you are? You don't know anything, and you cannot do all the amazing things that I can do." However, Job's knowledge of God's creative power was never an issue in the first place—God's power has been obvious to Job all along. Here we wonder if God's sarcastic questioning is an accusation, an indictment of a secret inflation in Job of which he had not been conscious. In retrospect, then, we wonder if the initial wager between

God and Satan was actually a subtle challenge to Job's arrogance, not a questioning of his piety as such. Perhaps "Satan" is an unconscious sector of Job's personality that accuses Job of arrogance.

God ends his speech with a final attack: "Shall a faultfinder contend with the Almighty?" (40:2). In other words, God says, "*You* are the problem, not I." In response to God's speech, Job becomes submissive and admits that God knows best: "Behold, I am of small account; what shall I answer thee? / I lay my hand upon my mouth" (40:40). It is difficult to know what this means. It may be that Job agrees with God, or it may simply indicate that the power differential between them is too great for him to argue with God, or that the experience of awe is so great that it overpowers Job's questions about God's injustice. In any case, Job's response does not appear to satisfy God, so, in case he has not made his point completely, God continues, apparently unable to contain his indignation and outrage. In this section, God adds some further impossible questions: "Will you even put me in the wrong? / Will you condemn me that you may be justified? / Have you an arm like God, and can you thunder with a voice like his?" (40:8-9). In other words, "Don't question what you don't understand. What I do does not conform to your categories of right and wrong." There follows another list of how strong God is and how much he can do, as if Job were still in any doubt. Job responds: "I know that thou canst do all things, / and that no purpose of thine can be thwarted .... Therefore I have uttered what I did not understand, / things too wonderful for me, which I did not know" (42:2-3). Then the important lines: "I had heard of thee by the hearing of the ear, / but now my eye sees thee; / therefore I despise myself, / and repent in dust and ashes" (42:5-6). Until now Job had a traditional idea of God, based on what he has been told, but now he has a personal experience. Typically, the real thing is quite different from our expectations based on hearsay. I suspect Job is still enraged about the injustice, but he is willing to accept it because it comes from a God that he can experience directly.

Job's final act of contrition seems to pacify God, who now agrees that Job was right, after all, and his friends were wrong. God condemns Job's friends, presumably because they tried to fit God into their own categories of morality. Interestingly, God commands Job's friends to ask Job to sacrifice and appeal to God on their behalf. This must be an acknowledgment of the importance of the connection between Job and his friends and their need to be reconciled. The drama ends as God tries to make it up to Job by restoring his material possessions and giving him new children, as if this would somehow make up for the death of his first family—a monstrous implication. No comment is made on the fact that Job's children were simply innocent bystanders in the wager between God and Satan. That God must have felt guilty is suggested by his giving Job twice what he possessed before, and his allowing Job a very long life. This rather sad attempt at a happy ending may have been added by a different writer in an attempt to salvage his own God-image, but it misses the point of what Job has gone through. The real benefit is Job's direct experience of the numinosum—he is given a new vision of the Self. This vision is personal and directly relevant to his psychology. As is often the case, it took tremendous suffering to bring about this experience of the numinosum, and the experience addressed Job's psychological difficulties, to which I would now like to turn. These difficulties reveal themselves both in Job's lament during his suffering and also in the context of his dialogue with God.

JOB'S PROJECTION ONTO HIS GOD-IMAGE

God's might is right whirlwind speech can be understood in various ways. At first glance, it seems to be evidence merely of the narcissism of the divine, since God never says that he is just, only that he is omnipotent, as if his sheer physical power justifies his behavior. Since it would be meaningless to attribute narcissism to the divine itself, it makes more sense to assume that the narcissistic, self-important, power-drenched aspects of this speech are the ways that Job (again, the writer) has colored his God-image with his own difficulty by projecting these qualities into Job's dialogue with the divine. Similarly, "Satan's" doubts about the reason for Job's piety could well represent something in Job's mind, a sector of his unconscious in which he is filled with self-doubt, which he defends against with self-importance. It is no accident that, during his laments, Job stresses his wealth, his high position in the community, his charity, and his righteousness. He appears to be dimly aware that these are the ways in which he held himself together and maintained his self-esteem. When he loses all these supports, and with them the power that his wealth made possible, he has to re-evaluate the way he thought of himself.

187

Job's God-image stresses power over the world. In those days, it was taken for granted that the divine would be characterized by dominion and domination. Power formed part of the collective God-image, because human rulers were interested in power. Job may have assumed that power is an aspect of the divine because power over others is so important to him personally. People who are oppressed experience God differently from those who are among the élite; to the oppressed, qualities such as justice, rather than power, are important. Job's suffering makes him more aware of the limitations of power, more empathic towards the suffering of others, less grandiose, and less self-important. Perhaps this was the point all along. The process was intended to change his values, deflate his self importance, and thereby speed up the maturation of his personality. This argument would be weak if it implied that intense suffering is the only way for this to happen, but for Job this may have been the case, since many people with narcissistic character disorders develop compassion for others only when they have suffered themselves. By all accounts, it took a good deal of suffering to deflate Job's grandiosity. Perhaps God's earlier attempts to reach Job in a gentler manner had failed.

A display of power is also seen in the appearance of the divine as a whirlwind. This intimidating imagery is a well-known part of the Biblical tradition and was part of the collective God-image at the time the Book of Job was written. Yahweh had appeared on Mt. Sinai in thunder, lightning, and a thick cloud, which terrified the people (Ex. 19:16-19). Jeremiah had portrayed the divine attack as a "whirling tempest" (Jer. 23:19) or a "whirlwind" (Jer. 4:13), and Hosea had spoken of God's vengeance as "reaping the whirlwind" (Hos. 8:7). Many scholars think that the Biblical Yahweh was originally a local storm god in the Sinai desert. The mythic storm gods tend to be gods of war as well as judges and law givers.[9] Yahweh is often depicted as a merciless warlord who helps his people fight battles and conquer cities. He tells them to kill all the inhabitants and keeps the spoils for himself (Josh. 6:16-24; 1 Chron. 26:27). In other words, it is very dangerous to cross him. In addition to these cultural roots of Job's God-image, if Job were living today we would probably find that there were also factors in his personal history that reinforce this angry God-image.

SATAN AS A SECTOR OF JOB'S PERSONALITY:
JOB'S FATHER COMPLEX

Instead of thinking of God and Satan as being "out there" in the experience of Job, we can read the story as a psychological drama, as something happening *within* the consciousness of Job itself. Satan is then not an outer figure, but rather, a representation of a painful complex or an emotional difficulty that afflicts Job. With good reason, Satan is traditionally known as the Adversary (the literal meaning of his name), and indeed "he" (this sector of Job's psyche) challenges Job's conscious attitudes. As a character in the plot, Satan drops out of the drama as Job's experience gradually resolves the problem that the figure of Satan represents. But also, as an aspect of Job's psyche, "Satan" remains dormant or unconscious until it is activated by the loss of Job's children and possessions, which plunges him into grief and depression. The story has it that Satan and God make their wager before these disasters happen, although this is the kind of idea that may have occurred to Job *after* these tragedies had occurred, in a retrospective attempt to make sense of *why* they happened to him. Before the disaster, Job had been constantly worried about whether God was displeased with him or his children, as evidenced by his constant sacrificing, so that he would naturally consider the severe thunderstorm that killed his children to be an act of divine retribution that he had failed to ward off.

If Job were our contemporary, we might be tempted to say that his anxiety about God's behavior towards him tells us more about his experience with his personal father than it does about the divine itself, since our fantasies about the reasons for God's actions are often colored by our experience with our childhood caregivers (see note 12). Theories about God that are not based on experience or direct revelation are always speculations, since all we can do is project onto the mystery, or attempt to describe how it affects us. It is often possible to understand the content of a fantasy about God by looking at the life story of the individual, because our God-images are shaped by our life experiences.

One line of evidence for the importance of the role of the father comes from the meaning of Job's name. According to the *Jewish Encyclopedia*,[10] the name Job has two possible origins: one, a verb meaning to bear ill-will; the other, a contraction of the phrase "where is the divine father?"

It is possible to see some psychological significance in these suggested derivations. Job's own behavior as a father, and his worry about the ill-will of the divine Father, both appear early in the story. Job's sons were in the habit of giving parties, and after each one of these Job would offer sacrifices to God, "… for Job said, 'It may be that my sons have sinned, and cursed God in their hearts.' Thus did Job continually" (1:5). Even though it was common practice in Job's day to offer sacrifices for sins, Job comes across as an extremely overanxious parent with his "continual" sacrificing. If Job were living today, we might see in his repeated ritual an obsessive-compulsive quality. From Freud we have learned that such rituals are attempts to manage guilt over a forbidden impulse. The obsessive-compulsive ritual tries to contain and bind aggression and fear so that they do not flood the personality. A modern-day Job who constantly worried about whether his sons had offended the divine Father might well be projecting onto God his fear of his own personal father. Such a person's concern about his sons' guilt could well stem from his own guilt, which he wards off with sacrifices and other appeasements to prevent divine retribution. All this suggests that there is a good deal of fear behind Job's piety, and it helps to explain Job's God-image of an angry sky father who must be placated with sacrifices. In addition to its other significances, then, the story is also a depiction of the way Job experiences the divine through the lens of his personal psychology. This is not to say that he does not experience anything real, as the traditional psychoanalytic explanation would have it; rather, he experiences the numinosum in a particular way that is radically colored by his cultural expectations and his personal psychology. Job experiences the archetypal sky Father in a negative form; at least for our contemporary Job, the devastating maker of storms is an image of the archetypal Father at the center of the father complex.

Job's God-image is clearly ambivalent. On the one hand, he is able to appeal to God as an honest judge who is approachable and fair, someone before whom he can plead his case. On the other hand, his experience of God in the whirlwind and his need to sacrifice constantly to prevent divine retribution suggest that he also sees God as overbearing and harsh. Typically, such a God-image is a projection produced by childhood experiences with a harsh parent.[11] Job's statement of repentance in his concession speech—"I have uttered what I did not understand … I despise myself and repent in dust and ashes"—can be understood on various levels. From the point of view of a child confronted by a powerful, angry father, an apology is the safest tack to take. Job's expression of utter humility is further evidence that the relationship is based on submission rather than love and connection. Consider the uncanny parallels between Job's experience of God and the experience of a small child dealing with an angry father. During his ordeal, Job constantly complains that God is unreasonable, and he wants to hear God's own explanation for what is happening, although when God finally speaks from the whirlwind he does not really address Job's concerns. Instead, God lectures majestically about how he created everything and about how small and ignorant Job is in comparison. It is often pointed out that this is all irrelevant to Job, since he never questioned God's power in the first place. In fact, early on in the poem, Job acknowledged that God alone "stretched out the heavens" and "made the Bear and Orion" (9:8-9), so the whirlwind speech does not reply to Job's indictment of God's justice. However, I think that God's lecture *is* in fact a kind of reply, and it constitutes circumstantial evidence that Job has colored his image of the divine with his feelings toward his own father. Understood as a projection, God's speech is the typical comment of an angry father in response to his child's complaints of unfairness. If we read the speech from this point of view, we may paraphrase God's reply thus: "Who do you think you are, you little brat? What do you know about life? You wouldn't even be here without me! Just do as you are told— you cannot understand what I'm doing since everything I do is hopelessly beyond your abilities." Job replies to God that he is "of small account," and, just like a child confronted by an angry father, backs away from further confrontation. God (the Father) proclaims that the facts of his wonderful creation justify his actions and make Job's questions irrelevant. But this wonderful creation is the container for the very problem of suffering and injustice that Job is complaining about, so God's response actually sidesteps the real issue.

To the clinician, the self-deprecation in Job's phrase "I despise myself" suggests that Job is depressed, a state of mind reflected in his wish to die (3:17) or to have not even been born (3:11-12). Like many depressed people, Job feels that he is a burden to God (7:20), just as many neglected children are made to feel that they are a burden to their parents. Job feels that God will not listen to him (9:16), that he is cut off from God (30:19-

20) and that God has become his enemy (13:24; 16:9). This depressive state of mind is typical of the way a child feels when his or her relationship with an angry parent has been severed and the child cannot find a way to re-establish the connection. In order to try to reconnect, the child is often forced to ignore his or her feelings, or simply bottle them up. The text says that Job did not sin "with his lips," meaning that he did not express his outrage verbally. But Job's feelings are expressed quite clearly in his physical body. Although Job is usually portrayed as a model of resignation to the will of God, if we look at his somatic afflictions as an expression of what is going on inside him, we see a different picture. He breaks out in a terrible skin inflammation, which covers his body from head to foot. It is well recognized that the skin is an organ of the soul—witness how our skin blushes with embarrassment or tingles with excitement. Job's angry skin eruptions are a bodily statement of his unexpressed rage at what has happened; he is not as resigned as he is made out to be after all. I suspect that many contemporary Jobs would, as children, have felt too unsafe to express their anger; this is common when the child is made to feel that his or her anger is unacceptable and that expressing it will threaten the connection with his or her parent(s). For the sake of self-preservation, the child has to repress his or her rage, which then expresses itself automatically through the body. Job is angry with God, and he assumes that God is angry with him. The abused child often projects his own reactions onto a parent, so that "I am angry with father because he has withdrawn from me" is converted into "father has withdrawn because he is angry with me." Or, "if father withdraws his love, he is bad" is transformed into "if father withdraws from me, I must be bad and unlovable."

If Job is obsessive about offering sacrifices, it is because he wants to ward off disaster and thus control his anxiety, which for many people is produced by a father complex. When tragedy strikes, he realizes that his obsessive sacrificing has not worked. Then, the underlying complex breaks out in full force, leading to Job's fantasy that his suffering is the result of divine retribution, which he has been trying to prevent with his rituals. When catastrophic losses are combined with a father complex they can plunge a person into a depression. This opens the way for "Satan" to appear. In psychological terms, Satan is a force within an individual's personality, possibly an aspect of his or her father complex, which may be more or less under control, but which produces psychological havoc when it breaks loose. Satan is an internal critic that torments Job, an inner voice that tells him his piety is not genuine, that he is not really as good as he thinks he is. Through contemporary eyes, Job's need to find a new way to relate to God is a central theme of the story; we realize that his friends miss the point when they focus on suffering as a punishment for sin. They are bound by a traditional reward-and-punishment God-image from which I believe Job is trying to escape.

The "Satan" sector of Job's personality disrupts his everyday consciousness so that he is forced to develop a new God-image. For this purpose, Satan is essential. This sector of his personality remains unconscious, or dormant, until it is activated by his losses, which he takes to be a punishment. Gripped by such a complex, a modern-day Job would then be plunged into the childhood experience of being cut off from his father and bewildered about why he is being punished. Making a harmonious re-connection with his father (or with God) will be a difficult task, because our Job feels persecuted. Here, he or she may be repeating a childhood experience; it is not unusual for a young child to try to do whatever it takes to keep connected to a raging, dangerous parent. Children often sacrifice themselves to maintain a needed relationship and scrape together whatever love is available to them.

Satan's initial accusation is that Job behaves well only because he has been bribed with material possessions. The implication is that loyalty can be bought, a fantasy that may also reflect a person's relationship with his or her father. We might imagine Job's father as someone who is hard to please, who becomes angry suddenly and arbitrarily, and treats his child unjustly, ignores his good behavior, and punishes him excessively with little justification. The father might then regret what he has done, and try to make it up to the child by giving him or her gifts, to buy back the child's love and make reparation. It seems as if Job projects these dynamics onto his God-image. He unconsciously assumes that God, like a human father, has to be constantly placated because his anger can be triggered at any moment. Eventually, after the tantrum is over, Job is given gifts by a now pacified and guilty God (father). But because this father projection onto God is unconscious, Job feels like a victim of the divine while he is under attack, with no idea as to why terrible things are happening to him. Nevertheless, the story goes on to say that Job recovers and lives a long life, so we can assume that this experience was also regenerative and helpful to him. One may wonder how this happened, since at first sight it may seem that nothing about the quality of the relationship has changed. However, what one finds in practice is that contact with the numinosum is itself restorative. Job has had an experience of divine reality that puts his everyday ego concerns into a radically different perspective.

As a result of Job's numinous whirlwind vision, he becomes silent because he realizes what he has been dealing with all along. We might say that he sees an image of the archetype at the center of the father complex. When he exclaims "but now mine eyes see thee," it is as if he is saying: "Now I have my own experience of you, I can see what you are really like, which is not what I have been told to believe about you." Job's experience is typical of the encounter with the dark side of the Self, and illustrates how suffering may be transformative.

The awesome experience of the numinosum at the core of the father complex is a typical example of the healing potential of contact with the numinosum, even when this is experienced as unpleasant. Job's experience reveals how important it is to inquire into the meaning of suffering and to maintain one's own position rather than follow collective wisdom. Job's vision of the numinosum is much more meaningful than simply hearing about the divine second hand. As a result of his numinous vision, Job is reassured that there is an Intelligence, a greater Consciousness, behind what has happened. His suffering was not meaningless; it was a dark night of the soul, a period of great spiritual importance. As a result, the "Satanic" sectors of his personality, his depression, anxiety, and narcissism are transformed.

TRADITIONAL AND PSYCHOLOGICAL APPROACHES COMPARED

The psychological approach can be contrasted with traditional explanations of Job's suffering, such as the idea that piety is its own reward, or that God was testing Job's piety. To me, this explanation reflects an aspect of the collective God-image that is based on projections of the parent-child or teacher-child relationship. The very problem that we are dealing with is that Job's relationship with his God is based more on fear-based obedience than on love, and God's behavior is hardly calculated to change this feeling.

To our ears, a God who would allow terrible suffering just to see whether Job loves him for his own sake sounds like a God-image with issues of self-esteem—obviously a human concern. This view of God projects the behavior of human rulers onto the God-image. *Human* rulers are concerned about how they are viewed by their subjects, even when they are more interested in power than in justice. The dark side of Job's God-image therefore reflects cultural factors combined with Job's personal problems. God's whirlwind speech is all about submission and domination, which suggests that (at least our modern-day) Job had been projecting his power shadow onto his God-image. Satan's accusation forces Job to become conscious of a God-image that contains elements of Job's own difficulty. In fact, the story of Job can be seen as an example of the transformation of a narcissistic shadow by suffering. Since Job's shadow must include a partial incarnation of the transpersonal shadow, Jung would say that the story could also be seen as the Self's attempt at self-transformation through Job.

Here I am obviously discussing images of the divine as they are portrayed in a story. It is useful to discuss the dynamics of the Self in this way, as long as we remember that we are not discussing the divine itself, but the way it affects us. It is not very satisfying to be told that God is an impenetrable mystery. Are there some things we are allowed to understand and some things that we cannot grasp? If so, where is the dividing line? Perhaps we *should* ask questions about the mystery of God, since we ask questions about every other type of natural phenomenon. It may seem silly, or even arrogant, for a human being to ask these questions, but I think they are legitimate, since the ego seems to be at the receiving end of a deal that it never consciously signed on to. Indeed it is quite plausible that we were designed to ask these very questions, which we must ask even as we realize that the answer is beyond thought. Only experience and insight take us where we need to go, and these can never fully be put into words. But the story of Job shows us how a person's questioning may lead to a deeper experience of the sacred. All of Job's earlier sacrificing, worshipping, obedience, and fear of God produced nothing more than a piety based on the standard model. Not until his suffering began his inquiry did he have a direct experience of the numinosum. In this way are born personal God-images.

The hard fact is that there often is no discernible relationship between a person's character and his or her fortunes in life. To insist that God rewards and punishes according to the way we behave is to deny reality; the traditional emphasis on God's justice is simply the projection of a human value onto the collective God-image. God admits as much when he says in his whirlwind speech that Job's friends were wrong to insist that suffering is the result of sin. Job's example tells us that while we are suffering we must ask questions about what the suffering means. If we are fortunate, we may then experience an entirely new God-image based on a personal experience of the numinosum. What happened to Job also happens on the collective level, because our culture continues to suffer; in a post-Holocaust, post-Hiroshima world our God-image has to change in response to our cultural suffering. These kinds of events are the reason why Jung insists that the Self has a dark side to it. Here begins Jung's controversy with the theologians, who did not appreciate Jung's making a distinction between the divine itself, about which Jung was consistently silent, and the Biblical God-image in his *Answer to Job*.

A RESPONSE TO JUNG'S *ANSWER TO JOB*[12]

To understand Jung's approach to the Book of Job, it is important to realize that although Jung was steeped in the Christian tradition, he did not read the Bible through the lens of Christian doctrine. He often said that he was not concerned with theology. Rather, as a psychologist, he dealt with "the layman's picture of theological concepts," or "people's common beliefs" rather than theological concepts of Truth.[13] For this reason, Jung did not get involved in Biblical scholarship or the analysis of Biblical language; the layman deals with the text that we have, and Jung felt that he was addressing the typical questions of the layman.

Jung suggested that the Book of Job depicts the beginning of the dissolution of the all-good God-image, because the people of that time realized that they could not rely on the divine promise that evil would be punished and good rewarded. In spite of this promise, the God of the Hebrew Bible could behave in unpredictable, often outrageous ways. In his *Answer to Job*, Jung points out that throughout his ordeal Job maintains his integrity, whereas the story reveals an abominable God-image. Job's personal ethical standards had evolved beyond those of the collective God-image that he inherited from an earlier era of history, so that Job came out of this encounter looking better than this God-image. To deal with what happened to him, Job's God-image had to change radically from its earlier form, which Job's friends keep insisting on, into something he could use. At the same time, there was also a need for a transformation of the collective God-image. Jung suggested that in order to catch up to the level that humanity (in this case Job) had reached, the collective God-image had to become more human. Therefore, according to Jung, God's incarnation in Jesus was the answer to Job. If the story of Jesus' incarnation had not emerged, the collective God-image might have become increasingly degraded, as the old images were seen to be less and less useful. Instead, Jung believed, Job's story forced a radical change in the collective God-image from that of an angry storm God into a God of love. Because he was a loving man, Jesus was able to embody love, something that had previously not been possible in the culture; in contrast to the Old Testament view of God as a warlord or a judge, Christ's God-image was that of a loving heavenly Father, and he was thus able to incarnate that loving aspect of the Self.

The Gospel story implies that when Jesus was crucified, God experienced what it is like to be mortal, and he realized how he had caused Job (who represents humanity) to suffer. That is to say, the new God-image that began with Christ takes into account human suffering in a way that does not radically split the human and the divine. Thus began a new mythology[14] based on the idea of the humanization of the divine. Job suggested the idea of God's becoming human when he protested to God: "Hast thou eyes of flesh? / Dost thou see as man sees? / Are thy days as the days of man, / or thy years as man's years?" (10:4-5). But, Jung insisted, this incarnation is not confined to Jesus—it happens within all of us. The incarnation of the Self into a conscious, empirical personality inevitably causes suffering. This suffering in turn forces us, Job-like, to a new consciousness of the Self, and this new consciousness itself is a form of incarnation. Jesus became fully conscious of the Self—in Eastern terms, he was a God-realized man—but now the development of this consciousness is a task for all of us.

Jung goes on to point out that the change in the collective God-image brought about by Job's experience was only partial; although Job became conscious of the dark side of the Self, this dark side was not integrated into the Christian God-image, which concerned itself with only the light side of the divine. Nevertheless, the process by which Job developed his new consciousness of the Self is a useful model. Job forced the Self into a dialogue with him by maintaining his own position and by refusing to take the collective God-image for granted. He even forced the Self to acknowledge its own darkness in relation to humanity. For Jung, Job acted as a reflecting consciousness for the Self, which made the Self conscious of its treatment of Job.

According to Jung, the capacity for self-reflection is essential for self-consciousness. However, we cannot be fully self-conscious without being in relationship with another consciousness. Jung thought that even the Self needs a reflecting consciousness, and this is why God's doubts about Job are personified as an "other," that is, as Satan; the confrontation with Satan is thus God's own inner dialogue as he wonders about Job. Without Satan and Job, it seems, God would not have been able to reflect on what he was doing. This is why Jung made the startling comment (which got him in trouble with the theologians) that God's behavior is so atrocious that he must be unconscious, or at least he must be unconscious of the split between light and dark in his own nature. The theologians who were outraged at Jung's idea of an "unconscious God" could not appreciate that Jung was speaking psychologically, not theologically, but even so, what Jung meant by the statement is not absolutely clear. When he said that "God becomes conscious in the act of human reflection,"[15] he could have meant that the Self becomes conscious in us when we reflect on it, or he could have meant that the Self itself is unconscious until it is able to see itself reflected in human consciousness. I prefer the first reading, but some scholars believe that Jung meant literally that the Self needs human consciousness to be aware of itself. For me this is a dubious proposition, since I regard the Self as Consciousness itself, so in the last analysis it is only the Self that is conscious of anything. I therefore read Jung to mean that *our* God-image is unconscious, as far as the human ego is concerned. Until we begin to experience our God-image and think about it, our God-image is inaccessible or incomprehensible to us. The Self is always active in us, but we are unaware of it until we start to experience it directly rather than project it outwards onto a figure such as Jesus.

For Jung, the story of Job is a model for a certain type of (dualistic) relationship between the ego and the Self. He speculated that the Self seeks to become conscious and to differentiate itself through humanity.

This occurs in various ways. Every time we work on any manifestation of the unconscious, be it a dream or a symptom, we are making some aspect of the Self conscious within us. Our developing consciousness of the Self occurs by means of human reflection on its workings. This work assists in its incarnation, and also in our discernment of its different aspects. The unconscious is an undivided unity until someone reflects on it, since within the Self opposite qualities such as good and evil, light and dark, are united, not split as they are in human consciousness. For Jung therefore, the Self becomes aware of the opposites within its nature by becoming incarnated in a human being. This idea cannot be proved—it is a mythic image that reflects Jung's personal approach, based on his own need to stress the importance of ego-consciousness. My own view is that we have no need to further inflate the importance of the ego. In any case, since the Self, for Jung, is also the totality of consciousness, the ego is actually contained within the Self and is not a separate entity.

Jung makes this suggestion in order to address the mystery of why the Self would want to incarnate in us, and why God would create the world in the first place if he is already perfect. The ideas for Jung's theory are found within various mystical traditions, which hold that the divine expresses itself by means of humanity and becomes manifest in the human act of reflection. The mystics of several traditions have taught that not only does God create humanity, but humanity creates God, in the sense that it takes human consciousness to *realize* that God is God. It is in this sense that the divine becomes conscious when we become conscious of it. This is a highly personal way of thinking about the divine; other people's God-image may be quite different, because such an image has to evolve out of one's own experience and reflection. Consciousness or Psyche produces images of itself that we experience, and Jung attached great importance to making Self-images conscious because he found that he could help his patients by doing so. In the process, he found that the Judeo-Christian God-image did not work for everyone, and he voiced his criticism of this God-image in his controversial *Answer to Job*.

Jung was criticized by the theologian Victor White[16] for not dealing with Job's obvious shadow material. Jung[17] acknowledges this omission, but points out that if Job had dealt with the situation at the personal level of his complacency, his self-righteousness, his literal-mindedness, and the like, he would have been deeply ashamed. Job may even have thought that it was delusional to imagine that his vanity could cause divine intervention. He would then have been less inclined to think he had heard the voice of God—it would be as if he were given a psychoanalytic explanation that removed God altogether, leading to nothing but disillusionment and resignation. Therefore, Jung says, he preferred to deal with the situation at the archetypal level. However, Jung also admits that he was possessed by intense emotions—mostly angry—as he wrote his commentary on the Book of Job. If Jung had not been so personally involved with the story, I think he would in fact have commented on Job's shadow and his rather one-sided, virtuous persona, and not just on the canonical God-image.

My focus on Job's shadow follows the lead of the poet William Blake, who believed that Job's problem was his self-righteousness—his imperial ego. For Blake, Job's piety was pretentious and excessive, and he was spiritually asleep. But Blake's account does not deal with *God's* injustice, just as Jung's does not deal with Job's narcissistic shadow. Before his losses, Job sounds as if he was rather smug and self-satisfied, so why does Jung ignore Job's own contribution to the situation and blame everything on God? In Jung's anger at the Biblical God-image, we can hear an echo of his problem with his father, who was a great disappointment to the young Jung. He felt that his father had foundered on the rock of his Christianity: he saw his father continually plagued by doubts about the doctrines of the Church, of which he himself was a minister. Jung tried to resolve his father's spiritual crisis in his own mind by dealing with religion psychologically. He focused on personal experience of the numinosum because he saw from his father's life that reliance on belief and doctrinal assertions without direct experience of the divine could lead to despair. Jung's passionate criticism of the Christian God-image in his *Answer to Job* sounds like a long-pent up reaction to the fact that his father was painfully hurt by his adherence to the God-image that his Church dictated. The elder Jung had to preach a set of ideas about God that were often meaningless to him and of no help during his crisis of faith. I believe that Job's plight reminded Jung of the difficulties that his father suffered in relation to God. Just as Job's friends offered the standard approach to religion, there was much prayer and preaching in his father's church, but these practices gave no real comfort. Jung vented his anger by attacking the Biblical image of God the Father, an image that contributed to the unhappiness of Jung's early home life by making his father miserable. Jung seems to identify with the suffering Job as he rails at God, as if Job speaks what is also in Jung's heart. Driven by his father's failure to answer Jung's questions about the meaning of Christian doctrine, Jung developed his own approach to the Christian story, an approach that requires us to become more conscious of the traditional God-image so that we can see how it needs to be changed to be of use to us today. This is why Jung insisted that we include a dark side to our God-image, an aspect that is by-passed in most traditional interpretations of the story of Job.

Unfortunately, the Church Fathers intensified the split between the light and dark aspects of the Self when they made Christ all good and Satan his adversary, as if they were two opposing principles rather than two aspects of a single image. This led Jung to point out that the Christ of Christian theology is an incomplete image of the Self: Christ is depicted without any shadow elements. Jung believed that the Self is a totality that must include everything in creation, including qualities that were traditionally excluded from the Christian God-image, such as evil, the body, and the feminine. According to Jung, the Antichrist represents the missing aspect of the Christian Self-image, its dark aspect. Our contemporary task is to unite these aspects of the Self in our own mythic image of the divine. This could be done in two stages. First, we can stop splitting off and projecting the shadow onto the figure of Satan, and acknowledge that the shadow is in us. Then, we can recognize that this shadow has an archetypal as well as a human component to it, because both the light and the dark side of the Self are incarnated in us, and the dark side produces the core of the human shadow. By acknowledging that the shadow is both personal and transpersonal we will develop a more accurate God-image, one that does not require the defense mechanism of splitting off what is too terrifying to deal with. We will then be less prone to color our fantasies about the divine with human projections, and we will no longer equate our God-images with the divine itself. (This serious error within the monotheistic traditions has led to futile religious wars over competing God-images.)

Our changing ideas about good and evil contribute to the change in our God-image. Some traditionalists were outraged when Jung said that God behaved in an immoral manner towards Job, and that Job's morality was of a higher order than that of God. This is actually Jung's critique of a particular God-image. Job could no longer project onto his idea of God a moral code that was less developed than his own moral standards. Job had evolved beyond the collective projections about the way in which God is supposed to behave, projections that were based on current social thinking, so that he needed a new way to think about the Self. In the Bible, morality that is *attributed* to God is actually the *projection* onto a God-image of what people in that period thought God would want us to do. A present day prophet might speak about the rain forest, the degradation of the environment, homelessness, starving children, and other social and ecological problems.

Christian theologians have never been happy with Jung's distinction between the divine itself and our God-image; they have always suspected that Jung treated the image and the Reality as if they were the same, as if Jung thought that the divine itself has an evil aspect. Theologians also had difficulty with the wide variety of God-images that Jung described, because many of these did not fit into the traditional Judeo-Christian formulas. Even though Jung wrote that "none of my reflections touches the essence of the Unknowable,"[18] it was difficult for his critics to grasp the difference between the God-image as a psychological phenomenon and their doctrinal descriptions of the divine itself, especially when these did not coincide. Consequently, they believed that Jung was actually doing metaphysics or theology disguised as empirical psychology. There is some truth to this claim in those areas where Jung is clearly speculating. However, as long as we stay with our direct experience when we speak of the Self, we are entitled to call what we do psychology. A problem arises only if we try to explain the *origin* of numinous experience—here we would drift into theory and speculation. Jung is clearly speculating when he suggests that the divine creates human consciousness so that it can become conscious of itself, or that the Self becomes self-conscious within human consciousness.[19] He is speculating when he suggests that because qualities such as good and evil are not separate within the wholeness of the Self we somehow render the divine a service when we suffer the tension of these apparent opposites. Whether the divine needs our help in this respect (a monumentally inflated idea) or not, experience does confirm that an encounter with the numinous helps us resolve and unify this tension within ourselves. This is a way of saying that, like Job, we have to ask

God for help with God: the source of a problem is also the source of the solution to the problem.

Jung's focus on the experience of the Self is unacceptable to theologians for various other reasons. It contradicts the claims of some Christians that there is no way to know God other than through the specifically Christian form of revelation. As well, for some theologians (such as Martin Buber[20]) Jung's description of the Self as a God-image within the psyche makes the divine seem rather too immanent, too intimate, not transcendent enough, and "only psychological," as if to say that it is not fully real. This critique ignores the fact that, for Jung, the psyche is real, and the experience of the numinous is an experience of something real. Furthermore, it is claimed that the suggestion that we can experience the Self in many ways threatens the principle of monotheism (but note that there are, ironically, many variants of monotheism, each claiming to be true, each offering its own God-image). The believer in a particular dogmatic God-image may protest that we cannot know the objective truth about God if we rely only on personal experience, since each person's experience of the divine may be different. Reliable information about the divine can come only through divine revelation as contained in the scriptures. However, only the fundamentalist can insist that the scriptures are purely objective.

It is no longer possible to argue seriously that there is only one true version of revelation, which tells us all we need to know about the Unknowable. Various conflicting assertions of metaphysical truth exist; which one shall we trust? Who has such authority? Today we are suspicious of "Truth," because we recognize that what is called truth is often only a tool in the hands of those in power, and is often determined by their beliefs and tailored to their requirements. We find it difficult to accept arguments based on divine inspiration from people who advocate partisan religious politics. Metaphysical assertions are often anthropomorphisms, human fantasies, and opinions about the divine, and may or may not correspond to the divine reality. We know that our beliefs about the physical world change constantly as they are shown to be incorrect, so why should our beliefs about the divine be any different? One can insist on having faith in a particular divine revelation, or one can take the position that what really matters is our experience of the divine as it is mediated by the psyche. Christians generally object to the latter approach on the grounds that individual experience is *too* personal; it cannot be given greater value than the accumulated religious insights of the human race. For them it is clear that they have to continue the work that Jesus began because he told them to do so.

Theologians who argued in these ways resented *Answer to Job* because it devalues tradition, the authority of the Church, and the consensus of the faithful. From the traditional point of view, Jung's interpretation of Job is far too idiosyncratic. But Jung is clear that he is not trying to be objective. He deliberately offers us his subjective reaction, his fantasy about Job's experience. Theologians felt that this method of reading Job obscured a more objective reading of the book in terms of its own historical background and in terms of received truth. Father Victor White angrily suggested that Jung's protest about God's apparent injustice to Job was an immature reaction, the tantrum of a spoiled child, as if Jung were fixated at the infantile level in which "'love' means the egotistic 'I want' ...."[21] White went on to suggest that this book reveals a "paranoid system which rationalizes and conceals an even more unbearable grief and resentment." However, to accuse Jung of being immature and disturbed is not to refute his argument that there is a dark side of the Self, an idea that gives us a deepened perspective on horrors such as Auschwitz and Hiroshima. Indeed, the psychologist could retort that, in the face of the suffering and radical evil that exists in the world, it is immature for the theologian to hold on to an outdated image of an all-loving sky Father who benevolently takes care of us.

Given the evidence of history, it seems that the theologians who were critical of the notion of the dark side of the Self were trying to preserve their doctrine and the validity of their sacred texts at all costs, to the extent that they were even prepared to disavow reality. They could not tolerate the idea that their God-image was at odds with the facts. From the perspective of the psychologist, the theologians also made the mistake of confusing their God-image with the divine itself. Jung is quite definite about this distinction in his book: "It will probably have become clear to the reader that the account I have given of the development of symbolic entities corresponds to a process of differentiation of human consciousness."[22] That is, as our consciousness evolves, so must our God-images. It *is* terrible (for an ego) to fall into the hands of the living God, because this God is experienced as a mixture of qualities that feel *both* benign and loving and *also* very dangerous.

JOB AS A MODEL OF THE TRANSFORMATIVE EFFECTS
OF SUFFERING

Our God-image affects the way we think about suffering. As discussed in Chapter 5, the traditional approach argues that suffering disciplines us, teaches us, tests our faith, promotes spiritual development, and strengthens our relationship to God, as is suggested by the fact that in the end Job's rewards seem to make up for his suffering. However, this is not everyone's experience. Sometimes suffering has none of these effects. Suffering may merely ravage people, causing them to become bitter and angry. On the other hand, we do see people like Job, whose suffering increases their empathy for other people, allows them deeper self-knowledge, and produces a radical change of values. Suffering may force a turning to the divine that otherwise would not take place. Even as Job yearned for an answer from God as he questioned what was happening, we sense that his yearning and questioning were themselves a form of connection. In the circumstances, this was the best he could do. Job's suffering led to his demand that God deal directly with him, and this at least allowed the potential for a different kind of relationship.

Job's story is therefore a mythic model of the potentially transformative effects of suffering on both character structure and one's God-image. Judging from Job's initial reaction to his losses, which he could only express through his body, it might be concluded that our (contemporary) Job had felt rage in his childhood that he was unable to express directly. When children who suffered in this way reach adulthood, they are able to view their childhood difficulties in a new way, because they are able to bring to bear their mature thoughts and feelings to the situation. They also have a new opportunity to develop a personal connection to the divine that is not confined to collective attitudes. Our modern-day Job may realize that something is going on that demands a deepening of his spirituality. The psychological importance of Job's experience is that it suggests we seek new meaning in what is happening to us without being satisfied with traditional explanations.

The eruption of the numinosum that Job experienced may only occur during periods of intense suffering and turmoil. When it does so, Job's experience shows us that the experience of the numinosum imposes order and meaning in the midst of a confusing situation. We realize that a larger

Consciousness is involved in the situation. Given this Presence, when suffering cannot be alleviated, our task is to develop an attitude that makes it possible for us to let go of what we think *ought* to happen (a function of the ego's conditioning) in favor of an attempt to understand and accept what *is* happening. This is why the question of meaning is often so crucial. Job constantly wants to understand why he is suffering, in keeping with the idea of psychologists like Jung and Frankl, who believed strongly that unbearable suffering can be made bearable if it is meaningful.

To conclude, I would like to mention an ancient Indian myth that also describes the archetypal theme of transformative suffering. In *The Greatness of Saturn,*[23] King Vikramaditya suffers terribly at the will of the divine, personified as the planet Saturn. In this mythology, Saturn is sometimes called the Lord of the Oil Mill, because he grinds people down and extracts their true essence, leaving behind a residue of what was false. Saturn does this by making us experience what *must* happen to us. He is portrayed as especially dangerous to arrogant people. Like Job, Vikramaditya is philanthropic, religiously observant, protective of his subjects, and well thought of, but also a rather self-righteous and self-centered personality. Although Saturn makes him suffer, the King learns to accept and embrace what happens as necessary for his development. He forgives all the people who hurt him during his period of suffering because he realizes that they too had to live out the roles that were given to them. Like Job, King Vikramaditya finally has the experience of a direct encounter with the divinity that tormented him, whereupon the King asks Saturn to be compassionate to others, because, as in the case of Job, suffering has produced a radical transformation of the King's capacity for empathy. One meaning of a mythic tale such as this is that we can think of the process of suffering as a kind of purging of what the Self does not regard as essential. We typically resist this process, and our resistance to radical change adds to our suffering—without resistance, our experience might be painful but not necessarily cause suffering.

CHAPTER SEVEN

A Sense of the Sacred: Spirituality beyond Religion

SPIRITUALITY AND RELIGIOUS INSTITUTIONS

Spirituality is a state of mind, an attitude to life, a way of being in the world that enables us to be aware of the presence of Ultimate Reality in daily life. Our spirituality may be caring, reverent, and life-affirming without being tied to any scripture or specific way of thinking about God. The established religious traditions are simply the ways that our spiritual instincts have been channeled by historical circumstance. These traditions arose during particular eras, and so were colored by local mythologies and cultural beliefs, a great many of which are no longer relevant. At their best, tradition religions act as containers for our spirituality; at their worst, the dogmas of the traditions do not express what is really important to us. If the latter is the case, it is important for us to know that a traditional container is not essential for our spirituality to express itself. There is no need for a complex philosophical, hierarchical, and theological superstructure.

When our spirituality is not limited to organized religions, we still have access to our original spiritual heritage, which springs from an innate human capacity that came into existence long before the development of the world's monotheistic traditions. This instinctive spirituality is "organic," by which

I mean it is free of dogmatic preservatives. It does not favor men over women, it includes animals and the natural world, and it does not seek to frighten people into obedience by threats of eternal punishment. It does not renounce the body or the enjoyment of the material world, it offers helpful approaches to everyday situations, and it recognizes that there is no such thing as an exclusively valid approach to the sacred. Although this spirituality acknowledges that there are transcendent levels of reality, it avoids meaningless speculation about them.

To be user-friendly, our spirituality must be psychologically relevant, non-dogmatic, not based on any particular scripture, not a matter of belief or opinion, and not uncritical, but able to doubt when necessary. It takes into account, and is not threatened by, new information from science and psychology. A practical spirituality allows a radical acceptance of life as it is, and affirms life's essential goodness. Such a spirituality acknowledges that our world is not separate from the realm of the sacred and sees that there is an intrinsic fullness, order, and harmony to life that includes the inevitability of suffering. Our native capacity for spirituality allows us to be aware of transcendent values such as love, compassion, and beauty. We sense the interconnectedness of all beings and the planet, which we recognize to be expressions of the divine. This spirituality is synonymous with a sense of wonder at the mystery of the universe. If we pay attention to this mystery, no matter how we do it, we are "being spiritual."

It is not surprising that many of us do not find this type of spirituality within conventional religious systems. Although it is generally agreed that the sacred is beyond conceptual thought, the Western religious institutions are loaded with elaborations of the experiences of Moses, Jesus, and Mohammed. The resulting conceptual superstructure is far removed from the spiritual source of the tradition. In addition, much of organized religion is simply the product of generations of convention, or the exercise of human religious "authority," with its implication that some people have special access to the divine intention. Such convention and authoritarianism are the products of human needs and preferences and have nothing to do with the sacred.

What about Sacred Texts?

The very notion of a religious authority, such as a Church hierarchy, implies that our spirituality needs a structure to interpret and contain it. For this purpose, religious authorities claim to have the power to explain the sacred texts, which are said to be the product of divine revelation, as if the divine were unable to make itself clear without the help of their interpretation. Thus, the Bible has been revised and edited by many people, translated into various languages, filtered through the human mind with all its prejudices and fears, its contents decided upon by the decisions of councils and committees. Could such a text actually reflect the Reality that is beyond thought? Since there are many sacred books from many competing traditions, how do we decide which book is the true revelation of the divine? Since there is no satisfactory answer to this question, we must conclude that the divine does not reveal itself in one exclusive manner and that the original authors of these texts wrote either in order to record their personal encounter with the sacred or to propagate their beliefs. Subsequent generations projected their sense of the sacred onto whichever book was handed down to them by their elders, so the books became increasingly hallowed by tradition and time. For the most part, people accepted as sacred the book that their culture told them was sacred, because they were brought up with it and because the book provided them with a set of beliefs that served as a ready-made container for their spiritual potential.

At best, sacred books contain some valuable spiritual teaching and accounts of authentic contact with the numinosum. However, they also reflect the very human opinions and prejudices of their authors, not to mention the mythology that was current at the time and place in which they originated. At their worst, these books are used for institutional propaganda or simply to justify theological opinion or certain social and religious practices.

ARE TRADITIONAL PRACTICES NECESSARY?

To be "spiritual" we do not have to go to a special building, read prescribed prayers, light candles, burn incense, listen to sermons, or believe in a set of doctrines. We may do these things if we enjoy them, or if they are helpful in inducing the mood or atmosphere that we seek, by making us more receptive or by helping us to express our intention more clearly. However, they may also prevent us from experiencing the sacred when they clutter our consciousness with preconceptions or dull our mind with repetition. Traditional religious practices can be a vehicle for authentic spirituality only when they act as a deeply felt, symbolic means of connection to the sacred. Otherwise, they may actually prevent us from discovering our real spirituality. It is also possible to carry out these practices and not be spiritual at all. Countless people have self-righteously attended a religious service, performed the required behavior in public, then gone home and abused their children, cheated in business, exploited the helpless, tortured "heretics," and violated the norms of social justice. The hearts and minds of these adherents to religion were not transformed in any way by their religious observance. Their rituals and prayers were merely prescriptions that did not touch the condition they were meant to cure. Their worship services did not open the door to the soul—they did not even approach this door. Their rituals were empty repetitions.

Traditional practices may feel useful simply because they give us social cover, soothe our bad conscience, or support our persona, the mask we show the world. They create the illusion that we are doing something spiritual, but they don't necessarily touch that special place in the heart, the place that yearns for a felt connection to the sacred. We may be using the wrong approach to this place, or it may feel simply too frightening to touch. A spirituality of the heart makes us vulnerable, both because it makes us very open to others and also because it requires a surrender of the sense that we are in charge of what happens to us. It is difficult to acknowledge that whatever happens is supposed to happen, no matter how painful to the ego, because a larger Intelligence is operating. The traditions teach this surrender, but they also encumber us with an unnecessary mythology that is often based on political considerations such as competition with rival sects or the need to preserve orthodoxy by combating heresy.

Sometimes collective spiritual practices are simply a way of belonging to a group of people who support each other's sense of self by sharing the same opinions and values. At times, these practices are superstitious attempts to ward off evil and attract benefits, a type of spiritual bribery of the divine. Much of this kind of "religious" behavior arises from fear. It is designed to produce a sense of security, either by trying to placate what is imagined to be an angry God who is taking notes about our behavior, or to reinforce an atavistic tribalism based on the need to belong to a group in order to feel safe from predators. If our spirituality is based on a sense of insecurity, then fear is likely to contaminate our spiritual experience.

As a result, our spiritual practices become largely a means of shoring up our sense of self rather than a means of relating to the sacred.

What actually happens when we follow formal spiritual practices? Is it possible to approach the divine using a specific method? If the divine is transcendent, then any method we use will be limited in its effectiveness, and so at most could afford us only a glimpse of the totality. Spiritual practices are limited to time, and so cannot take us to the Timeless.[1] Yet, to acknowledge the limitations of these practices is not necessarily to dismiss them completely, since a spiritual practice may be useful for temporarily softening or quieting the ego, expanding its awareness, and making it more conscious of the larger Reality. The shadow side of spiritual practice is that it may actually be a subtle way of inflating the ego's sense of its own importance. For example, ministering to the needy may arise from authentic compassion, but it may also arise from a need to impress others or reassure oneself that one is a good person. Meditation techniques that require physical discipline may degenerate into a masochistic exercise in self-inflicted pain, or a means of feeling spiritually superior to those who do not meditate. There is, therefore, a risk that the very act of spiritual seeking, so hallowed by tradition, will impede the discovery of spiritual truth by reinforcing the ego, especially when we personally have a great deal invested in the tenets of a particular creed. The ego often secretly hopes to enhance itself or feel better by means of the search, and being "on a spiritual path" makes the ego feel important compared to those who are not. To counter this tendency, some of the Eastern traditions remind us that what we are looking for does not need to be sought after because it is always immediately present. However, this is a rather philosophical view for most people, and not of much practical value. As long as we feel an inner dissatisfaction, spiritual seeking will occur spontaneously.

At times, although we are ostensibly on a spiritual path, what we want may be what the ego finds attractive, so we find what we are looking for rather than what we actually need. A true spiritual quest requires us to be receptive to the promptings of the Self rather than seeking to satisfy the demands of the ego. As the desire for a spiritual connection arises, an appropriate path opens up before us, and this may not necessarily be a traditional one. We are invited to follow it, often with no idea of what it will be like—the process is not under our control. The particular path to which we are drawn is determined by a deep, intuitive resonance we feel with something inside us, a felt sense that is difficult to articulate. All we know is that we have an intimation of the presence of Something to which we feel called or drawn. People have felt the need to give this Presence a name—"God," for example—but the name is relatively unimportant; it is the experience of a connection with the Presence that matters. The problem is how to go about establishing this connection. We may try various approaches until one of them really resonates, but nothing we do in our search is ever wasted; it is useful to know what works and what does not. In the end, if nothing in particular appears, it is reassuring to know that there is no need for a specific method.

Unfortunately, the beneficial effects of certain spiritual practices, such as prayer and meditation, may be transitory, wearing off quickly under the pressures of daily life, so that the practitioner often ends up feeling unfulfilled, even after several repetitions. This effect is only to be expected, since no method created by the ego and practiced by an ego can take us to the Reality that is beyond the ego. Yet, the various priesthoods have traditionally maintained that they are the exclusive means by which to gain complete access to the divine.

ON SPIRITUAL TEACHERS

Traditionally, the spiritual teacher is thought to embody a consciousness or knowledge of divinity that can be transmitted to his or her disciples. The implication is always that this awareness is less accessible to the seeker by other means. It is not unusual for spiritual aspirants to experience profound emotional reactions in the presence of a charismatic spiritual teacher, reactions that are usually explained in terms of the mythology of the system. The teacher is sometimes said to transmit spiritual energy or power. At its best, such a relationship can initiate the seeker into an experience of the sacred or a new state of consciousness, but some disciples are attracted to a powerful teacher because of a sense of their own fragility, which creates in them a need to idealize[2] a strong figure. By idealizing the teacher, the seeker is trying to fill a psychological deficit, perhaps caused by the absence of an internal sense of direction, a lack of personal goals and values, or an inability to soothe oneself. This issue is better addressed with ordinary psychotherapy, because as long as one idealizes a teacher there is no incentive to understand the origin of the feelings and find what is missing within oneself. (In technical terms, the idealizing transference cannot be resolved.) The seeker is looking for a sense of the sacred, or an experience of the Self; but rather than experiencing it internally, he or she finds it in a projection onto the teacher, whom he or she sees as above ordinary humans. Such idealization can have devastating results, as when the spiritual teacher falls off his or her pedestal due to a sexual or financial scandal, and the seeker is left with nothing but crushing disillusionment. A further problem is that looking to someone as a teacher immediately puts one in the position of a follower, and this state of dependency, inertia, laziness, or insecurity may prevent the seeker from developing his or her own brand of spirituality, based on his or her own experience. Teachers tend to have a personal stake in the systems and disciplines they teach, and expect loyalty from their followers, but being tied to a specific system may get in the way of one's own exploration and the discovery of one's own mode of connection to the sacred.

For this reason, it is important to not invest too much authority in spiritual teachers. They can be of great benefit if they arouse an interest in spirituality, awaken the seeker to Truth, or act as a temporary guidepost or support, but only if they are genuine. In recent years, there has been a notable increase in the number of self-styled "gurus," some actually quite dangerous, others harmless, but more interested in financial gain than in their disciples' spiritual development. Almost all make exaggerated claims to enlightenment or a high level of spiritual attainment. Most have a narcissistic certainty about the correctness of their own point of view, and need to have followers in order to enhance their own standing. Overall, they cause division and conflict by insisting that only they have all the answers. Generally, they offer some kind of reward to faithful followers— enlightenment, heaven, salvation—although offering such rewards in exchange for devotion or loyalty really amounts to spiritual bribery and exploits the insecurity of the vulnerable.

What is Authentic Spirituality?

For many of us, spirituality can no longer be found by following the traditional paths. More and more we realize the truth of Krishnamurti's assertion that "truth is a pathless land." He never tired of pointing out that one path can take us to only one place, but Truth is never fixed or static. If we block out everything that presumes to tell us all we need to know about That which is beyond thought and image, if we rid ourselves of the superstructure of organized religion, perhaps in the space and silence that results we may come across the Ultimate. The potential to encounter the Ultimate lies in all of us, often dormant. Our awareness that there is a larger reality is wired into the very fabric of our being, so that we have an instinctive sense of the sacred, a sense that reveals itself in our creativity, our love, our relationships, our exploration, our imagination, our desire to be whole, our passion for life, and our gratitude. Acknowledged or not, hidden by cynicism or not, our longing for peace and unity is still there. Even if we are not ready to admit it, everything else—our toys, our achievements—is a substitute. In the long run, nothing else will satisfy us. Unfortunately, however, our pain, fear, and ignorance blind us to the real nature of this yearning. Even when we realize that we are looking for spiritual satisfaction, time and again we never quite seem to get there. Often, this happens simply because we are trying to force our natural spirituality into an unsuitable, artificial container.

It is surely a mistake to think that "being spiritual" means living according to a set of rules or precepts. To force oneself to do so is to set up either resentment or a compensatory resistance to following the rules, and this leads to internal conflict. Nor is it necessary to follow a set of rules. Compassionate behavior towards others arises from our natural spiritual sensibility, as is evidenced by the fact that it is found among believers and non-believers alike. One cannot simply teach this behavior from the pulpit and expect it to be an automatic path to spiritual fulfillment. If we try to live according to the ideology of a particular creed, we may find that its teachings are antithetical to our instinctive spirituality, as might be the case with traditions that devalue women, the body, or the material world. Very often, adherence to doctrine is merely a psychological prop, not a living connection to our spiritual Source. Doctrinal formulas arose in part to buttress the politics and ideology of a particular tradition or to preserve the power of its institutions. However, an authentic spiritual connection to the Source cannot be experienced through theological statements alone, without an *experience* of the Source itself, through the heart and the instincts, through relationships and knowledge of oneself. Spiritual understanding cannot be handed down to us, but we can be pointed in the right direction, and we must then discover it for ourselves.

Whatever form it takes, spirituality includes the intuition or insight that there is another level of reality beyond our ordinary perception of the world. We realize that our everyday personality is not the deepest part of ourselves, that there is something More to us. We recognize the spiritual importance of relationships and the profound mystery of the other, which is not separate from us or from That Which Is. We treat animals and the environment with respect because we instinctively recognize that they too are manifestations of the Source. We recognize that our creative work happens *through* us and does not originate within our ego. We notice and value beauty, which expands our sense of self to include more than ourselves. We realize the dangers of sectarianism, competitiveness, and exclusivity. This attitude is simple to articulate but difficult to live, so we must accept that in practice we will repeatedly forget to live it, at which times we have to remember and begin again, with compassion for ourselves and without recrimination or judgment.

All the traditions have encouraged this perspective, but we lose sight of it easily in the stresses of daily life. The fragility of our sense of self makes us respond to everyday events in ways that are defensive, self-protective, or self-centered. It is difficult to set aside our own preferences and accept that a larger Wisdom is running the show,[3] even if we accept this idea in principle. If there really is a greater Intelligence determining our lives, then whatever happens to us cannot have happened any other way. Still, we try to bend reality to the way we would like it to be. Because the demands of the ego are so intense, we may first have to try a life of ambition, competition, self-aggrandizement, and aggressive self-promotion before we realize that these are all too often purchased at the cost of inner conflict and emotional estrangement from others. The very structures of our society prove this point; everywhere, people who live in this way—and their victims—are miserable and self-destructive.

It is easy to *say* that we are deeply interconnected, but this idea undercuts our cultural mythology of nationalism and individualism, which are instrumental in making people feel important and special. To say that we are really not separate from others—and from the earth—is an offense to these cultural values, which reject the idea of the unity of all things. Nationalism and individualism are the quintessential attitudes of the isolated ego, triumphant in its castle, convinced that "my" religion is the only real one and my values are universally applicable. But the very need for the castle's thick walls betrays the vulnerability of the ego, which must always take a defensive posture. We are not truly free until we are free in ourselves, that is, until we understanding the structures of our personality and the demands of the unconscious. When we see how we have been conditioned by family, society, religious traditions, and our ethnic and national identification, we are better able to let go of this conditioning. This in turn enables us to embrace life in a way that demands nothing in return. When a new center such as this is found, inner peace is possible.

Spiritual peace cannot be found at the extremes of being completely entangled in the world or ignoring the world completely. Neither is peace necessarily found in special "holy" places or activities. Spiritual peace is to be found in a sense of the sacred that is so clear that we know we are safe, no matter what happens. In the end, the mystics are correct: it is necessary to surrender our will completely—but this is easier said than done. As will be discussed below, surrender can occur at different levels. At the personality level, we must recognize and accept the particular spiritual or archetypal patterns that are demanded by each type of personality: serving, healing, ministering, teaching, etc. These manifest themselves to us as a sense of having a vocation; the call comes to us in dreams, in visions, through fascination with certain kinds of work, in synchronistic events, or as gnosis (a profound interior knowing). Our task, though it is not always easy, is to discern these patterns and be true to them while living in a culture that may make it difficult for us to do so. This discernment must be done consciously, not simply by allowing ourselves to fall into collective values. It is achieved by following the scent or flavor of that which grips the personality. As Jung[4] pointed out, a shining exemplar of this single-minded response to the call of destiny is Jesus, who rejected imperial power in favor of spiritual service. Unfortunately, many of his followers today fail to follow his example and instead conform to conventional group thinking. His life is the ultimate answer to the objection that following one's own calling is narcissistic and potentially antisocial. His life demonstrates to us that one's vocation need not be a product of the ego; it can come from the Intelligence of the universe, and whether or not it will lead to ruin in the sight of others is not for us to judge.

Dualism and Monism: Two Approaches to Spirituality

When Jesus said, "I and the Father are one," (John 10:29) or "Truly, truly, I say to you, before Abraham was, I am" (John 8: 58), he was actually giving voice to a type of spirituality that recognizes the oneness of all things, including God—an idea known as "monism" (sometimes called "nonduality"). This form of spirituality, which is found in many Eastern religions and mystic traditions, teaches that human beings, like the rest of the cosmos, are actually an expression of the divine, not separate from it. The most well-known declaration of monism is the statement made by an Eastern sage to his son: "Thou art That."[5] In it we hear a strange echo *in reverse* of God's declaration to Moses out of the burning bush: "I AM THAT I AM" (Exod. 3:14), a declaration of the divine-human dualism, or dichotomy (a splitting into two), that characterizes the Judeo-Christian tradition. In keeping with this declaration, Christianity has traditionally interpreted Jesus' statements in a dualistic manner, on the understanding that the human and the divine are separate from each other. However, the monistic, or unitary (sometimes referred to as "nondual"), approach to spirituality is gradually gaining a foothold in the West and so deserves mention here.

In what way is it true that humanity and divinity are a unity? And if it is true, why are we not constantly aware of it? What prevents us from experiencing such a unity directly? Many thinkers have suggested that the barrier is the interference caused by the human sense of selfhood, otherwise know as the ego, the sense that I am a discreet individual, different from everyone else. In the West, we are trained to think of ourselves as self-contained entities with an isolated mind and body. We are told that we have relationships with other people who are essentially separate from us. Our social, legal, and political institutions try to balance the rights of the individual with the rights of society as a whole, treating the two as separate domains. We speak of the value and dignity of the individual, who is said to be independent and unique. Yet, paradoxically, from the moment we are born, we exist in a matrix of relationships, without which we could not exist at all.

Our sense of selfhood (the ego), begins in childhood as our genetic endowment interacts with our early relationships. Our sense of being a discreet self is reinforced in childhood because we are called continually by a particular name and treated as if we were a separate entity. Our culture trains us to believe that we are individuals who make choices about how to behave. In fact, we are intensely conditioned creatures, shaped by a set of culturally imposed beliefs—a mythology—about the nature of reality. This conditioning arises from the family, education, religious training, ethnic identification, and so on. Over time, we develop a story, a particular version of events that allows us to give a coherent account of what has happened, and we develop a certain image of ourselves. We are told that we are intelligent or stupid, beautiful or ugly, talented or ordinary, lovable or hateful, wanted or unwanted, important or insignificant. These ideas are all based on social norms and on the prejudice and needs of the other members of our family, who project their own problems and beliefs onto us and induce us to share their perceptions of reality. As children, we tend to accept these beliefs as if they really reflect who we are. We take in distortions, which become beliefs about ourselves, beliefs that form the contents of our personal consciousness. As we grow up, we develop likes and dislikes, based on sensations that are judged to be good or bad in relation to "me," depending on whether the experience causes pleasure or pain. We are also subjected to forces in the unconscious, such as complexes, that radically affect our behavior. Because we are afraid of painful sensations, we struggle to avoid them, and we try to experience as many pleasant sensations as possible. The ego is also bound by prevailing social values and ideals. Thus, in our society the ego wants to become important. The more inadequate we feel, the more important we have to make ourselves, often at any cost to others and to our own well-being. One of the worst sources of agitation and unhappiness in our lives is our feeling of being separate from others, a feeling that leaves the ego desperately lonely. As a result of all this, frustration of one kind or another sets in, and this leads to an internal sense of dissatisfaction, restlessness, and the need for change. The only way to escape from the demands of the ego seems to be through the distractions that we call "entertainment," or by drowning our discomfort in drugs or alcohol.

Even though the ego may torture us with its demands for pleasure and safety, it is not necessarily bad or unnecessary. There is a common misunderstanding that the Eastern religious traditions advocate getting rid of the ego altogether. That would lead to disaster; we would then be either unconscious or psychotic. What we call the ego is actually the name we give to a set of essential functions, such as perceiving and testing reality, remembering, thinking symbolically, regulating tension, delaying the discharge of impulses, organizing ourselves, making judgments, and dealing with anxiety, to mention only a few. Obviously, we need these functions and mental processes to carry out ordinary daily tasks.[6] The problem occurs when we think of the ego as a kind of solid entity, or when we forget that our sense of personal identity is an acquired mental image and does not represent what we are at the deepest level of our nature. We forget that the sense of "me" is simply the name we give to the collection of feelings, memories, knowledge, thoughts, and ideas that arise continually within our personal consciousness. Because we are brought up to identify with feelings that arise in us, when a feeling such as anger arises we immediately think, "I am angry," rather than "anger is arising." What happens in our minds seems to happen to a "me." It seems as if there must be someone doing all this thinking and feeling, so we identify the contents of our mind with a "me." But this is an illusion; there is no little person sitting in our brain in front of a control panel! If it is raining outside, there is no "rainer" who is doing the raining; there is just rain happening. Similarly, thoughts and feelings happen, and consciousness is aware of them. Similarly, we are trained to believe that our minds are contained in a body that is radically distinct from other bodies, forgetting that our bodies and the environment are interconnected, part of a unitary system. At first, it sounds counterintuitive, or just too strange, to suggest that we exist in a system in which apparently separate entities are dialectically related within an underlying unity. Yet not only does quantum physics acknowledge such deep interconnectedness, but in fact all of science reveals the gap between perception and reality. Many ideas that society once took for granted are shown to be false as science looks at them more closely. It sounds odd to hear that there are empty spaces between the atoms of a material that feels solid to us. All things considered, it is not too farfetched to suggest that our vision of ourselves as distinct entities is an illusion. We have had many mistaken notions about reality that have not stood up to closer investigation. Our notion of radically separate individuals is just such a concept. The isolated ego is simply our way of participating in consensual reality, but it begins to look less and less substantial as we examine it more closely.

We can understand and be compassionate towards any ego only if we realize that, fundamentally, it suffers from profound vulnerabilities. The ego is afraid of loss and pain, tends to reject what is happening if it is unpleasant, and hopes for a better future, based on desires and memories from the past that it would like to re-experience. When the ego is faced with a threat to its survival, fear arises, and aggression is the typical response to fear. This makes the ego dangerous. Much violent behavior arises out of the ego's need to protect itself. Tens of millions of people were killed by egos in the last century alone, and this century has begun to repeat the same pattern. Because we are afraid of death, we live in constant fear of annihilation, and we annihilate others to protect ourselves. Because we are afraid of being the victims of others, we become victimizers. Because the ego has the illusion of being distinct from others, we do not realize that any harm or violence we inflict on others is also damaging to ourselves—at the level of the Totality, the other and the self are one.

An alternative view to the illusion that we are insular entities is the realization that what seems to be our personal consciousness is actually a part of the larger Consciousness of the Self, somewhat the way in which currents of water exist within an ocean—the individual currents are inseparable from the totality of the ocean. The larger Consciousness is the source of our mental life, but we are so identified with the individual contents of our minds that we ignore or take for granted the underlying ground of Consciousness in which our minds exists. Consciousness is not divisible, so the Consciousness of the Self is the same Consciousness in all of us. At that level we are not separate. Our real nature, the spiritual aspect of the human being, is the underlying Consciousness that is the uniform matrix of our existence. This Consciousness allows the experience of experience, the sense of being, the feeling of "I am," whereas the sense of "I am so-and-so and my story is …" arises from the conditioned level of the mind, from the storehouse of experiences that are held in our memory. Because the ego is *made up of* the accumulation of what has already happened, it perceives and evaluates reality through the veil of the past. Therefore, the ego can never be fully in the present moment, not to mention the fact that, at the unitary level of the Totality, there is no individual to be in the now. In fact, the very notion of "now" depends on the ego's sense of time.

Unfortunately, we often lose touch with the Consciousness that is the deep level of our nature, because the ego is basically a kind of autopilot or robot that allows us to get through daily life mechanically, without full awareness of what we are doing. Our cultural attitudes rarely promote much introspection or self-reflection about who we really are. Instead, we are encouraged to focus outward, by means of an avalanche of advertising which implies that happiness is about consuming more or being entertained. We are also directed outward by constant warnings about the presence of enemies. With a few exceptions, even our religious institutions tend to be externally oriented towards worship services and reading the Bible, rather than seeking the Light inside ourselves. How then may we access this light?

BEING SPIRITUAL WITHOUT ANY RELIGION

Traditional spiritual practices, such as formal prayer or meditation, are motivated by various factors besides the usually stated goals. Some of these motives are quite unconscious, so that there is inevitably a shadow aspect to such spirituality. As we have seen, some spiritual practices are pretentious, an attempt to bolster one's sense of self by making oneself feel self-righteous. Some are superstitious, an attempt to bribe the divine or ward off disaster. Or, spiritual practice may serve as a disguise for sectarianism, especially when it is tied to a tradition that insists on its own version of the truth. Even when spiritual practices are authentic, people cannot always say why they are carrying them out; it just feels necessary to do so, because we know instinctively that there is something beyond the ego with which we need to connect.

To maintain a constant connection to the sacred, we need ways of being in the world that are applicable everywhere, at all times in our daily lives. The following suggestions are useful because they require no predetermined theology, no congregation, and no specific prayers, priests, robes, or special buildings. They are not based on the tenets of any particular creed or religious system, and they are the work of this world, not directed towards gaining some future heavenly existence.

1. Attention

There is a level of transcendent Consciousness within us that is always accessible. This Consciousness is like the sky, and our emotions and

221

thoughts are like clouds that form in the sky and may obscure our vision of it, but do not eliminate it. We take this background Consciousness for granted, but it comes to the foreground if we stop everything, close our eyes and look inward for a moment. When we let go of everything else, we find a silent Space of awareness, which is the Consciousness of the Self. This practice may not come naturally to us because our brains seem to need stimulation, so we constantly occupy ourselves with ideas, sensations, entertainment, memories, fantasies, and so on, lest we feel bored. But behind all that is a Presence that is accessible if we pay attention and relax into it. This is the unconditional Ground of our being, which is not affected by our activity; it remains untouched by all of that. This Ground is not a thing; indeed it is sometimes called No-thing, or a full emptiness.

We have been told by some traditions that we can be in touch with this level only by formal spiritual practices, since it is unknowable and unattainable by any other means. To help us get there, the traditions have produced experts, teachers, books, and methods galore. None of them is necessary for us to get in touch with this subtle level of Awareness, which I believe Jesus was referring to when he said that "the kingdom of heaven is within you" (Luke 17:21). A simple and direct way to experience this Consciousness has been taught by Douglas Harding,[7] who describes a series of exercises that help us attend to pure Awareness. Harding points out that what we look like to other people is not what we are and not what we actually experience. He recommends that instead of looking outward only, which is the way we have been trained to look, we can also become aware of what we are looking out of. If we look inward instead of outward, we find that rather than experiencing ourselves as looking out of two holes in a sphere of flesh, we seem to be looking out of a colorless, perfectly transparent "window" that is totally open. We then realize that there is an Awareness that is doing the looking. This Awareness is not a thing; it has no boundaries, it is timeless, ageless, silent, still, and can contain everything. It is the final Witness of everything that happens.

Many spiritual traditions stress the practice of awareness, mindfulness, or attention to what we are doing, rather than behaving automatically. We can be aware in various domains; we can be conscious of what we are doing in the outer world, we can watch thoughts and feelings arise in the mind, and we can be aware of our breathing and the energy field of the body. This practice cultivates the experience of Witness Consciousness.

A potential mistake here is to *try* to be mindful, since this sets up a conflict between the part of me that is trying and the part of me that resists doing so. Without trying, there is simply attention happening.

There is no need to criticize the everyday mind as we watch it working. We can simply observe the constant stream of judging, commenting, liking, and disliking that goes on in the mind. When we observe these processes, we are less trapped within them. We can say to ourselves "thinking about dinner" before we automatically begin cooking. If a strong emotion arises, we can be aware that anger or fear is arising. There is no need to verbally label or judge what we observe; we just notice it happening. Caught in a traffic jam or a slow elevator, we notice that the ego's conditioned response is to become frustrated. If someone cuts us off in traffic, our usual reaction is irritation because our self-esteem has been wounded. Anger arises to re-establish the ego's sense of importance—"who does he think he is, cutting *me* off like that?" A story line might then develop in one's mind—"I'll show him," and so on. But attention to our reaction cuts off the story before it gets very far, and makes it possible not to act automatically. Gradually, this work of self-observation frees us from automatic bondage to the ego's demands. Witness Consciousness can simply watch this mental chatter going on in the everyday mind. Watching it prevents our being unconsciously caught up in it, and allows us to realize that while all this is happening it does not involve the deepest level of our being. This practice of observation—and it takes practice to develop the skill—is a process of "de-conditioning" that eventually allows the experience of peace amidst turmoil.

There is no need to try to deliberately control the mind using some kind of device such as a *mantram*. In fact, constant repetition may actually dull the mind or merely place it on a different kind of auto-pilot. One simply observes the mind with an attitude of interest that does not condemn, judge, or justify what we see. Methods that require effort and intense concentration strengthen the ego that is making the effort, whereas simple observation of the mind is not carried out by an ego; it is the process of Consciousness being aware of itself.[8]

The body is an important place in which to pay attention. Many religious traditions have tried to escape from the body, by denying it in some way, calling it "merely physical." However, the body is a place in which the Totality is expressing itself, in a particular way at a particular time. Attention to the body helps us to stop being focused exclusively on the mind, which has become such an automatic habit for most of us. In most situations, we can at least for a moment become conscious of the body's intrinsic energy, which may be felt as warmth, tingling, or just a sense of aliveness. No matter what we are busy with in the world, we can usually pay attention briefly to the state of this energy. We may then respond to the situation from a different place than we would if we stayed purely within conditioned thought. We can attend to the body when waiting for elevators or in lines in shops and traffic jams, as an alternative to simply feeling irritable. In these situations, we can attend to the way irritation feels in the body—usually as some kind of sensation such as muscle tension, a pounding heart, frowning, and so on. If we constantly return to the felt sense within the body, we stay aware, and we are less likely to be gripped by a complex. This practice is made easier if we learn to breathe into the uncomfortable body sensations that accompany painful emotions. Attention to breathing alone is itself a method of relaxation. These approaches are useful because, since Consciousness is not separate from the body, the body is a portal for the experience of the Self. By paying attention to the body we become less dominated by mental chatter. This kind of attention is especially useful in situations that would otherwise be boring or routine.

The work environment can be used as a place where one can deepen one's spiritual commitment by practicing values such as service to others. While this seems idealistic in a setting whose mission is profit, research shows that when personal and spiritual values are integrated into the workplace, it is possible to achieve increased growth, creativity, customer service, and other business values. It is therefore not surprising that many businesses have tried to introduce spiritual values (not organized religion) into the workplace, sometimes as a component of employee wellness programs. Some organizations are open to spiritually-based approaches that can lead to constructive change, if only because there are economic advantages to spiritually-oriented businesses, not the least of which is their ability to attract the right kind of people.

Even when we wish to bring our spiritual values into the workplace, it is difficult to maintain a "spiritual" attitude at work if one is harassed, stressed by deadlines, and under constant pressure to perform. Our good intentions are then quickly forgotten unless we first develop the capacity to observe ourselves. This means paying attention to our thoughts, feelings, and behavior, rather than being on auto-pilot. This takes practice because we are so accustomed to behaving automatically and *identifying* with the contents of the mind rather than *watching* them. When we first try to practice awareness, we forget ourselves over and over again. It is then important to be kind to ourselves, without judgment, and simply start again.

2. Attention to Feelings

Very often, we are told that destructive and painful feelings such as rage or hatred are inimical to spiritual development. To experience the sacred we are told to be loving, receptive, open, and so on. When this is possible it is pleasant, but it is not essential. Even though we feel that we have so much confusion, anger, or fear in us that there is no room for spirituality, painful feelings are, in fact, themselves spiritual energies; they are the way the sacred is manifesting itself at that moment. Unpleasant feelings and painful states of mind are not just obstacles that get in the way of our spiritual connection. They are a *type* of connection. Many of our negative feelings originate within our complexes, and as we saw in Chapter 2, our complexes have an archetypal—that is, a spiritual—core. Complexes are activated in any situation that corresponds to our conditioning, and we quickly become unconsciously possessed by the feeling-tone of the complex. It helps if we can notice the arising of the feeling early on, as a witness; the act of watching the feeling softens our automatic responses to it and we are less controlled by it.

Feelings, whether joyful or painful, are an experience of the numinosum in the body. Feelings are not just a concern of the everyday personality; feelings represent the Self expressing itself through the body. Feelings are therefore sacred energy, Presence in the body, an incarnation, part of the flow of nature, not merely a moral failing or a sign of weakness. Unfortunately, millennia of social conditioning have taught us that feelings such as envy, lust, and greed should be thought of as somehow wrong. This attitude does no good at all; it merely adds guilt to the mix by telling me that I should not feel the way I feel. It is preferable simply to see our feelings as signals that something in our lives needs attention.

It is important to accept painful feelings without judgment about whether or not we should be having them. Acceptance is not the same as acting them out or approving of them. Acceptance means that we acknowledge the feeling, feel it fully, and allow it to be in the body, knowing that it is necessary. A feeling is a guide to what is happening, a part of our innate intelligence that expands our understanding of a situation.

Our *interpretation* of a feeling is based on our conditioning. For example, if we were exposed to a particularly critical parent in childhood, and were often humiliated, we may then develop a complex that is activated whenever we feel we are wronged or under attack. We then feel intolerable shame or depression, which may lead to rage, hurt, and retaliation at the one who has done this to us. With practice at paying attention to our internal state, we notice that such a situation has arisen, and we become aware of those feelings as they arise without resisting them and without being possessed by them. It is then possible to let go of our insistence on the rightness of our opinion and not be so concerned about buttressing our self-esteem at all cost. We can feel the hurt at being criticized but realize that this is our personal problem, so that we do not need to fight with our critic. By contrast, if we are not fully conscious of our feelings, or if we try to resist them, we induce painful feelings in others, trying to make them feel as badly as we do.[9] We then poison the atmosphere around us, as people react to these feelings. Similarly, blaming others, feeling sorry for oneself, and retaliating keep us stuck in the situation and add to it. Instead, aware that this is happening, we can realize that we are worried about the self-esteem of a mental image we have of ourselves, and this image is not who we are. We can let go of the need to protect this image.

Unfortunately, acceptance of one's feelings is not always possible. It is common in childhood to be told that some feelings, such as anger or sadness, are not acceptable to the family. These feelings have to be disavowed in order to stay connected to a parent who cannot tolerate them. Such feelings are then buried somewhere, so that we are not conscious of them. The result is a life-long tendency to deny specific feelings, using a strategy such as eating, watching television, shopping, working, having sex, or some other activity. Once we realize this, it helps to sit down, stop what we are doing, and be with the feeling as fully as possible. There are two aspects to this process; one is to pay attention to the movement of the emotion in the body, perhaps as muscle tension, a pounding heart, a gripping in the belly, tightness in the chest, a flow of energy, or however it manifests itself. The other is to look at the image of oneself that the feelings have challenged.

Buddhism tries to replace harmful feelings and tendencies with the quality opposite to the negative feeling, so that anger is replaced with tolerance or patience, cruelty with compassion. In that tradition, the realization of the ultimate emptiness of negative feelings is a kind of final antidote to all of them. However, for many people there has to be a preliminary step, which is to understand the childhood origin of these feelings. I may be angry because someone is hurting me in a way that reminds me of the way I was hurt in childhood. I may be depressed because I cannot meet the standards of success my family wanted me to live up to. Or, I feel I am not good enough because I was treated with contempt as a child. Usually these feelings have in common a wound to one's sense of self, or a sense that something must be wrong with me. When such feelings are intense, in a situation of conflict there is a tendency to blame others to avoid feeling any personal responsibility, so that we do not have to attack ourselves. From a spiritual point of view, it is important that the problem begin and end with ourselves. The other person, the one who has hurt me, has simply revealed some area of fragility in me—not something bad, rather an area of the personality that needs care, forgiveness, and compassion. My mental image of myself has been hurt, but that image is not my true nature. If one looks at the problem from this point of view, there really is no need to make enemies.

As children, we develop strategies to maintain self-esteem and prevent shame and fear. All children need to feel that they are wanted, lovable, and special. To the extent that these needs were never met, they remain more or less intense throughout our lives. The more we are involuntarily gripped by these needs, the more vulnerable we are to feeling hurt by others if they behave in ways that wound us. We may defend against this possibility by being outwardly arrogant, confident, and controlling. But in the end our need to be right, or our need to have power and to be important, only heighten our sense of separation from others and cause conflict. Our needs to be superior to or in control of others are simply strategies of the ego as it tries to protect itself against its own vulnerability. Authentic power and authority do not arise as defenses against fear; they arise from contact with the Self.

3. Attention to What-Is

Here I borrow from the insights of Krishnamurti on the importance of attention to what-is. By this term, he means what actually exists in contrast to what the ego thinks should be, or what we expect and desire. We need an unprejudiced mind to see what-is; we cannot see what-is and respond to it if the mind is trying to change or suppress it.[10] We resist what-is because we are afraid of the unknown, or because what-is contradicts what we have been conditioned to believe, or because it threatens us. The resulting fear prevents from us accepting what-is.[11] Resistance to what-is may look like strength, but actually arises from fear, whereas it is powerful and freeing to accept what-is. It is important to stress that such surrender does not mean passivity, resignation, irresponsibility, or failure to deal with a situation, and it does not mean splitting off feelings. Surrender means allowing life to happen rather than opposing the flow of life, accepting the present moment without resistance. The necessary action will then arise, but when we act out of acceptance rather than resistance, we act without negativity or judgment. Action that arises out of acceptance is different from action that arises out of rage and hatred. Action that arises from a state of surrender is less contaminated with judgment and the need to hurt others. We simply do what needs to be done without labeling the situation as good or bad according to the ego's criteria.

4. Letting Go

Most religious traditions have stressed the importance of letting go, meaning surrendering one's will to the will of the divine. Yet the psychological barriers to this process are formidable if one's sense of self is fragile, because of the fear that one will not be safe if one is not in control. Again we see the effects of early child rearing; a close, safe relationship with early caregivers gives us an internal sense that the world can be trusted. Otherwise one is thrust back on one's own resources, dependent only on oneself. One's anxiety about survival is then repressed or disavowed but always lurking in the background. Or, if one's early caregivers were devouring and possessive, one is afraid of losing oneself if one is too open to the world. If one's self-esteem is fragile, one cannot let go because one needs to maintain one's own judgments and opinions as a way of shoring up an uncertain sense of self. True letting go then becomes much more difficult. Given these difficulties, it is nevertheless true that once we risk letting go by accepting what-is, we find a fullness that supports and renews us, and we discover an order to our lives and a sense of connection to a deep reality.

Real letting go is a form of non-resistance to what is happening, at the same time as we are fully present to the situation. This process is peaceful, and is not the same as aloof withdrawal, which is a defensive retreat to protect oneself from psychological hurt. The process of surrender to what-is acknowledges that the ego is not controlling events, and thus frees us from bondage to the priorities of the ego. This philosophy is not merely fatalistic, and it does not imply a mechanical, indifferent universe. Quite the contrary, surrender to what-is means that we trust the way life unfolds because events are not meaningless or the result of chance, and they depend on the larger Intelligence rather than on what we decide to do. This way of thinking contradicts the commonsense notion of free will, because it is based on the notion that at the deepest level of reality there are no individuals separate from the Totality. At this level there cannot be free will in the usual sense, because there are no discrete agents acting on a world distinct from them. We cannot be separated from Nature as a whole because we *are* Nature, manifest in the form of people. There is no "objective" world apart from its living subjects who are acting on it. There are no static or self-contained entities, only interactions and processes that are part of a unified continuum. Concern with free will is a result of the Western tendency to divide the indivisible into a series of successive, causal events that have lost their connection to the whole. In fact, there is only the totality of what-is-happening, so that the actions that we take in response to a situation are inextricably a part of it. Any action is a part of the totality of action; it is not simply "mine" or "yours." The Western traditions' emphasis on free will, and the New-Age attitude of "we can do anything we can imagine," result from a combination of terror at being helpless, a hubris that refuses to see our radical interconnectedness, and a deep lack of faith.

We see the problem of letting go mirrored in our physical posture. We are not letting go if we have hunched-up shoulders that expect attack, a clenched jaw indicating our determination to express our will, a perpetually furrowed brow from chronic concern, or shallow breathing limited to the upper chest. This kind of holding on is an expression of our lack of a sense of safety and a feeling that we must rely on our own mind. No amount of yoga or other attempts at relaxation will release these bodily constrictions until our *attitude* surrenders. Without a surrender of attitude, the body is always sensing danger. Properly understood as a gesture of surrender to what-is, to breath deeply and relax the body fully is a powerful statement of trust in the Ground.

5. Ritual

As discussed in Chapter 2, some people find that ritual helps them to connect to or remember the sacred. They prefer to emphasize the body, or gestures, rather than words alone. A personal ritual is often more meaningful than a collective ritual that has little emotional resonance. If one's intention is to pay attention to the sacred, ritual is helpful; if one is trying to exert power, or force something to happen, ritual merely reinforces the ego rather than surrendering it.

6. Prayer

Countless people and all religious traditions attest to the value of prayer, which has both positive and problematic aspects to it. In its helpful aspect, prayer is an important aspect of our spiritual life. For many people, prayer is a reflex, an almost involuntary response either to serious difficulty, to awe and gratitude, or to the feeling of being overwhelmed and needing help. Or, prayer simply arises as the result of an inner beckoning. In either case, prayer makes the ego realize its limitations. In order to pray, the ego has to surrender, stop what it is doing and remember the sacred. At the same time, prayer seems to have a strengthening and orienting effect on the ego. Overall, therefore, whether or not prayer is "answered" is not as important as its effect on the person. At the very least, prayer seems to activate the unconscious.

In spite of its benefits, prayer can be problematic for various reasons. At the strictly unitary level, prayer is not necessary, since we are not separate from that to which we pray. Some of the other problems are obvious: we might be on a power trip, bargaining, asking for magic, avoiding responsibility, or unconsciously imagining that we are talking to a very big version of a human parent. Does the divine not already know what we need? When is asking necessary? Might we be asking for something that is actually not in the best interests of all concerned? Can words describe how we feel? Do we really know what should happen in a given situation? Is it not the case that the universe unfolds the way it should? However, these are rather intellectual responses to what feels like an undeniable need for a sense of connection to the transpersonal. We can simplify our response to this need in two ways. One is to practice the continuous awareness of divine Presence, which is a form of constant prayer, or sometimes the most powerful prayer is just silence. Most of the time there is no need for anything more specific. Or, if you prefer, the great fourteenth-century mystic Meister Eckhart said that "if the only prayer you say in your life is 'thank you,' that would suffice."[12]

7. Gratitude

An attitude of thankfulness develops humility, opens the heart, and brings our attention back to the Source, whether or not we personify this as a personal God. Gratitude acknowledges that life is meaningful and valuable, prevents our taking life for granted, prevents the ego feeling inflated or self-important, and reminds us of our interconnectedness.

8. Be Wary of Beliefs Based on Traditional Doctrines

Belief in doctrines and dogmas about God becomes important when we have no internal sense of direction, so we need an outward structure to follow. Even when well intentioned, most doctrines and dogmas are ideologies invented by religious establishments to control the thought and behavior of their followers. These attempts to legislate or franchise the sacred are divisive and lead to wars. They are not necessary. When we believe what we have been *told* to believe, we may not find our own experience of the Truth. Even worse, beliefs or preconceived ideas may get in the way of our understanding the meaning of an important spiritual experience.

In the liturgies of both traditional Judaism and Christianity, the divine is portrayed as a benevolent father, a heavenly king or shepherd, and so on. Our metaphors have become less sexist and more sophisticated over time, but nevertheless these are all fairytale images that we have surely outgrown. Clearly, the divine does not correspond to any notion that we can create out of the human imagination, based on our fears and wants. The divine is not something that can be conceptualized, so to think we can give it a name or affect it with elaborate worship services simply reflects what we wish were the case. Surely it is preferable to be receptive to the way the sacred actually manifests itself, even if it does so in an unpleasant form.

9. Creativity

Real creativity does not come out of the ego or the personal self. Creative products are given through us. Consequently, we may produce something and wonder where it came from. Our task is to learn whatever technique is necessary to get the energy of creation into a particular medium. The ideas themselves emerge from the Self. In other words, creativity is a form of revelation in which we participate. This means that we can treat creative work as a form of personal ritual, during which we enter sacred space and time.

In this way, our creativity becomes an essential aspect of our spirituality; but again we find that there may be psychological blocks to its expression. Typically this happens because when we were children an envious parent, teacher, or sibling attacked our creative work, or made us feel ashamed if we felt proud of it. The envious, attacking figure seems to live on inside us, so that every time we create something an inner voice says, "That's no good. Who do you think you are?" This internal critic is a potent cause of creative block, or it makes us devalue our work. It helps to realize that there is something or someone in our mind that wants to sabotage us. We may then imagine that figure in the mind's eye, either the actual person or some other image, and say, "Thank you for your opinion. I prefer my way of looking at it." It is important to remember that as adults we can handle these internal attacking figures in more realistic ways than is possible when we are children.

10. Continual Inquiry

It is useful to wonder continually about the meaning of life, about fear, tragedy, suffering, and evil. Struggling with these issues is a profoundly spiritual pursuit.

11. Pay Attention to the Question of Death

The fact of death heightens the importance of our spirituality and makes it particularly important for us to live our lives fully. Our spirituality must include some way of thinking about death that does not romanticize it. To invoke the notion of an immortal soul merely invites questions about the relationship of the soul to the mind and body. Traditional ideas of heaven, or the notion that consciousness continues in some form after death, or the doctrine of reincarnation, may all arise from our death anxiety. We cannot easily tolerate the idea that everything we have become will be gone. Our fear of death is partly a function of the ego's fear of loss, nothingness, separation, and abandonment, and is a reminder of our vulnerability. One has to acknowledge these concerns and come to terms with them. In the end, like life, death has to be consciously accepted. The way we accept death is very much connected to the way we think about life.

12. Find a Way to Lose Yourself

It does not matter whether we are swept away by music or gardening, dancing or surfing. Anything that takes us out of the ego into a state of flow and out of ordinary time is a spiritual pursuit.

13. Make Everyday Life Your Practice

Everyday life can become an expression of our spirituality. To make it so requires a good deal of remembering; remembering to pay attention, remembering to be grateful, remembering to look at people, animals, and the natural world as expressions of the same Totality, and remembering that comparisons and judgments come out of the ego. We also have to remind ourselves that things must be the way they are because the universe as a whole is in harmony, and part of that harmony involves our doing what needs to be done. To do so with a spiritual sensibility is to realize that, once we have done what we can do, we can let go, because the outcome is not in our hands.

Everyday life does not impede our relationship with the sacred, since the sacred is always present. The problem is to stabilize our awareness of that fact, which is something we remember and forget, over and over again. Because this practice, which is a form of attention to what-is, can be going on continually, for many people it is more important than formal prayers or worship services.

14. Don't be afraid to be different

Although our culture pays lip service to individuality, a certain degree of conformity is expected, and this makes many people uncomfortable about being too different. This becomes an issue when certain of our social values come into conflict with spiritual values, such as humility and forgiveness. There is enormous cultural investment in profit, celebrity, appearances, competitive striving, and acquisitiveness, which have become a kind of collective mythology that is taken for granted as being inherent in human nature. They are reinforced by the media's constant focus on them, which induces a collective trance. Overall, therefore, our culture does not support the development of a personal spirituality significantly different from that of the mainstream. If we did develop our own personal spirituality, we might feel alone or find ourselves swimming against the cultural tide. However, this should not stop us from taking a critical look at our culture's standards of spirituality and rejecting them if necessary. For example, our personal spirituality may reject competitiveness and acquisitiveness, even though these behaviors are accepted as normal in our society. There is nothing more inimical to spirituality than the struggle for superiority, since this leads to the constant fear of hostility and retaliation from others, the fear of failure, and a sense of isolation. Competition rather than cooperation is a culturally determined spiritual disorder rather than an inherent aspect of human nature.

On the Psychology of Some Traditional Spiritual Virtues

Our religious traditions have typically encouraged certain virtues, such as faith, hope, and charity. However, from a psychological point of view, it is unrealistic to merely recommend such qualities and practices, since they require a good deal of psychological maturity and a reasonably solid sense of self before they can be implemented. In what follows I hope to show how these spiritual virtues are inextricably connected with our psychology.

Faith and Trust

Besides its obvious religious connotation, faith is a complex psychological phenomenon. Faith is closely related to trust, since it involves the sense that we can rely on unseen forces. But trust is possible only if one has had a reasonably safe childhood with dependable caregivers, so that the child has had the experience of reliable help arriving when it is needed.[13] If such positive experiences are repeated often enough, the expectation of timely help becomes a part of one's self, and we develop a built-in sense of confidence that what we need will be provided. In the absence of such basic trust, although one may assert that one "has faith" that God will provide, one may have no experience of what it really means to trust anything, including divine providence. Given a childhood in which trust could not develop, one can only fall back on narcissistic entitlement, a sense that I will get what I need because I am special, a feeling that arises to defend against a sense of inadequacy. Or one may feel an aggrieved sense that says: Since I've had a painful childhood, I must get my needs met because the universe just owes me. Similarly, one hears some believers say that because of their faith they will be rewarded by God with eternal life or salvation—a reward-punishment psychology by any standards, and surely more a matter of barter or bribery than faith. Mature faith and trust are not based on the expectation of rewards or on naïve gullibility or passivity. They require an acceptance of vulnerability and loss of control even though these are frightening. Such acceptance is possible when one feels that there is an Ultimate Ground to reality and one understands that whatever happens is ultimately supposed to happen. Even so, an ego that is essentially terrified and needs to be in control can never really trust. Trust is so deeply rooted in character structure that it is not something we can *decide* to do; it is something that arises autonomously if we have the developmental potential for it. The benefit of trust is peace of mind.

In spite of events such as the Holocaust, faith persists because the call from the Self persists. There seems to be something in us that just knows there is a Ground, and indeed there is an interesting and tangled relationship between faith and knowledge. If I jump into the deep end of a swimming pool, I know that I will rise to the surface in a few seconds, based on prior experience. If I've had a convincing numinous experience, I know with certainty that there is a spiritual reality, and faith arises from this knowledge. Faith therefore may be based on experience. Yet faith is itself an intangible form of knowledge, a conviction that we are correct when we have no evidence to support what we sense inwardly to be true. This knowing does not originate in the conscious personality; it is as if something reaches out and holds us, even as the ego doubts. Such faith is especially important in a crisis, or when we must take action in an uncertain situation. In contrast to faith, belief that is not based on experience, such as belief in a set of doctrines, tends to be influenced by personal preferences—what I like to think is true. Presumably this is why many believers feel threatened by people with beliefs contrary to theirs. Here lies the shadow side of both belief and faith. They may prevent inquiry, they tend to be divisive, and they may be defensive or illusory, based on denial.

Hope

Hope is often thought of as a spiritual virtue, but hope is actually a mixed blessing; this is why there are two trends in our cultural attitudes to hope, one affirming and the other dismissing its importance. On the positive side, hope is praised as inspiring and is regarded as perhaps the only thing that sustains life and increases our probability of survival in desperate situations. At the same time, although hopelessness is debilitating, hope can be impractical, illusory, or false, distracting us from the present reality of our situation or facilitating denial.

One's attitude to hope is very much a function of one's psychological make-up. Mature hope is a function of confidence in oneself and the world, and is born in childhood when we encounter caregivers whose dealings with us lead us to expect that hope has the possibility of being fulfilled. Mature hope does not deny reality, and is based on a reasonable appraisal of the situation. Only when it is unrealistic does hope merge with egocentric or naïve optimism. Hope is particularly necessary during adversity, so one's attitude to hope is a function of one's way of coping with adversity in general. Perhaps, given their history of persecution, this is why the Jews have eulogized hope since Biblical times. Hope has also been valued by Christian authors since St. Paul, who expressed hope in the Second Coming of Jesus. It is testimony to the power of hope that although this expectation for the End Times promised in the Bible has never been fulfilled, it is restated by each successive generation.

However, hope for the relief of suffering can also be a failure of surrender. From this point of view, if hope arises, it is a gift, but it is not necessary. Of course, depending on one's personality, when hope is offered we may refuse it, as we may refuse love.[14] I suspect that whether we accept or deny hope is often a matter of mood; when we are depressive in our outlook or when life seems meaningless, it is difficult to be hopeful. This is important, not least because our expectations often have a way of influencing what actually happens.

Charity

Our capacity to give to others is related to our psychological health, because it is difficult to be truly generous if one is internally empty. If we are empty on the inside, we tend to acquire and hold onto external possessions, as if they were extensions of our body and essential for our psychological equilibrium. It is as if by holding on to them we prevent ourselves slipping away, or we use them to hold ourselves together. Consequently, apart from realistic concerns about income, much desperation about money is the result of a fragile sense of self, a self that feels safe only if it has money. One cannot give freely unless one can also receive, but receiving feels humiliating when it implies that we are needy. A shadow side of giving is that charity to others can be merely a way of making ourselves feel important. In such a personality, giving is really a form of getting. Charity is most authentic if one realizes that "ownership" is really stewardship, so that one can give without resentment or pride in giving.

Honesty

Honesty is always recommended by the spiritual traditions, but various anxieties make honesty a difficult practice. If one suffers from fragile self-esteem or intense shame, one may need to sidestep the truth to avoid painful feelings of humiliation. The truth about oneself may be too difficult to look at because it means confronting one's shadow. It is difficult to be honest if the truth is frightening or threatening. So, we typically rationalize our behavior and make excuses for ourselves; it is a truism that there is no deception quite as effective as self-deception. What helps in the process of self-examination is to remember that the image we have of ourselves, which we are trying to shore up and protect at all costs, is just that—an image in our mind. It is not our absolute nature. The more unpleasant aspects of our personality that are difficult to face are usually coping mechanisms that we used in order to survive childhood. Honesty about these shadow traits can therefore be combined with empathy for ourselves, and eventually with self-forgiveness.

Love

Love is much spoken about by religious traditions, but it is difficult to know exactly what "love" means, since it is obviously impossible to love more than a few people in the everyday sense of the word. Few words are more subject to a corruption of meaning and usage. Thus, we misuse the word "love" (when we really mean "fascination" or "idealization") when speaking either of qualities that we lack in ourselves or of our own attributes that we project onto another.

Love in its true sense is indefinable. Its nature cannot be put into words because it is a quality of the Ground of existence, and language is too fragmentary to capture such wholeness. Krishnamurti[15] suggests that even though we cannot define love positively, we can approach it by saying what love is not. Love is not desire, possessiveness, or sexual passion, nor is love the performance of actions out of a sense of duty or responsibility. Love is not attachment based on the fear of loss or a need for security. Such personality factors may radically interfere with the emergence of love, so that it cannot be present if one is aggressive, jealous, ambitious, greedy, or hateful.

While romantic love is intoxicating, even a taste of the ecstasy of union with the divine, it is transitory. More permanently but less intensely, love is the true ground of emotional intimacy, communion with others, and receptivity. These qualities are not always available to us because a subtle personality factor may intervene. This factor seems to be a product of the unconscious, since we cannot always articulate it. The unconscious level of connection between people manifests itself as a mysterious energetic quality, colloquially referred to as "vibes," that is sometimes pleasant and sometimes unpleasant. In the latter case, we may try to fall back on the traditional Christian *agapé*, or spiritual love, which requires that we put ourselves aside. For most of us, this is possible only when we are not self-absorbed, exhausted, afraid, or on the brink of falling apart. If we are experiencing any of these conditions, it is too difficult to surrender to love. In that case, perhaps the best we can do is appreciate the profound mystery of the other, and be as kind as possible, given the limitations of the ego.

Our traditions are full of advice such as: "Love thy neighbor as thyself." What does this mean in practice? Is it feasible? To follow this teaching in its ultimate sense is enormously difficult, especially for people who cannot set aside their own needs because these needs are too intense. Here empathy is crucial, including empathy with oneself. If we can tolerate our own vulnerability, we can imagine how others feel, or how we would feel in their place. Compassion then arises spontaneously. However, if we have to deny our own vulnerability because it is too painful, we cannot afford to feel the pain of others. In that case, can there be love if our own pain produces a sense of separation from others? Alternatively, it is possible to use our own pain to develop the awareness that all human beings feel the same pain, the same sorrow and fear. Real love for our neighbor may also arise if we realize that we are not separate entities, but part of a unified continuum. Perhaps this is why the philosopher Søren Kierkegaard[16] suggested that to love oneself in the right way and to love one's neighbor are one and the same. He pointed out however that many of us do not love ourselves, and indeed psychotherapists see the suffering produced by self-hatred quite often in their practice. Is it of any value to love others as ourselves if we hate ourselves?

Humility

Humility is often recommended by spiritual teachers, but it is possible only if one does not need to be grandiose to bolster a fragile sense of self, and if at the same time one is tolerant of one's limitations. There is no point in washing another's feet if one is secretly resentful of having to do so, or if it makes one feel smug because one is nursing fantasies of spiritual superiority that enable one to "stoop" to this practice. Sometimes a fear-based God-image contributes to producing what looks like humility, but in reality is cowering rather than truly loving surrender. Being *afraid* of God (rather than in awe) is a perverse form of relationship to the divine. True love of God is humble by nature, but the fear of God is angry and resentful.

To develop real humility, it helps to notice how the ego constantly needs to feel important, special, and right. Once we *really* see this—it is often easier to see it in others first—we realize how we have been hanging on to a certain image of ourselves. Humility follows naturally as we remind ourselves of the limitations of the ego. Attention to our grandiosity begins a process of dissolving our need to be important; gentle humor at our own self-importance also helps, until eventually our attempts at being

239

important actually appear funny. This development is crucial, because inflation and self-importance are sure signs of a lack of spiritual awareness.

Forgiveness

Most religious traditions recommend forgiveness.[17] In practice, there are formidable emotional barriers to forgiving those who hurt us. Real forgiveness requires strength and courage. Because the psychology of forgiveness is little understood, many religious people feel ashamed that their anger at an offender prevents them from feeling forgiveness, and such shame adds to the pain of their original injury. Consequently, although the rewards of forgiveness are great, it cannot be achieved without conscious work. Forgiveness means that we give up bitterness and the need for revenge, and we let go of blame and anger towards the offender. We try to achieve reconciliation with, and avoid retaliation against, a person who has hurt or offended us. To achieve this position, we have to let go of what we think is our right to resentment and negative judgments about that person. It is as if the offense has produced an interpersonal debt, and to forgive means that we cancel the debt. This means we have to let go of playing the role of victim, though this is not easy since there are often advantages to this role—the aggressor's continued indebtedness to us, for example. We may prefer the leverage and the sense of moral superiority that comes with being a victim. We may prefer to stay angry because that makes it possible for us to feel self-righteous and important, elicits support from others, absolves us of any responsibility and therefore any personal guilt or shame in the situation of conflict, and even provides us with an excuse for our own transgressions. Besides, we may feel that forgiveness puts us at risk, since it opens us up to future transgressions, or it may encourage the abuser to keep on abusing. We wonder if we will be hurt again if we forgive, or even whether we are condoning the abuse by forgiving. For some people, forgiveness is seen as a loss of face, or as giving the appearance of weakness, especially if the offender does not apologize; thus, pride makes the victim hold on to the grudge. We may see our anger at being treated unfairly as a mark of self-respect, which we feel may be hard to maintain if we let go of the anger.

When injury or betrayal in adulthood taps into memories of similar childhood experiences, the injury or betrayal arouses a dormant reservoir of pain; this is why the response to an interpersonal injury may seem disproportionate in intensity and duration to the injury itself. When our sense of self has been injured, rage and fantasies of revenge surface. This may happen even if the injury is not serious, but our fragile ego has been hurt because someone has made us feel unimportant or devalued. Such injury to one's narcissism, such an affront to one's sense of self, is the enemy of forgiveness. One is then too self-absorbed to consider the motives of the aggressor, his or her reasons for acting as he or she did.

Severely narcissistic people cannot acknowledge their own contribution to a situation of conflict. When they are the aggressor, they cannot handle their shame at their actions, and must maintain an internal sense of self-approval at all costs. Since other people are less important to them than their need to maintain their own equilibrium, it is difficult for them to express remorse because admitting to a personal fault would shatter their illusion of their perfection. Even when it is given, the apology of the narcissist is designed to maintain personal self-esteem or deflect blame from themselves. When the narcissistic individual is the victim, he or she is too angry and hurt to forgive, and typically nurses unforgiving rage and a wish for revenge. One cannot turn the other cheek if one is possessed by hatred and vengeful fantasies.

Revenge is said to be "sweet" because hurting others *seems* to make us feel better. However, apart from the spiritual benefits of forgiveness, bearing a chronic grudge and remaining vengeful perpetuates one's own suffering. If we exact revenge on the one who hurts us, all we have really done is evacuate our rage and helplessness onto that person, trying to make him or her feel the pain that he or she made us feel, so that we do not have to keep feeling it ourselves. To identify oneself as a perpetual victim means that suffering becomes a part of one's identity and prevents us from ever being content. Constant blaming and fantasies of revenge are associated with poorer physical and emotional health, whereas forgiveness has a healing effect and leads to peace of mind. If someone causes us to suffer in a such way that the wounds take a long time to heal, for example by murdering someone close to us, chronic suffering may act as a barrier to forgiveness, which then becomes possible only after a period of mourning. Forgiveness must not be attempted too soon after an injury, while the individual's wounds are still fresh.

Another barrier to forgiveness arises when the person who has offended us has behaved in a way that reminds us too much of our own behavior—

he or she carries the projection of our own shadow. This may be difficult to acknowledge, but realizing that we too are capable of doing hurtful things to others can be a powerful aid in letting go of our resentment. Forgiveness may begin with the attempt to understand ourselves and the aggressor. It is therefore useful to use our empathic ability to imagine what may have prompted our tormentor to behave in that way towards us. Did he or she act out of some kind of pain or desperation? Did he or she perceive some provocation, even if none was intended? If so, his or her behavior is easier to forgive. We can also ask ourselves whether the hurtful behavior reminds us of the harsh behavior of one of our parents. If it does, then we may realize that we are reacting to the new situation with emotions that we needed to protect ourselves as children, but that we can approach things in a different way as adults.

Sometimes it is easier to forgive others than to forgive oneself. Acceptance of oneself is difficult if one has been raised in an atmosphere that fostered guilt and shame, so that some people are able to be gentle and accepting of others while remaining harsh towards themselves. It helps if we can become curious about our feelings rather than self-critical. It is worth looking in detail at one's childhood wounding and viewing it in the light of one's adult perspective. For example, if we had a father who made us feel unworthy or inadequate, we may realize that he was projecting his own unbearable sense of badness or worthlessness onto us, making us feel like the problem so that he might feel better about himself. None of this means that to forgive is to forget, and it certainly does not condone hurtful behavior. Neither does forgiveness mean that we are naïve about the possibility of future danger from the person or institution that has hurt us. Forgiveness is a state of mind and heart that must not be confused with the concept of pardon; one can forgive an offender and at the same time require him or her to make restitution.

Understanding others is made easier if we remember that human beings have different temperaments, and thus different approaches to the world, different standpoints and preferences. It is well worth looking at various ways of describing people such as the Enneagram or the Myers-Briggs typology.[18] Remembering that no temperament is better or worse than any other and that people see the world differently helps in developing forgiveness, smoothing relations, and easing impatience. However we arrive at it, in the last analysis forgiveness becomes an act of radical surrender.

A CAUTIONARY NOTE ABOUT THE SPIRITUAL JOURNEY

Spirituality requires a sincere, lifelong commitment; it is not an easy or quick pursuit.[19] To adopt a spiritual life requires nothing less than a reorientation of consciousness. A spiritual attitude cannot be handed to us; teachers can help, but ultimately spirituality involves the cultivation of awareness, both of one's own mind and of the minds of others within one's relationships. Spirituality includes the struggle with human frailties and the mystery of suffering. This journey often begins with an initial awakening or opening, provided by a numinous experience, followed by a period of clarity or even bliss. Occasionally, the initial transformation is permanent, but a period of disillusionment often follows as life's tensions and problems re-assert themselves, sometimes even more intensely than before. It is as if we have had a glimpse of Reality and have somehow been given a promise that everything will be different from now on. We then find ourselves slipping back into our daily grind. At first, it may seem as if our turn to the sacred was a mistake, or we may feel discouraged because it looks like much hard work will be needed to re-establish our sense of connection to it.

Re-connecting to the sacred can be a long and slow, even painful, process, with only the memory of the initial experience to guide us. Some people lose faith, give up in despair, and later proclaim that they tried spirituality and it did not work. In fact, a powerful numinous experience that produces a spiritual awakening is often simply a window through which we see a goal. A numinous experience makes us realize just how deeply egocentric we are or how completely disconnected from a stable sense of the sacred, and it invites us to do the work necessary to re-connect. However, our religious institutions often do not prepare us for this sequence, promising instead that if we profess to be "born again" (in the contemporary Christian sense), or "obey the commandments" we will be instantly and permanently changed. However, these formulas may serve as a barrier both to confronting the shadow as well as to becoming aware of the personality transformation that is necessary for authentic spiritual growth.

THE QUESTION OF STAGES

Spiritual illumination may be instantaneous or gradual. Those who believe it is gradual (the majority) insist that spiritual development takes time and occurs in stages, because the goal is distant. Instantaneous illumination is said to incorporate into itself all the stages of the gradual path, and seems to accomplish them at once. There is then a permanent realization of the Truth. Both varieties of spiritual illumination are valid, and it is not clear why the process happens one way or the other.

Those who feel they are on a gradual path often wonder how far along they have come on their spiritual journey, but the problem with trying to assess this is that stages imply a fixed sequence, as if things are supposed to happen in a prescribed order. In fact, no two journeys are alike. Although it is true that there are some aspects of spiritual development that can be identified, it is a mistake to think of them as necessarily occurring in a progression. They happen at different times, in any order. Sometimes they seem to be happening in parallel, and the same process may recur at different levels.

In the traditional view of the gradual path, the spiritual journey often begins with an experience such as an eruption of the numinosum. Or a serious life crisis makes us realize that there is something more to life than we have been aware of, and only a spiritual solution to the problem will suffice. There follows what used to be called a "purgation," that is, a confrontation with the shadow, with our problematic personality traits such as narcissism, grandiosity, self-importance, possessiveness, greed, fear, and envy. It is important to explore these difficulties gently with compassion for oneself. Painful feelings are not obstacles but signposts that indicate where we need to work; they are the doorways into the soul's deeper places. During these periods, one re-evaluates one's values and beliefs, and may either re-commit to one's religious tradition or leave it entirely.

Gradually, our emotional responses are less governed by past resentments and hurts, we stop responding automatically, and there is less need to respond in a way that defends a fragile sense of self. We become more sensitive to the suffering of others, and often to the environment as well. These developments lead to the realization that the image we had of ourselves is not our real identity. We have developed a "false self" to satisfy the family and the culture—we had to pretend to be someone we were not, in order to survive. Eventually we no longer strive to maintain this image.

We make a conscious decision to turn towards the Self when we realize that we are looking for something beyond our day-to-day striving, something more meaningful than the distractions provided by our culture. Unfortunately, we may know no better than to make do with images of the divine that we have unconsciously carried with us from childhood. Occasionally these images are useful, but often our personal development has outstripped them. Here is where we must depend on our own experience of the numinous and our own intuition about the sacred.

In the process of "illumination," which may follow purgation, we begin to apprehend the Reality we have been seeking as we begin to see everything as a manifestation of the divine, and we have more experiences of divine companionship and love. At this point in our journey, the apparent disharmonies of life seem to resolve themselves, and we feel that we stand on the edge of another plane of being. We are in a more passive state, in which we become more and more receptive, and our longing for the presence of the divine becomes a preoccupation.

The journey culminates in unity. This process brings a stable sense of direct contact with, or absorption into, the Absolute, as well as the realization of the unity of oneself with others and with the earth. Not much can be said about this experience because it involves a loss of the sense of a separate, personal self, although individuals who have achieved this state function normally in consensual reality.[20] Having arrived at this experience, the developed mystic is involved in ordinary social life with a renewed consciousness, often teaching or involved in socially useful movements. Such an individual may be highly evolved yet live in total obscurity, simply because there is no need to do anything else.

However one views the spiritual journey, there are fundamentally only two outcomes. One leads to the experience of union with the divine such that there remains no concern with individual uniqueness, just as a drop of water is lost in a glass of wine. The everyday personality persists but is not particularly important. In the other outcome, the goal may be one of relationship to the divine, which requires a full development of the authentic personality in a conscious relation to the sacred. Total surrender may then occur. It is often said about such surrender that one can give only what one has: if the personality or the ego is not developed, it can never really surrender. However, I find that this is not true; one can give whatever one has to offer of oneself. Many emotionally disturbed people have a profound spirituality and great faith.

A spiritually-oriented life should not be mistaken for an easy life. What makes it spiritual is our attitude to the situations that arise, not the absence of difficulties. If we know that the painful things that happen are the workings of the Intelligence of the universe, we can accept what happens at the same time as we deal with it. In that frame of mind, which is admittedly difficult to achieve in the midst of a storm, things simply are the way they are. Rather than cursing fate, we realize that difficult situations are presented to us because there are certain things that need our attention. The difficult part is making *sure* that there really is a larger pattern to our lives, and that the painful things that happen are not random accidents. One of the benefits of numinous experiences is that they help us realize that we are not solitary specks of meaningless matter floating within an indifferent cosmos. Once one is convinced that there is a larger Intelligence working, it is easier to relax and trust. It is also easier to open the heart and give to others without having to be self-protective. One cannot just *decide* that one is going to be like that, but one can look at the psychological obstacles to being more loving and tolerant of others and of life in general. This self-examination may be carried out as a solitary, introspective task, or, if necessary, with the aid of another person. I suggest here some exercises that are useful for fostering the process.

DISCERNMENT EXERCISES

In addition to the self-observation discussed above, there are entertaining exercises that help us to discover some of the organizing principles within the personality that may govern our behavior without our realizing it.

Imagine that you are free of all cultural, financial, and family restrictions on your behavior. Then, in your mind's eye, indulge in an untrammeled fantasy of who you might be, and what you might do, based on what you really want out of life or on your wildest escape fantasy. You may discover that you want power over others, or that you crave safety above all else. You may imagine great wealth, beauty, luxury, fame and glory, artistic or professional achievement. Whatever our fantasy, it helps us to acknowledge some of the driving forces in our lives.

We may also ask ourselves: What is my greatest fear? What would be so terrible that I could hardly bear to imagine it? Often this fear represents a situation that the ego must defend itself against at all cost. It may involve public disgrace, loss of security, loss of loved ones, a massive blow to one's self-esteem, or the loss of power and prestige. By looking honestly at this fantasy, we can see how much of our behavior was directed towards self-defense. Typically, the individual who is driven to control others sees the underlying fear and vulnerability that makes him or her seek power. The arrogant individual sees the helpless, shame-filled child that must be protected. Those who are attractive see their concern about their intelligence; those who are intelligent see their concern about their attractiveness.

These are not exercises in morality. They are ways of looking into the ego's conditioning so that it may be brought into the light and allowed to fade in intensity. When a particular trait is identified, it is important not to try deliberately to make the problem go away. Such attempts often reinforce the problem by constantly reminding us that we have it. It is generally more useful simply to be constantly aware of the trait, constantly seeing it in operation. Understanding and observation help to dissolve it. Here I recommend Krishnamurti's suggestion that we just see ourselves as we are, without trying to make ourselves into what we want to become. Whatever this reality is like, see it clearly, without judgment or condemnation. When we see reality in this way, the right action will follow. Above all, accept yourself; allow who you are to emerge, rather than adopt some image of yourself that was foisted on you by family and society. If we accept what-is, instead of being in a compulsive, ego-driven urge to change things, a new attitude often emerges spontaneously.

How Does the Future Look?

The old-time religion with its hellfire and damnation has lost its hold on us, but the psyche does not tolerate a spiritual vacuum. Religious traditions are becoming increasingly receptive to depth psychology, and psychological language is proving useful as a way of speaking about the sacred. Since the divine mystery chooses to reveal itself by means of the psyche, it is entirely appropriate for us to focus on the psyche's manifestations in our spiritual life. The numinosum is so intimately a part of our psyche that, in the end, our spirituality and our psychology are synonymous.[21]

Notes

INTRODUCTION

1. See David and Susan Larson, *The Forgotten Factor in Physical and Mental Health: What Does the Research Show?* (Rockville, MD: National Institute for Healthcare Research, 1994).
2. Harold G. Koenig, M.D. and his colleagues at Duke University conducted a study which followed almost 4,000 people between the ages of 64 and 101 over a six-year period, to determine whether church attendance had any effect on longevity. They found that the risk of dying (during the duration of the study) among those who attended a religious service at least once a week was 46% lower than it was among those who attended less often or not at all. Even after adjusting for other factors that might influence longevity, the figure was still relatively high at 28%. See David B. Larson, Susan S. Larson, and Harold G. Koenig, "Longevity and Mortality," *Psychiatric Times*, XVII, No. 8 (August 2000).

CHAPTER 1—THE NUMINOSUM: DIRECT EXPERIENCE OF THE SACRED

1. Richard M. Bucke, *Cosmic Consciousness* (Secaucus, NJ: Citadel Press, 1961), p. 214.
2. *Ibid.*, p. 272.
3. Rudolf Otto, *The Idea of the Holy* (New York: Oxford University Press, 1958). Some thinkers make a distinction between the holy and the sacred: holiness is an intrinsic property of events, places or experiences, whereas sacredness is a quality with which people *invest* the event, place, or experience. Thus it is that certain places or events can be sacred to one person or tradition but have no special significance to others. In this book, however, I use the terms "sacred" and "holy" as approximately synonymous descriptors for an experience of transcendent reality. That is, I assume that everything has the intrinsic property of holiness because of the interconnectedness of all things and the connection of all things to the divine. Thus, anything that is understood to be an aspect of the divine is sacred.
4. From the Latin word *numen*, meaning a divinity, and the verb *nuere*, to nod or beckon. Thus, the sense of the word numinous is of a divine beckoning or divine

approval. In this book, I will assume that spontaneous numinous experience is of transpersonal origin, or at least that what we describe as numinous can be our response to an experience of the transcendent realm. This qualification is necessary because we may sometimes invest an experience with numinosity for purely personal reasons, and certain events may seem uncanny or supernatural merely because we do not understand them. In spite of such objections, there do seem to be occasions when transcendent reality irrupts into our experience.

5. Many Christian theologians object to the idea of the numinous as wholly other, since it seems to make religion something less than rational and so pre-Christian. However, the forces that live in the psyche are clearly not rational if judged by the standards of the conscious personality, and they do not feel as if they are a part of it. In pre-Christian times, these forces, which we now call archetypal processes, were thought to be the pagan gods. They are still alive and well, even if they are not acknowledged to be divinities by the theologians. Perhaps a more serious objection to the notion of the numinous as Otherness is the fact that this is a dualistic perspective that radically splits the human and the transcendent realm. From a unitary viewpoint, the divine is not other than ourselves. For a discussion of Otto's work, see Philip C. Almond, *Rudolf Otto: An Introduction to his Philosophical Theology* (Chapel Hill, NC: University of North Carolina Press, 1984), and Robert F. Davidson, *Rudolf Otto's Interpretation of Religion* (Princeton, NJ: Princeton University Press, 1947). For a discussion of Jung and Otto, see Leon Schlamm, "The Holy: A Meeting-Point between Analytical Psychology and Religion," *Jung and the Monotheisms,* ed. J. Ryce-Menuhin (New York: Routledge, 1994). For a general discussion of the depth psychological approach to numinous experience, see Lionel Corbett, *The Religious Function of the Psyche* (New York: Routledge, 1996). For a discussion of numinous experience in psychotherapy, see Lionel Corbett's "Varieties of Numinous Experience," *The Idea of the Numinous: Jungian and Psychoanalytic Perspectives* (London: Brunner-Routledge, 2006).

6. See for example Andrew M. Greely, *Ecstasy: A Way of Knowing* (Englewood Cliffs, NJ: Prentice-Hall Inc., 1977), and Alister Hardy, *The Spiritual Nature of Man* (New York: Oxford University Press, 1979), which contain many examples of numinous experiences.

7. Gen. 14: 18-20, Psalm 110:4.

8. See John A. Sanford, *Dreams: God's Forgotten Language* (San Francisco, CA: HarperSanFrancisco, 1989).

9. A traditional Freudian criticism of Jung's notion of the archetypal or transpersonal level of the psyche is given in Nandor Fodor's *Freud, Jung, and Occultism* (New Hyde Park, NY: University Books, 1971). His claim is that all unconscious material can be accounted for in terms of the individual's personal history, without the need for anything transpersonal. Fodor (p. 177) insists that the apparently spiritual

element in dreams is "a beautiful unconscious fantasy. The Jungian contribution is only verbal—but it is stimulating and appeals to the imagination." The Kleinian school would understand numinous phenomena as originating from introjected part-objects, such as the mother's breast, while a modern psychoanalytic understanding would reduce them to the activation of infantile images of the self and others. According to George Atwood and Robert Stolorow, their appearances are "indices of narcissistic regression and decompensation"—*Faces in a Cloud: Intersubjectivity in Personality Theory* (Northvale, NJ: Jason Aronson, 1999, p. 74). The Jungian response to such critiques is to point out the collective features of archetypal experiences that cannot be explained purely in terms of individual development, which does not adequately account for their phenomenology. Perhaps these arguments boil down to different assumptions about the nature of the human condition, since in the end it is impossible to prove that there is a spiritual dimension to experience. I should add here that some theologians are also unhappy with Jung's theory, which they regard as an illegitimate reduction of the transcendent concerns of religion to mere psychology. As Josef Goldbrunner puts it: "… [T]his thinking of Jung must be called psychologism, the leveling down of supra-psychic realities to the level of purely psychic reality"—*Individuation: A Study of the Depth Psychology of Carl Gustav Jung* (Notre Dame, IN: University of Notre Dame Press, 1964, p. 172). These theologians object to Jung's use of the theory of archetypes to understand religious experience in a psychological way, even though this theory is metaphysically neutral with regard to issues such as the existence of a transcendent divinity beyond the psyche. Jung would say that his theory is empirically based, while the assertion that there is a transcendent God remains a matter of faith. An important source of this disagreement seems to be that if Jung's theory of the archetypal origin of numinous experience is correct, then traditional religious assertions would be only a limited example of such experience, rather than the supreme truth. Perhaps all religious experience, since it is fundamentally psychological, could then be included within his theory, which would indeed be to over-apply it. Finally, I should mention that it is possible to think of the archetypes as not purely psychological but as transcendent metaphysical processes in their own right, in which case the psyche is only one place in which they manifest themselves. For a discussion of this view, see James Hillman's "Why 'Archetypal' Psychology?" *Spring*, 1970, p. 216.

10. C. G. Jung, *The Undiscovered Self* (Princeton, NJ: Princeton University Press, 1990).

11. C. G. Jung, *Psychology and Religion: West and East*, *CW*, vol. 11 (Princeton, NJ: Princeton University Press, 1969), p. 6.

12. Jung pointed this out, and made it crucial to his theory of psychotherapy. See C. G. Jung, *Letters, Volume 1: 1906-1950*, ed. G. Adler (Princeton, NJ: Princeton University Press, 1973), p. 377.

13. I can attest to this woman's sanity on the basis of many years of working with very disturbed psychiatric patients. For the skeptic, I would also point to Andrew Greeley's *The Sociology of the Paranormal* (Beverley Hills, CA: Sage Publications, 1975) which reveals that paranormal experiences are quite frequent. People who have them, rather than being disturbed, are often emotionally healthy. In Greeley's survey, 35% of respondents reported at least one mystical experience, and 5% reported them "often." In any case, there is no reason that mentally ill people should not have authentic numinous experiences.

14. William James, *The Varieties of Religious Experience* (Cambridge, MA: Harvard University Press, 1985), pp. 340-341.

15. *Ibid.*, p. 66.

16. Alister Hardy, *The Spiritual Nature of Man* (New York: Oxford University Press, 1979).

17. *Ibid.*, p. 39.

18. Perhaps because our society does not allow profound feelings about nature to be spoken of in spiritual terms, they emerge politically as the secular movement called environmentalism, or as deep ecology, eco-feminism, or the Gaia Hypothesis.

19. William Blake, "Auguries of Innocence," *William Blake: Selected Poetry*, ed. W. H. Stevenson (London: Penguin Books, 1988).

20. Walt Whitman, "Starting From Paumanok," *Leaves of Grass* (New York: Bantam Classics, 1983).

21. See for example Matthew Fox, "Meister Eckhart on the Fourfold Path of a Creation Centered Spiritual Journey," *Western Spirituality: Historical Roots, Ecumenical Routes*, ed. Matthew Fox (Santa Fe, NM: Bear and Company, 1981).

22. Quoted in Howard H. Brinton, *Mystic Will: Based Upon a Study of the Philosophy of Jacob Boehme* (Whitefish, MT: Kessinger Publishing, 1997).

23. William Wordsworth, "Tintern Abbey," *The Pedlar, Tintern Abbey, the Two-Part Prelude* (New York: Cambridge University Press, 2005).

24. Walt Whitman, "Song of the Redwood Tree," *Leaves of Grass* (New York: Bantam Classics, 1983).

25. Thomas Traherne, "Vision of Childhood," *Traherne: Selected Poems and Prose* (London: Penguin Classics, 1992).

26. Richard Jefferies, *The Story of My Heart* (Dartington, UK: Green Books, 1883/2003), p. 71.

27. There is a large body of literature on the question of what constitutes religious experience. Some people believe that religious experience is an actual perception of the transpersonal realm. Another theory says that this experience is simply a strong emotion that is interpreted spiritually. There are distinctions between prophetic experiences, devotional experiences, liturgical experiences, and experiences of mystical unity, all of which may be intermingled. All this is complicated by the

fact that there is no agreement on exactly what constitutes "religion." The word "experience" itself also has various meanings; it may mean the perception of something that originates from within, or the perception of something in the outer world. For a full discussion of religious experience within various traditions, see Ralph W. Hood, ed. *Handbook of Religious Experience* (Birmingham, AL: Religious Education Press, 1995).

28. Cicero thought that the word "religion" derived from the Latin *relegere*, suggesting that which one goes over and over again in reading or in thought. Jung adopted this usage because it fit with his own view of what religion should be—see C. G. Jung, *Letters, Vol. 2, 1951-1961*, ed. G. Adler (Princeton, NJ: Princeton University Press), p. 272, and "On the Nature of the Psyche," in C. G. Jung, *The Structure and Dynamics of the Psyche* (Princeton, NJ: Princeton University Press, 1978), § 427. Few subsequent Latin scholars agreed with Cicero. The *Catholic Encyclopedia* points out that the practice of religion dates back to long before humans could read, so it is unlikely that the word was derived from anything to do with reading. Cicero's derivation was influenced by religion as it was practiced ritually by the Romans of the 1ˢᵗ century B.C.E. It calls to mind the reading of entrails and the careful performance of rituals. Another possibility is that the word "religion" derives from the Latin *religare*, meaning to bind together, a derivation that recalls the Sanskrit word yoga, meaning to unite or join—thus, what connects us to the divine.

29. p. 2.

30. C. G. Jung, *Psychological Reflections*, ed. J. Jacobi and R. F. C. Hull (Princeton, NJ: Princeton University Press, 1978), p. 105.

31. Georg Feuerstein, *Sacred Sexuality* (New York: Jeremy Tarcher, 1992), p. 29.

32. Jiddu Krishnamurti, *You are the World* (Chennai, India: Vasanta Vihar, 1972), p. 37.

33. Our spiritual sameness has important implications; when people behave badly towards us, or say something hurtful, the simplest response is to remember that this person is not different from me. This perspective helps us to see something in the situation that needs attention. Judgment or condemnation are not necessary, and arise only to soothe our wounded sense of self. Out of this awareness, compassion may arise.

34. See for example John Gribbin, *Schrödinger's Kittens and the Search for Reality* (New York: Back Bay Books, 1995).

35. The knowledge that is imparted during numinous or mystical experience, such as the conviction that the universe is permeated with love, cannot be verified or disproved by means of positivistic empiricism. It is up to the individual whether to take such claims seriously or to ignore them.

36. John A. Coleman, "Mel Gibson Meets Marc Chagall: How Christians and Jews Approach the Cross," *Commonweal* 131 (Feb. 27, 2004).

37. Of course, this is not a materialistic view of consciousness. Consciousness is seen

here as an irreducible principle, not something created by the brain.

38. Presumably there are brain events that correlate with numinous experience, since there are brain events that correlate with all our experience, but this is not to say that the brain is the primary originator of the experience. When the brain is frankly disordered, for example, because of a high fever or a metabolic disturbance, a numinous experience may result because the brain is unable to maintain its usual level of order and sustain the functions of the ego, so that other dimensions of reality are more accessible.

39. In the psychiatric literature, numinous experience that prevents suicide is typically reduced, for example to "residual primary narcissism," or a return to the original feeling of blissful merger with mother at birth. See, for example, Paul C. Horton, "The Mystical Experience as a Suicide Preventive," *American Journal of Psychiatry*, 130, no. 3 (1973): 294–296.

40. I believe this phenomenon is identical with what Mihaly Csikszentmihalyi calls a "flow" experience, which provides a sense of discovery, a creative feeling of being transported into a new reality, which may lead to previously undreamed-of states of consciousness.

41. Many alcoholics agree with Jung's prescription for treating alcoholism: *spiritus contra spiritam*, meaning that an authentic or healthy spirituality can replace the compulsion to find the spirit in the concrete form of alcohol.

42. The psychologist Abraham Maslow coined the term "peak experience" to describe feelings such as intense happiness and well-being, sometimes accompanied by a sense of ultimate truth and the unity of all things. He regarded these as normal but transcendent experiences that have a beneficial effect. He stressed that they might not occur in the context of organized religion. Maslow was clearly describing a type of numinous experience, using a different term. He understood that spirituality in this sense is really a state of mind that can arise in any walk of life. See Abraham Maslow, "Religious Aspects of Peak-Experiences," *Personality and Religion*, ed. W. A. Sadler (New York: Harper & Row, 1970).

43. The problem of psychosis is a special case. The psychotic is not believed because his or her behavior, speech, and thinking are too disorganized to be taken seriously.

44. Such an interpretation was given to a patient of mine when she told her minister that she dreamed of Jesus as a woman.

45. John Dourley, *Strategy for a Loss of Faith: Jung's Proposal* (Toronto: Inner City Books, 1992), p. 75.

46. Philip Rieff, "C. G. Jung's Confession: Psychology as a Language of Faith," *Encounter* 22 (May 1964): 47.

47. Philip Rieff, *The Triumph of the Therapeutic: Uses of Faith After Freud* (New York: Harper and Row, 1966), p. 114.

48. Edward Burchard, "Mystical and Scientific Aspect of the Psychoanalytic Theories

of Freud, Adler, and Jung," *American Journal of Psychotherapy* 14 (April 1960): 306.

49. Paul Friedman and Jacob Goldstein, "Some Comments on the Psychology of C. G. Jung," *Psychoanalytic Quarterly* 33 (April 1964): 196. The question of the scientific validity of Jung's approach is discussed by Walter A. Shelburne, *Mythos and Logos in the Thought of Carl Jung* (Albany, NY: State University of New York Press, 1988).

CHAPTER 2—THE REALITY OF THE PSYCHE: THE ARCHETYPE AS A SPIRITUAL PRINCIPLE

1. There is a contemporary move away from experience itself towards a stress on the primacy of language. We must acknowledge that experience is permeated with language, and we reflect on experience by means of language. However, I do not believe that human experience is possible only *because* we have language. There are states of consciousness that are prior to language and states of consciousness that cannot be articulated at all, and to call them a language in themselves would be meaningless. I regard language as a product of consciousness.

2. C. G. Jung, *Modern Man in Search of a Soul* (New York: Harvest Books, 1955, pp. 190-191). The question of illusion and sense-deception arises here. However, even the delusion or hallucination of a mentally ill person is perfectly real to him or her, even if it does not correspond to the reality that the rest of us experience.

3. The existence of such prophetic or prospective dreams suggests that there are realms of consciousness that are outside of time and space.

4. C. G. Jung, "On the Nature of the Psyche," *The Structure and Dynamics of the Psyche* (Princeton, NJ: Princeton University Press, 1978, p. 215).

5. Paul Kugler, "Psychic Imaging: a Bridge Between Subject and Object," *The Cambridge Companion to Jung*, ed. P. Young-Eisendrath and T. Dawson (New York: Cambridge University Press, 1997, p. 84).

6. C. G. Jung, *Letters, Vol. 2*, ed. G. Adler and A. Jaffé, trans. R. F. C. Hull (Princeton, NJ: Princeton University Press, 1975), pp. 371-2.

7. It is probably just an anthropomorphism to think of the divine as having a "mind," except in a metaphorical sense.

8. C. G. Jung, *Alchemical Studies*, *CW*, vol. 13 (Princeton, NJ: Princeton University Press, 1976), p. 70, note 4.

9. C. G. Jung, *Two Essays on Analytical Psychology* (Princeton, NJ: Princeton University Press, 1966), p. 160.

10. C. G. Jung, *Alchemical Studies*, *CW*, vol. 13 (Princeton, NJ: Princeton University Press, 1976), p. 346.

11. C. G. Jung, *Symbols of Transformation*, *CW*, vol. 5 (Princeton, NJ: Princeton University Press, 1967), p. 102. See also C. G. Jung, "Psychological Aspects of the Mother Archetype," *The Archetypes and the Collective Unconscious*, *CW*, 9i (Princeton,

NJ: Princeton University Press, 1968), p. 79.

12. C. G. Jung, "Mind and Earth," *Civilization in Transition, CW,* vol. 10 (Princeton, NJ: Princeton University Press, 1970), p. 31.

13. C. G. Jung, *Two Essays on Analytical Psychology*, vol. 7 (Princeton, NJ: Princeton University Press, 1966), p. 69.

14. C. G. Jung, "Psychological Aspects of the Mother Archetype," *The Archetypes and the Collective Unconscious*, CW vol. 9i (Princeton: NJ: Princeton University Press, 1968), pp. 101; 69, note 27.

15. C. G. Jung, "A Psychological Approach to the Trinity," *Psychology and Religion, West and East, CW*, vol. 11 (Princeton, NJ: Princeton University Press, 1942, p. 149), note 2.

16. C. G. Jung, *Man and His Symbols* (Garden City, NY: Doubleday & Company, 1964), p. 96.

17. In animals, we clearly see examples of instinctual behavior such as nest building. To what extent human behavior is truly instinctual in that sense is controversial, because human behavior is not usually as automatic and stereotyped as the fixed action patterns of animals. It is difficult to separate behavior that might be inborn from behavior that is acquired. But, even empiricists such as Edward O. Wilson believe that the human mind has "moral instincts," although he thinks they arise from the interplay of biology and culture—see: "The Biological Basis of Morality," *The Atlantic Monthly* 281, no. 4 (April 1998): 53-70. The archetype is not, however, fully located in the genes; if it were, spirit would be reduced to biology. Rather, the genes are an expression of archetypal organization in the body. Either something organized the genes, or the whole system simply evolved that way and there is no superordinate spiritual principle.

18. For example, babies are oriented towards searching for their mother's face—the baby expects a face and has an innate preference for looking at faces. For a full discussion of this issue, see Maxson J. McDowell, "The Three Gorillas: An Archetype Orders a Dynamic System," *Journal of Analytical Psychology*, 46, no. 4 (2001).

19. The archetypes as a spiritual ordering principle perhaps correspond to the idea of God as the Eternal Order of Things or the Creative Order of the universe.

20. For most Protestant theologians, the woman described in Rev. 12:1-6 represents the Church.

21. Many pre-Christian, pagan mythologies had virgin goddesses, and Catholicism no doubt draws upon this tradition.

22. The mythologies of many religious traditions contain the same archetypal themes. There is often the theme of a Golden Age, such as that enjoyed by Adam and Eve in the Garden of Eden, when things were perfect on the earth. The notion of a world axis that connects this world with the world of the gods is also common. In the Hebrew Bible we have an image, in one of Jacob's dreams, of a ladder stretching

up to heaven; in Norse mythology a great tree fulfills the same function. All traditions have sacred buildings, such as churches and temples, which symbolically represent the notion of a spiritual center that links heaven and earth. Their domes and spires represent spiritual aspiration or a reaching upward in order to establish a heavenly connection. Every culture has sacred trees, such as the Tree of Life in the Garden of Eden, the Wisdom Tree of Buddhism, and the sacred groves of the goddess. These examples could be multiplied at great length. See Mircea Eliade, *The Sacred and the Profane* (New York: Harvest/Harcourt Brace, 1959).

23. For a detailed review of many Cinderella stories, see Ann Baring, "Cinderella: An Interpretation," *Psyche's Stories: Modern Jungian Interpretations of Fairy Tales,* Vol. 1, ed. Murray Stein and Lionel Corbett (Willmette, IL: Chiron Publications, 1991).

24. The obvious mythic example is ritual circumcision among the ancient Israelites and contemporary Jews, stipulated in Genesis 17:10-14. The origins of this ritual are not clear. In the Israelite mythology circumcision was specifically a mark of the covenant, which had to do specifically with the "seed" of Abraham, which had been chosen by God. One could enter into the covenant with God only through birth; one had to be of Abraham's seed to qualify. The phallus as the organ of generation and reproduction was therefore of primary importance in membership in the covenant, and circumcision dedicated the penis to the perpetuation of the covenant. A major part of the covenant involved producing progeny who would inherit the promises of the covenant. Circumcision then was a sanctification of the penis, which was the locus of all future generations. The covenant was a perpetual covenant, and involved all future generations in perpetuity, and the only way to ensure the perpetuity of the covenant was to dedicate the penis to its perpetuation. Every time an Israelite man looked at his penis, he was reminded of his commitment to the covenant and his duty to perpetuate it through his seed. Every time he had sex, he was reminded that he was performing an act on behalf of the covenant, namely, providing progeny who would inherit the blessings of the covenant. In the Bible, the locus of reproduction and generation was referred to as the "loins," and sons (1 Kings 8:19; 2 Chron. 6:9), kings (Gen. 35:11), and descendents (Gen. 46:26; Ex. 1:5; Acts 2:30; Heb. 7:5, 10) were said to come from fathers' loins. The loins were also the locus of strength (Job 40:16; Pr. 31:17; Nah. 2:1). Inasmuch as the covenant involved blessings to future generations and inasmuch as future generations were thought to be in the male loins, the covenant had to be associated with the loins, and the mark of the covenant would then be located there, in the organ that would ensure the production of progeny.

25. Mircea Eleade, *The Sacred and the Profane: The Nature of Religion* (Fort Washington, PA: Harvest Books, 1968).

26. It is not an accident that many native American rituals, such as vision quests and sweat lodges, are becoming increasingly popular among the general population.

27. Arnold van Gennep, *The Rites of Passage*, trans. Monika B. Vizedom and Gabrielle L. Caffee (Chicago, IL: University of Chicago Press, 1960).

28. Victor Turner, *The Ritual Process* (London: Aldine, 1969).

29. Much of this material is found in Mircea Eliade, *Rites and Symbols of Initiation: The Mysteries of Birth and Rebirth* (San Francisco, CA: HarperCollins, 1980). For a review of initiation practices in contemporary culture, see also L. C. Mahdi, S. Foster, and M. Little, eds., *Betwixt and Between: Patterns of Masculine and Feminine Initiation* (La Salle, IL: Open Court Press, 1987).

30. Douglas Allen, "Eliade and History," *The Journal of Religion* 68, no. 4 (Oct. 1988): 545-65.

31. Anne Cameron, *Daughters of Copper Woman* (Vancouver, Canada: Press Gang Publishers, 1981), pp. 101-03.

32. Bruce Lincoln, *Emerging from the Chrysalis: Rituals of Women's Initiation* (New York: Oxford University Press, 1991).

33. Erich Neumann, "On the Psychological Meaning of Ritual," *Quadrant* 9, no. 2 (1976): 5-34.

34. Sigmund Freud, "Obsessive Actions and Religious Practices," *The Standard Edition*. Vol. IX, trans. J. A Strachey (London: The Hogarth Press, 1959, p. 119). See also Christopher A. Lewis, "Religiosity and Obsessionality: The Relationship between Freud's 'Religious Practices'," *The Journal of Psychology* 128.2 (March 1994): 189. This study used objective measures of religiosity and obsessional behavior among teenagers, and concluded that "the differences between religious practices and obsessive actions are greater than their similarities."

35. Sigmund Freud, "Obsessive Actions and Religious Practices," *The Standard Edition*, Vol. IX, trans. J. A Strachey (London: The Hogarth Press, 1959), p. 126.

36. Karl Abraham, "A Complicated Ceremony Found in Neurotic Women," in *Selected Papers of Karl Abraham*, trans. D. Bryan & A. Strachey (London: Hogarth Press, 1948), pp. 157-163. (Original work published 1912.)

37. One can never be quite sure to what extent these patients' associations were influenced by their knowledge of the analyst's theoretical commitment.

38. Rush Rehm, *Marriage to Death: The Conflation of Wedding and Funeral Rituals in Greek Tragedy* (Princeton, NJ: Princeton University Press, 1994).

39. Robert L. Moore, *The Archetype of Initiation: Sacred Space, Ritual Process, and Personal Transformation*, ed, Max J. Havlick, Jr. (Philadelphia, PA: Xlibris Publishing, 2001).

40. See http://www.uscobm.com.

41. Laura E. Berk, *Development Through the Lifespan*, 3rd ed. (Boston, MA: Allyn & Bacon, 2004).

42. Margaret T. Singer, *Cults in Our Midst: The Continuing Fight against Their Hidden Menace* (San Francisco, CA: Jossey-Bass, 1995).

43. As yet, insufficient research has been carried out into spirituality and religion among adolescents. What has been done suggests that spirituality and religion are important for many adolescents, and that greater levels of involvement with spirituality and religion are associated with better health and less involvement in high risk behavior. E.g., Christian Smith, "Theorizing Religious Effects Among American Adolescents," *Journal for the Scientific Study of Religion* 42, no. 1 (March 2003): 17-30.

44. Edward Edinger, *The Creation of Consciousness* (Toronto, Canada: Inner City Books, 1984).

CHAPTER 3—PERSONALITY, PSYCHOPATHOLOGY, AND PERSONAL SPIRITUALITY

1. Contemporary mainstream psychology calls these categories of experience "cognitive invariants," which are aspects of the archetypes by another name.

2. The word "personality" comes from the Greek *persona*, or mask. Personality refers to the way in which we present ourselves to the environment, the outer skin of the self that makes us think, feel, and behave in typical ways. Whereas "personality" is a term that refers mainly to social adaptation and appearances, the word "character" tends to refer to the permanent, deeply ingrained psychological organization of the person, such as the tendency to be excessively meticulous. The word "character" comes from the Greek "*charasso*," meaning to engrave or dig in, a root that is found in the English word "scratch." Character is often used to refer to moral qualities, but it need not have a moral connotation. "Temperament" usually refers to innate factors that are constitutional or genetic. We see temperament at birth when we say that some babies are born more irritable or placid than others.

3. Erich Schenk, *Mozart and His Times* (New York: Alfred A. Knopf, 1959).

4. Without going into a long discussion of the mind-brain problem, suffice it to say that I do not believe that spirituality or any other aspect of consciousness can be reduced to the workings of the brain. I also subscribe to the view that mind and body are two aspects of a unitary reality.

5. The problem is to explain the ways in which the links between these qualities are made. Other than the genetic contribution this is not clear, unless one resorts to explanations based on *karma* or past lives.

6. C. G. Jung, *The Structure and Dynamics of the Psyche, CW,* vol. 8, trans. R. F. C. Hull (Princeton, NJ: Princeton University Press, 1969) § 204.

7. James Hillman, *The Soul's Code* (New York: Random House, 1996).

8. For example, after hurricane Katrina, a sign outside a New England Baptist church declared: "New Orleans: Natural disaster? Or God's anger with sin?" Apparently, an organization known as Repent America took the position that Katrina was the result of the permissive attitude of New Orleans towards homosexuality.

Fundamentalist Christians blamed the attacks of Sept. 11 on abortion, "pagans," feminists, and homosexuality. (See for example, http://www.religioustolerance.org/tsunami04m.htm, and http://www.cadenhead.org/workbench/news/2733/pastor-god-destroyed-new-orleans).

9. See Ana-Marie Rizzuto, *The Birth of the Living God* (Chicago, IL: University of Chicago Press, 1979), Michael St. Clair, *Human Relations and the Experience of God* (Mahwah, NJ: Paulist Press, 1994), and John McDargh, *Psychoanalytic Object Relations Theory and the Study of Religion* (Lanham, MD: University Press of America, 1983).

10. William W. Meissner, *Psychoanalysis and Religious Experience* (New Haven, CT: Yale University Press, 1984).

11. John McDargh, "The Deep Structure of Religious Representations," *Object Relations Theory and Religion: Clinical Applications*, ed. M. Finn and J. Gartner (Westport, CT: Praeger Publishers, 1992) p. 3.

12. Francois Trochu, *St. Bernadette Soubirous* (Rockford, IL: Tan Books, 1985).

13. Mary F. Windeatt, *The Children of La Salette* (St. Paul, MN: Grail Publishing, 1951).

14. Renzo Allegro & Roberto Allegro, *Fatima: The Story Behind the Miracle* (Cincinnati, OH: St. Anthony Messenger Press, 2002).

15. Others who were with these children at the time of the apparitions did not see the Virgin.

16. Mary exhorted them to say the Rosary, do penance, and pray for the conversion of Russia. Various predictions and secrets were also said to have been revealed: a vision of hell, a prediction that the First World War would end but that another war would occur if people continued to offend God, and that Russia would eventually become Catholic. Controversy surrounds one of the secrets, and some people believe it has been censored by the Vatican.

17. Clinical practice confirms Jung's idea that an individual may have an archetypal experience that contains imagery from any religious or mythological tradition, not solely the one in which he or she was raised. Archetypal images are not simply inherited in the ordinary genetic sense of the word. Jungian theory suggests that, because the personal psyche is continuous with the objective psyche, the manifestations of the archetype do not always respect cultural boundaries.

18. I would like to acknowledge the invaluable help I received from Michael Mendis in the preparation of this section.

19. Sophie Jewett, *God's Troubadour: The Story of St. Francis of Assisi* (Chapel Hill, NC: Yesterday's Classics, 2005).

20. The temperament (or psychological type) of St. Francis of Assisi will be identified and discussed in a later section in this chapter.

21. Paul used the Greek word *sarx* (literally translated as "flesh") throughout his writings to talk about that part of himself that had a natural tendency to do things that

another part of himself felt were wrong. This other part he called "the spirit" (his "higher" nature). He wrote: "For the flesh sets its desire against the Spirit, and the Spirit against the flesh; for these are in opposition to one another, so that you may not do the things that you please" (Gal. 5:17—NASB). Of his own personal struggle with the "flesh," he wrote: "For we know that the Law is spiritual, but I am of flesh, sold into bondage to sin. For what I am doing, I do not understand; for I am not practicing what I would like to do, but I am doing the very thing I hate. ... For I know that nothing good dwells in me, that is, in my flesh; for the willing is present in me, but the doing of the good is not. For the good that I want, I do not do, but I practice the very evil that I do not want." (Rom. 7:14-19—NASB).

22. In the same passage where Paul talks about his zeal for the Jewish faith and his persecution of the Christians, he says, "God ... set me apart even from my mother's womb and called me through His grace ..." (Gal. 1:15—NASB). This might well be Paul's way of saying that he was born a "Christian" *by temperament*, even though he was born *into* the Jewish faith. The verse goes on to indicate that Paul was "set apart" and "called" to preach to the Gentiles (that is, non-Jews, who, by Jewish standards, were outcasts and unworthy to participate in Jewish rituals). It is an irony that someone who was so zealous about Judaism should be called to be the Apostle to the Gentiles, but Paul may have been a Gentile at heart from the very beginning. In fact, he became the fiercest opponent of the idea of retaining Jewish practices in Christianity among the early Christians, and he went out of his way to find a Christian equivalent for Jewish religious practices such as circumcision and animal sacrifices by spiritualizing and de-literalizing them.

23. Paul's personality type will be identified and discussed in a later section in this chapter.

24. Saint Augustine, Bishop of Hippo, *City of God*, trans. Marcus Dodds, George Wilson, and J. J. Smith (New York: Random House, 1950).

25. There was considerable controversy over the doctrine of Original Sin. A British monk by the name of Pelagius had challenged Augustine's view of the fundamentally sinful nature of human beings and his idea of inherited guilt. Pelagius taught that individuals were born fundamentally good and that they could achieve moral perfection in this life without the grace of God or the sacrifice of Christ. The issue was settled in C.E. 529 when the Council of Orange rejected Pelagianism and accepted Augustine's doctrine that Adam's sin corrupted both the body and the soul of the whole human race, and that sin and death are a result of Adam's disobedience.

26. It was introduced by Pope Pius IX in 1854.

27. "But I would have you without carefulness. He that is unmarried careth for the things that belong to the Lord, how he may please the Lord: But he that is married careth for the things that are of the world, how he may please his wife. There is difference also between a wife and a virgin. The unmarried woman careth for the

things of the Lord, that she may be holy both in body and in spirit: but she that is married careth for the things of the world, how she may please her husband" (1 Cor. 7:32-34, KJV).

28. 1 Tim. 2:11-15.

29. Rom. 5:12.

30. This figure is most suggestive of the Etruscan Diana, later identified with Artemis. There was a great temple to Diana at Ephesus, in modern-day Turkey. Her statue had many breasts, indicating her capacity to nourish all creatures. Here, devotion to her was so great that the early Christians considered her a great rival. She was known by many names including: Queen of Heaven; the Great Goddess; Lunar Virgin; Mother of Animals; Lady of Wild Creatures; the Huntress; Patroness of Childbirth, Nursing and Healing; and Queen of the Witches. Diana was the goddess of the moon, a protector of women, and in early times the great mother goddess of nature. I have no idea whether the dreamer had seen images of this goddess.

31. To understand fully the mythic connotations and nuances of the dream, one would have to look at the mythology of Kali. She re-creates life by first destroying what has to be eliminated. She assumes this terrible role to annihilate evil, but in her rage she devours all of existence. She symbolizes the power of the divine feminine (*Shakti* in Sanskrit) for action and change. She is uncompromising and direct, and she demands total surrender of the ego and detachment from materialism. She cannot tolerate complacency and arrogance, and she requires honesty. But she is also the Divine Mother, the nurturer and provider.

32. Concentrating on typical pairs of the first two functions described by Jung, Peter Richardson (*Four Spiritualities: Expressions of Self, Expressions of Spirit* [Palo Alto, CA: Davies-Black Publishing, 1996]) has described four spiritual paths that suit people of different types. All are equally valid, and they overlap. They partially correspond to the ancient Hindu system of the four main *yogas*, or ways of joining with the divine. However, the path of raja yoga does not easily lend itself to such correspondence.

33. Hippocrates believed that one's state of health or sickness depends on the balance of the "humors" (or fluids) in the body. In his thinking, each of the four humors—blood, black bile, yellow bile, and phlegm—was connected to one of the four elements—air, earth, fire, and water. To this scheme, Galen later added the four temperaments—sanguine, melancholic, choleric, and phlegmatic—that went along with the humors. Too much black bile (earth) made one melancholic or depressed. A predominance of blood (air) caused the sanguine, confident, optimistic character. Yellow bile (fire) produced the hot-tempered choleric individual, while an abundance of phlegm (water) produced the phlegmatic, imperturbable or placid character.

34. For a basic review of Jung's typology, see Daryl Sharp, *Personality Types: Jung's Model of Typology* (Toronto, Canada: Inner City Books, 1987). For a review of the Myers-Briggs approach to type, see Isabel B. Myers, *Gifts Differing: Understanding Personality Type* (Palo Alto, CA: Davies-Black Publishing, 1995).

35. The Enneagram must also be mentioned here as a valuable tool for understanding the relationship between personality and spirituality.

36. The *DSM* does have a category designated "Religious or Spiritual Problem," but the description applies it to situations in which the patient has had experiences that have produced a loss of faith, problems converting to a new faith, or the questioning of his or her spiritual values. This category could be used for situations such as a near-death or other numinous experience that are recognized to be non-pathological. The category was introduced in response to pressure from the transpersonal psychology movement.

37. Alice Miller, *For Your Own Good* (New York: Farrar Straus Giroux, 1990).

CHAPTER 4—A DEPTH PSYCHOLOGICAL VIEW OF SOME RELIGIOUS IDEAS

1. Heinz Kohut, "Forms and Transformations of Narcissism," *Self Psychology and the Humanities: Reflections on a New Psychoanalytic Approach* (New York: W. W. Norton and Co., 1985).

2. The archetypal image of the divine child is found in many mythologies. Typically, the child has a miraculous birth, often from a virgin, and performs miracles early on. The conception of the Buddha was announced by a numinous dream in which the Buddha entered his mother's womb in the form of a white elephant. Many miracles and healings then occurred. At his birth, the baby Buddha and his mother were refreshed by two streams of water from the sky. The baby then strode about, proclaiming his future glory. For an account of the birth of many divine children, see David A. Leeming, *Mythology: The Voyage of the Hero* (New York: Harper and Row, 1981).

3. Evangelical churches often downplay Jesus' emphasis on helping the poor and needy, and instead merge their theology with an emphasis on consumption and capitalism. In 2000, a best-selling book titled *The Prayer of Jabez* recommended that prayer be used for material success. This is a good example of the way in which we can find what we need in a religious tradition, turn it to the service of our own narcissism, and ignore its teachings that make us uncomfortable.

4. George H. Gallup Jr., *Religion in America: 1996 Report* (Princeton, NJ: Princeton Religious Research Center, 1996).

5. James M. Robinson *et al.*, *The Nag Hammadi Library in English*, 4th ed. (New York: E. J. Brill, 1996).

6. However, it is important to point out that the word meant something different to the ancient Greeks from what it means to us today. For Homer, the psyche was a sort of image of the deceased, complete with scars, that descended to Hades after death. It was not implicated in causing thoughtful behavior in the modern psychological sense until much later. Aristotle for example saw the soul as able to receive knowledge.

7. Evangelos Christou, *The Logos of the Soul* (Zürich: Spring Publications, 1976).

8. There is a potentially confusing overlap between the use of the words "ego" and "soul," since the term "ego" is often used to refer to anything that is conscious. In practice, we tend to use the word "soul" to imply that an experience has depth, genuineness, and emotional power, whereas we use the world "ego" to refer to any kind of conscious experience, even that which is purely conceptual, unimportant, or mechanical. Another difference is that the ego is one voice, but the soul has many voices, not all of which are conscious.

9. For the clinician, this means that "sticking to the image" is only half of what is necessary. Accurate emotional attunement, or keeping track of the patient's emotional state, is equally important, since emotions are an expression of the archetype in the body.

10. The work of psychotherapy is then analogous to the "soul retrieval" of the shamanic traditions.

CHAPTER 5—A DEPTH PSYCHOLOGY OF EVIL

1. Jesus' advice, "resist not evil" (Matt. 5:38), is particularly difficult to follow because it requires real trust and absolute faith in divine providence. Jesus must have been at that level himself. He must also have realized that resistance strengthens evil, and when we resist evil we risk becoming just like that which we resist. We see this effect when we go to war against what we perceive to be evil and our wars end up causing their own evil. Even our anti-war protestors can be war-like. But we fear that if we do not resist evil, it may spread instead of just burning out, like an untended fire. Unfortunately, Jesus' advice is widely ignored by nominally Christian politicians because following it would make them look weak.

2. Here I would like to draw attention to a useful discussion of good and evil by J. Krishnamurti, in his fourth Public Talk, 27th Feb. 1955, Mumbai (Bombay), India. For him, there is actually only one important thing: a mind that is attentive. He believes that there is no such thing as good and evil; there is only a state of mind that is or is not awakened. Goodness is then not a particular quality, not a virtue, but a state of love. Morality cannot be based simply on the need for social order and security; it must be based on the discovery of spiritual intelligence.

3. In the Zen tradition, a *koan* is an unanswerable question that forces the student to

get past conceptual thought. The student is tempted to give a rational response to the *koan*, but he or she must resist this temptation. His or her response must simply reflect reality, so action may be better than words.

4.   The depth-psychological approach is only one of many lenses through which to view the problem of evil. Each discipline brings its own methods to bear on what is clearly a problem with many levels. For the sake of perspective, here are some of these alternative approaches.

1. Following Darwin, most sociobiologists believe that evil behavior emerges because it contributes to the survival of individuals within the species. In some cases, it can help us adapt and reproduce more easily. Such behavior is embedded in our genes, our body chemistry, and the wiring of our brains; some people are born evil because they have a preponderance of genetic factors that predispose them to evil behavior. Thus, the way to eliminate such behavior is to root it out at the genetic level. In the spirit of Darwinism, Jean Baudrillard has suggested that evil is necessary to maintain the vitality of civilization. See: *The Transparency of Evil* (New York: Verso Books, 1992).

2. The medical model assumes that evil people such as serial killers are mentally ill or at least have a severe character disorder. These disorders result from malfunctions or malformations in the brain. Some such patients can be treated psychiatrically with medications that alter their behavior by correcting disordered brain chemistry.

3. Behavioral psychologists believe that evil behavior is learned during childhood development. The family and the culture in which we live reinforce evil behavior. Evil people need behavioral methods to re-program the way they behave.

4. Social scientists believe that evil behavior arises from the social environment in which we live and that inter-group conflicts are conditioned by history, geography, and economics. We are brought up by the society in which we are born to believe that our side is in the right, and that God or the good is on our side. Consequently, our enemies are evil, and they can therefore be destroyed; in this way we justify war and our own evil behavior towards those who disagree with us. In this view of evil, the way to deal with evil behavior is to promote better education, diplomatic efforts, peace treaties, and institutions such as the United Nations.

5. A legal or law-enforcement approach to evil takes the position that the question of how people become evil is less important than the fact that they have actually committed evil acts. The way to deal with evil is to deter evildoers by imposing stiff penalties and also to protect law-abiding citizens by isolating the evildoers from the rest of the community.

6. The religious perspective on life views evil as cosmic rather than located primarily in the human sphere. In the Judeo-Christian tradition, human beings are seen as prone to evil because human nature became corrupted when Adam and Eve yielded

to temptation in the Garden of Eden. In traditional Judaism, evil was dealt with through animal sacrifices. In Christianity, Christ is the ultimate antidote to evil; with his help, individual human beings can overcome the evil that has corrupted human nature.

5. In response to this challenge, Christians might invoke the idea of original sin, just as Hindus might appeal to the doctrine of *karma*. In regard to original sin, the Christian would say that in Biblical times, a person's primary identity was derived from the collective (or group) to which he or she belonged. Thus, his or her existence as a member of the human race took precedence over his or her existence as an individual. In such a world of collective (or corporate) identity, the disobedience of a single individual, such as Adam, would involve the collective responsibility of the whole human race and thus be deserving of collective punishment. In the psychology of collective identity, all innocent human babies, as descendants of Adam, share in the responsibility for his disobedience, and therefore inherit the consequences. One major consequence of Adam's disobedience was that the entire human race—including innocent human babies—became estranged from God. In this state of estrangement from God, human babies are subject to pain and suffering, even though they might themselves be innocent of any evildoing. St. Paul made the point that just as Adam's disobedience estranged the human race from God and brought sin and death upon all humans, so the death of Christ reverses the estrangement and reconciles the entire human race to God. That reconciliation is not yet complete, but when it is, innocent babies will not have to suffer any more. No doubt this explanation satisfied people in Biblical times, since it was addressed to their psychological makeup. However, our notions of identity and justice have changed considerably since then, and today it is difficult to see the justice in people being forced to bear the consequences of someone else's disobedience or being punished for it. Our sense of individual identity leads us to expect that we will be judged on our own individual merits, and on them alone. This is yet another indication of how necessary it is to develop a spirituality that speaks to the psychological needs of our times.

6. Process theology suggests that we are co-partners with God in the process of existence. The divine is best understood in relation to values such as truth, beauty, and goodness. To the extent that we prefer these values or choose them, we reflect the divine. This viewpoint places the divine within the context of time and space rather than in the transcendent realm of absolutes.

7. Harold S. Kushner, *When Bad Things Happen to Good People* (New York: Bantam Doubleday Dell Publishing Co., 2004).

8. This slaughter appears to have had divine sanction—see Deut. 20:16-17. And again, after the Israelite victory over the Midianites, Moses commands his people kill all the women—except the virgins—and children (Num. 31:16-17).

9. See Jeremiah 12:1-2.
10. To argue that the Holocaust is acceptable because it led to the establishment of the State of Israel is to invoke the "greater good" argument. This is not of much help to those who died in the Holocaust. The local Arabs who were displaced by the formation of the State of Israel would point out that there was no greater good from their point of view.
11. Jacob B. Agus, "Good and Evil," *Encyclopedia Judaica*, ed. Cecil Roth (Jerusalem: Keter Publishing House, 1972).
12. Among the ultra-orthodox, there is a strand of primitive reward-punishment thinking, according to which the Holocaust was a punishment for the Jews' failure to be sufficiently observant of the law.
13. Saint Augustine, *City of God*, trans. Marcus Dodds, George Wilson, and J. J. Smith (New York: Random House, 1950).
14. John Hick, *Evil and the God of Love*, 2nd ed. (San Francisco: Harper & Row, 1978).
15. In Simone Weil, *Simone Weil, An Anthology*, ed. Sian Miles (New York: Weidenfeld and Nicolson, 1986), p. 192.
16. Jane M. Trau, *The Co-Existence of God and Evil* (New York: Peter Lang Publishing, 1991).
17. Some Christians, such as the late Mother Teresa, believe that it is not only Christ's suffering on the Cross that is a prerequisite for a relationship with God, but our individual human suffering as well. The people who are brought to Mother Teresa's hospices for the dying are not given medical treatment for their pain, but are encouraged to endure their suffering as Christ endured his. The lack of proper medical care for terminally-ill inmates at Mother Teresa's Home for the Dying Destitute in Calcutta was documented by Dr. Robin Fox in an article published in the British medical journal *The Lancet* in 1994—see Robin Fox, "Mother Teresa's Care for the Dying," *The Lancet* 344, no. 8925 (Sept. 17, 1994): 807. At a press conference in Washington, D.C. in 1995, Mother Teresa declared, "I think it is very beautiful for the poor to accept their lot, to share it with the passion of Christ. I think the world is being much helped by the suffering of the poor people"— quoted in Christopher Hitchens, *The Missionary Position: Mother Teresa in Theory and Practice* (London: Verso, 1995), p. 11.
18. This way of thinking has its origins in the ancient Hebrew Yom Kippur (Day of Atonement) ritual (Lev. 16). In this ceremony, the sins of the entire community were ritually loaded by the High Priest onto a goat, which was then led off into the wilderness, bearing the sins of the people with it and thus cleansing the community.
19. Jesus is reported to have said: "... [E]veryone who looks at a woman with lust for her has already committed adultery with her in his heart" (Matt. 5:28—NASB).
20. This teaching is based on passages such as Eph. 5:22-23: "Wives, be subject to your husbands .... For the husband is the head of the wife ...."

21. Those who use the Bible to justify slavery or segregation draw upon the story of Noah's son Ham finding his father drunk and naked in his tent. Ham came out of the tent and made fun of his father to his brothers. They, however, out of respect for their father entered the tent backwards, so as not to see his naked body, and covered him. When Noah sobered up, he cursed Ham, saying, "A slave of slaves shall he be to his brothers" (Gen. 9:25). Supporters of slavery or racial segregation of Blacks claim that Noah's curse on Ham had God's seal of approval. Based on other Biblical passages, it is concluded that Africans are the descendants of Ham, and thus, the keeping of African slaves is merely the fulfillment of Noah's curse and in accordance with God's will. The Bible does appear to condone slavery in various places, such as Gen. 9:25; 1 Kings 9:21; 2 Kings 4:1, and passages such as these were used by Christians in the Old South in defense against the abolitionists, whom they accused of going against God's will.

22. Brian Davies, *An Introduction to the Philosophy of Religion* (New York: Oxford University Press, 2004).

23. By "religious forces" I mean the anti-Semitism that was endemic in Europe, fostered mainly by the various Christian denominations.

24. One of the main techniques of government propaganda is to degrade the enemy by making people think of them in terms of negative categories—categories immediately associated with evil. Communists spoke of the bourgeoisie, and the followers of Mao and Pol Pot destroyed the intelligentsia; putting these category labels on people somehow made them less than human.

25. In some churches, the altar cross was replaced by the swastika, and Hitler's *Mein Kampf* replaced the Bible. In some circles, prayers were offered to Hitler.

26. Stanley Milgram, *Obedience to Authority: An Experimental View* (Pittsburgh, PA: Harper Collins, 1974.)

27. Philip G. Zimbardo, "A Simulation Study of the Psychology of Imprisonment Conducted at Stanford University," Stanford Prison Experiment website, 1999-2007, retrieved January 2007 <http://www.prisonexp.org/>. See also the Holah Psychology website (http://www.holah.karoo.net/zimbardostudy.htm) for an analysis and critique of the original article in which the results of the experiment were first published. The original article is: Craig Haney, Curtis Banks, and Philip Zimbardo, "A Study of Prisoners and Guards in a Simulated Prison," *Naval Research Review* 30 (1973): 4-17.

28. It should be noted that the psychologist Erich Fromm disagreed with both Milgram's and Zimbardo's conclusions and had serious reservations about the manner in which the prison-simulation experiment was conducted. For his critique, see Erich Fromm, *The Anatomy of Human Destructiveness* (New York: Holt, Rinehart and Winston, 1973), pp. 76-90.

29. Kohut called empathy "value neutral," meaning that what we do with the

information that we obtain is up to us; empathy can be used to hurt or to help the other person. The sadist can be empathic with his victim in the sense that he knows exactly how he is making his victim feel.

30. Alice Miller, *For Your Own Good* (New York: Farrar, Straus and Giroux, 1990).

31. Some historians have suggested that Hitler believed he was doing good, no matter how evil he may seem to us. Perhaps they were influenced by Socrates, who thought that no one does evil for its own sake—we do evil because of a mistaken notion of what is good.

32. Ronald Fairbairn, *An Object Relations Theory of the Personality* (New York: Basic Books, 1952).

33. See for example Hannah Segal, *An Introduction to the Work of Melanie Klein* (New York: Basic Books, 1974).

34. Jean Piaget, *The Moral Judgment of the Child* (New York: Free Press, 1965).

35. Lawrence Kohlberg, Charles Levine, and Alexandra Hewer, *Moral Stages: A Current Formulation and a Response to Critics* (Basel, Switzerland: Karger Publishers, 1983).

36. Hannah Arendt, *Eichmann in Jerusalem: A Report on the Banality of Evil* (New York: Viking Press, 1963).

37. *Ibid.*, p. 126.

38. This particular individual was greatly distressed by a sermon he heard on Jesus' encounter with the rich man who was told that it is easier for a camel to pass through the eye of a needle than for a rich man to enter the kingdom of heaven (Mark 23:25). This is an example of the way in which a spiritual teaching may be totally at odds with an important aspect of the individual's personality, so that the teaching is useless or even alienating.

39. Berel Lang, *Act and Idea in the Nazi Genocide* (Syracuse, NY: Syracuse University Press, 2003).

40. Some theologians acknowledge this. In *The Darkness of God* (London: SCM-Canterbury Press, 1982), Jim Garrison points out that Hiroshima cannot be explained away as a purely human disaster—God was involved in the nuclear blast.

41. C. G. Jung, *C. G. Jung Speaking* (Princeton, NJ: Princeton University Press, 1987), p. 327.

42. *CW* 11, p. 357.

43. W. Robert McClelland, *God, Our Loving Enemy* (Nashville, TN: Abingdon, 1982).

44. C. S. Lewis, *A Grief Observed* (San Francisco, CA: Harper SanFrancisco, 2001).

45. See Judith Plaskow and Carol P. Christ, *Weaving the Visions: New Patterns in Feminist Spirituality* (New York: HarperCollins, 1989).

46. See for example Edward Edinger, *The Creation of Consciousness: Jung's Myth for Modern Man* (Toronto, Canada: Inner City Books, 1984).

47. This myth can be contrasted with two other mythic images of the struggle with the divine. In Christian mythology, Satan (or Lucifer) is said to have rebelled against

God because of pride and ambition. God casts him out of heaven for rebelling, and he resents this treatment. However, he does not give up easily. He recruits the human race to his side on the principle that there is strength in numbers. God intervenes indirectly through the incarnation of Christ and wins the human race back to his side, and Satan and evil are eventually destroyed once and for all. In a society that was organized hierarchically and saw the universe as a kind of a pyramid with God at the top, it made sense to think of rebellion against authority (especially the authority of the divine) as evil. However, the modern mind might find it more appealing to think of Lucifer's struggle with God as forcing the emergence of a new kind of consciousness in the divine. In Greek mythology, Prometheus rebels against Zeus by doing the forbidden and stealing fire from the gods. He does this for the benefit of humanity. His only motive is sympathy and a desire to help; unlike Lucifer, he has no wish for personal power over others, but offers them power instead. The power that Prometheus offers can be used for good or ill, and this suggests that rebellion against the divine may lead to something very useful. The fire that he brings can also be thought of as the light of a new consciousness.

48. William Blake, *The Complete Poetry and Prose of William Blake*, ed. David V. Erdman (New York: Doubleday Publishing, 1988).

CHAPTER 6—THE DARK SIDE OF THE SELF AND THE TRIALS OF JOB: TRANSFORMATION OF THE GOD-IMAGE

1. *CW* 11, § 557.
2. The book is generally divided into a "frame," Chapters 1, 2, and 42:7-17, and a center, based on major stylistic differences. These parts of the book were probably written at different times; for a full discussion see David Pechansky, *The Betrayal of God* (Louisville, KY: Westminster/John Knox Press, 1990).
3. The prophet Ezekiel (14:12-20) of the 6th century B.C.E., mentions Job and Hebrew legend has Job as the grandson of Jacob's brother Esau. An early Sumerian version of the story is thought to be from about 2000 B.C.E., and a Babylonian poem mentions the suffering of a pious king who has been called the Babylonian Job (John B. Gabel *et al.*, *The Bible as Literature* (New York: Oxford University Press, 1996). There is a rabbinic tradition that Job was a counselor to the Pharaoh of Egypt who imprisoned the Israelites, and this is why he was condemned to suffer— see James L. Kugel, *Traditions of the Bible* (Cambridge, MA: Harvard University Press, 1998). Later I will discuss some parallels between *Job* and an ancient Indian story about a legendary king called Vikramaditya.
4. For example, the New International Version translates Job 13:15 as: Though he slay me, yet I will hope in him; / I will surely defend my ways to his face. The

Revised Standard Version reads: Behold he will slay me; I have no hope; / yet I will defend my ways to his face. In the first case, Job can hope and trust God even if God kills him; in the second, Job defends himself defiantly even though he has no hope.

5. Jack Miles, *God: A Biography* (New York: Knopf, 1995), p. 311.

6. Miles ignores the possibility that the book is an allegory rather than an historical account of actual events. This would make the book rhetorical rather than an attempt to present a particular God-image. As a literary device, the dramatic irony in the allegory is that Job does not know he is the subject of a wager, and believes his suffering comes from God even though it does not. Job is faithful to God in spite of this mistaken belief, thus vindicating God and proving Satan wrong.

7. Presumably this scene is intended to remind us of Eve's temptation of Adam.

8. This section was probably added by a later editor to relieve the painful tension that has built up so far.

9. Like Zeus and Jupiter, the Norse Odin or the Aztec Huitzilopochtli.

10. *Encyclopaedia Judaica*, vol. 10, ed. Cecil Roth (Jerusalem: Keter Publishing House, 1972), p. 111.

11. See for example, Michael St. Clair, *Human Relationships and the Experience of God* (New York: Integration Books, 1994), and Ana-Maria Rizzuto "The Father and the Child's Representation of God: A Developmental Approach," in *Father and Child: Developmental and Clinical Perspectives*, ed. Stanley Cath, Alan Gurwitt, and John Ross (Boston, MA: Little, Brown and Co., 1982). Also, by the same author, *The Birth of the Living God: A Psychoanalytic Study* (Chicago, IL: University of Chicago Press, 1979).

12. Paul Bishop's *Jung's Answer to Job* (New York: Brunner-Routledge, 2002) is valuable in this area.

13. Howard L. Philp, *Jung and the Problem of Evil* (Boston, MA.: Sigo Press, 1993).

14. New only in the Western tradition—the idea of a divine incarnation had long existed in the East.

15. *CW* 11, § 238.

16. Victor White, Review of *Psychology and Religion* (*CW* 11), *Journal of Analytical Psychology*, 4:1 (Jan. 1959). For a full account of the relationship between Jung and White, see Ann C. Lammers, *In God's Shadow: The Collaboration of Victor White and C. G. Jung* (New York: Paulist Press, 1994).

17. C. G. Jung *Letters*, vol. 2., ed. G. Adler, trans. R. F. C. Hull (Princeton, N.J.: Princeton University Press, 1975), pp. 545-6.

18. *CW* 11, § 556.

19. Jung's emphasis on the importance of human consciousness in relation to the Self is radically different from those traditions that locate the divine in a transcendent realm that is beyond the human. Rather than being two distinct domains, the

transpersonal and the human levels of consciousness are continuous with each other, for example when we dream. Jung's notion that the Self becomes conscious of itself within human consciousness contrasts with the traditional idea of a God-image that is entirely self-sufficient and perfect as it is.

20. Martin Buber, *Eclipse of God* (London: Victor Gollancz, 1953).

21. Victor White, "Jung on Job," *Blackfriars* 36 (March 1955): 54 60. For a detailed account of their relationship, see Ann C. Lammers, *In God's Shadow: The Collaboration of Victor White and C. G. Jung* (New York: Paulist Press, 1994).

22. *CW* 11, § 758.

23. Robert Svoboda, *The Greatness of Saturn* (Tulsa, OK: Sadhana Publishers, 1997).

CHAPTER 7—A SENSE OF THE SACRED: SPIRITUALITY BEYOND RELIGION

1. Certain spiritual practices can simulate a sense of Timeless by causing us to have the experience of stepping outside of time or of losing consciousness of the passage of time. Religious practices that induce trance states and spiritual ecstasy are actually thought to transport the devotee to the realm of the Timeless. In Hinduism, yogic practices are though to be able to achieve such states, which is also the goal of some forms of Buddhist meditation.

2. Idealization means that we see the other as larger than life, even more than human, with no faults. The teacher is seen as a source of superior wisdom and strength, and the student wants to become a part of that greatness. Such a psychological merger with the power of the teacher has a soothing effect, and gives the student a sense of direction and purpose.

3. I think this is the meaning of Jesus' comment: "Whosoever shall lose his life shall preserve it." (Luke 17:33). "His life" would be a reference to the ego's opinions and preferences.

4. *CW* 17, § 309.

5. *Chandogya Upanishad*, 6.8.7.

6. Freud postulated the existence of the ego to explain these kinds of processes. Although its existence was never proven, in subsequent psychoanalytic thought the existence of the ego was not only taken for granted but actually used to explain mental processes. This has confused postulation with explanation.

7. Douglas Harding, *Look for Yourself* (Encinitas, CA: InnerDirections Publishing, 2000) and *Face to No-Face* (Encinitas, CA: InnerDirections Publishing, 2002).

8. This is why Krishnamurti distinguished between concentration, which is carried out by a center that deliberately tries to focus on a single point and exclude everything else, and attention, where there is only observation of what is happening with no center and no preferences. See Jiddu Krishnamurti, *The Flame of Attention*

(San Francisco, CA: Harper and Row, 1984.)

9. The process of inducing in others feelings that we cannot tolerate in ourselves is called "projective identification."

10. Jiddu Krishnamurti, *The Impossible Question* (San Francisco, CA: Harper and Row, 1972).

11. Jiddu Krishnamurti, *First and Last Freedom* (Wheaton, IL: The Theosophical Publishing House, 1971).

12. Meister Eckhart, *Treatises and Sermons of Meister Eckhart*, ed. and trans. James M. Clark and John V. Skinner (New York: Octagon Books, 1983).

13. The extreme example is the psychopath, who had an extremely dangerous and abusive childhood in which trust was impossible; there are no truly spiritual psychopaths.

14. I borrow this idea from Gabriel Marcel, *Homo Viator*, trans. Emma Craufurd (New York: Harper Torchbooks, 1962), p. 63.

15. Jiddu Krishnamurti, *On Love and Loneliness* (San Francisco, CA: HarperSanFrancisco, 1993).

16. Søren Kierkegaard, *Works of Love: Kierkegaard's Writing*, ed. and trans. Howard V. Hong and Edna H. Hong, vol. 16 (San Francisco, CA: Harper and Row, 1998).

17. Think for example of Matthew 18:21-22: "Then came Peter to him, and said, "Lord, how often shall my brother sin against me, and I forgive him? As many as seven times?" Jesus said to him, "I do not say to you seven times, but seventy times seven."

18. See for example Helen Palmer, *The Enneagram: Understanding Yourself and the Others in Your Life* (San Francisco, CA: Harper Collins, 1988) and Isabel B. Myers & Peter B. Myers, *Gifts Differing* (Palo Alto, CA: Consulting Psychologists Press, 1980).

19. The fifteenth-century mystic Thomas à Kempis wrote that the spiritual life "is not the work of one day, nor children's sport ...."—Thomas à Kempis, *The Imitation of Christ* (New York: Knopf Publishing, 1998).

20. It has been well described by Bernadette Roberts in *The Experience of No Self* (Boston, MA: Shambhala, 1984).

21. For an account of this idea in its application to psychotherapy, see Lionel Corbett and Murray Stein, "Contemporary Jungian Approaches to Spiritually Oriented Psychotherapy," *Spiritually Oriented Psychotherapy*, ed. Len Sperry and Edward P. Shafranske (Washington, D.C.: American Psychological Association, 2002).

Index

SPRING JOURNAL BOOKS

The book publishing imprint of *Spring Journal*,
the oldest Jungian psychology journal in the world

STUDIES IN ARCHETYPAL PSYCHOLOGY SERIES
Series Editor: Greg Mogenson

Collected English Papers, Wolfgang Giegerich
  Vol. 1: *The Neurosis of Psychology: Primary Papers Towards a Critical Psychology*, ISBN 978-882670-42-6, 284 pp., $20.00
  Vol. 2: *Technology and the Soul*, ISBN 978-882670-43-4, 375 pp., $ 25.00
  Vol. 3: *Soul-Violence* ISBN 978-882670-44-2
  Vol. 4: *The Soul Always Thinks* ISBN 978-882670-45-0

Dialectics & Analytical Psychology: The El Capitan Canyon Seminar, Wolfgang Giegerich, David L. Miller, and Greg Mogenson, ISBN 978-882670-92-2, 136 pp., $20.00

Northern Gnosis: Thor, Baldr, and the Volsungs in the Thought of Freud and Jung, Greg Mogenson, ISBN 1-882670-90-6, 140 pp., $20.00

Raids on the Unthinkable: Freudian and Jungian Psychoanalyses, Paul Kugler, ISBN 978-882670-91-4, 160 pp., $20.00

The Essentials of Style: A Handbook for Seeing and Being Seen, Benjamin Sells, ISBN 978-882670-68-X, 141 pp., $21.95

The Wounded Researcher: A Depth Psychological Approach to Research, Robert Romanyshyn, ISBN 1-882670-47-7

The Sunken Quest, the Wasted Fisher, the Pregnant Fish: Postmodern Reflections on Depth Psychology, Ronald Schenk, ISBN: 978-882670-48-5, $20.00

Fire in the Stone: The Alchemy of Desire, Stanton Marlan, ed., ISBN 978-882670-49-3, 206 pp., $22.95

Honoring David L. Miller

Disturbances in the Field: Essays in Honor of David L. Miller, Christine Downing, ed., ISBN 978-882670-37-X, 318 pp., $23.95

The David L. Miller Trilogy

Three Faces of God: Traces of the Trinity in Literature and Life, David L. Miller, ISBN 978-882670-94-9, 197 pp., $20.00

Christs: Meditations on Archetypal Images in Christian Theology, David L. Miller, ISBN 978-882670-93-0, 249 pp., $20.00

Hells and Holy Ghosts: A Theopoetics of Christian Belief, David L. Miller, ISBN 978-882670-99-3, 238 pp., $20.00

The Electra Series

Electra: Tracing a Feminine Myth through the Western Imagination, Nancy Cater, ISBN 978-882670-98-1, 137 pp., $20.00

Fathers' Daughters: Breaking the Ties That Bind, Maureen Murdock, ISBN 978-882670-31-0, 258 pp., $20.00

Daughters of Saturn: From Father's Daughter to Creative Woman, Patricia Reis, ISBN 978-882670-32-9, 361 pp., $23.95

Women's Mysteries: Twoard a Poetics of Gender, Christine Downing, ISBN 978-882670-99-XX, 237 pp., $20.00

Gods in Our Midst: Mythological Images of the Masculine—A Woman's View, Christine Downing, ISBN 978-882670-28-0, 152 pp., $20.00

Journey through Menopause: A Personal Rite of Passage, Christine Downing, ISBN 978-882670-33-7, 172 pp., $20.00

Portrait of the Blue Lady: The Character of Melancholy, Lyn Cowan, ISBN 978-882670-96-5, 314 pp., $23.95

MORE SPRING JOURNAL BOOKS

Field, Form, and Fate: Patterns in Mind, Nature, and Psyche, Michael Conforti, ISBN 978-882670-40-X, 181 pp., $20.00

Dark Voices: The Genesis of Roy Hart Theatre, Noah Pikes, ISBN 978-882670-19-1, 155 pp., $20.00

The World Turned Inside Out: Henry Corbin and Islamic Mysticism, Tom Cheetham, ISBN 978-882670-24-8, 210 pp., $20.00

Teachers of Myth: Interviews on Educational and Psychological Uses of Myth with Adolescents, Maren Tonder Hansen, ISBN 978-882670-89-2, 73 pp., $15.95

Following the Reindeer Woman: Path of Peace and Harmony, Linda Schierse Leonard, ISBN 1-882670-95-7, 229 pp., $20.00

An Oedipus—The Untold Story: A Ghostly Mythodrama in One Act, Armando Nascimento Rosa, ISBN 978-882670-38-8, 103 pp., $20.00

The Dreaming Way: Dreamwork and Art for Remembering and Recovery, Patricia Reis and Susan Snow, ISBN 978-882670-46-9, 174 pp. $24.95

Living with Jung: "Enterviews" with Jungian Analysts, Volume I, Robert and Janis Henderson, ISBN 978-882670-35-3, 225 pp., $21.95.

Terraspychology: Re-engaging the Soul of Place, Craig Chalquist, ISBN978-882670-65-5, 162 pp., $21.95.

HOW TO ORDER:

Write to us at: Spring Journal Books, 627 Ursulines Street # 7, New Orleans, Louisiana 70116, USA

Call us at: (504) 524-5117

Fax us at: (504) 558-0088

Visit our website at: www.springjournalandbooks.com